Contemporary Critical Theory

Contemporary Critical Theory
A Selective Bibliography

Donald G. Marshall

The Modern Language Association of America
New York   1993

© 1993 by The Modern Language Association of America. All rights reserved
Printed in the United States of America

Library of Congress Cataloging-in-Publication Data

Marshall, Donald G., 1943–
    Contemporary critical theory : a selective bibliography / Donald G. Marshall.
    p.   cm.
    Includes index.
    ISBN 0-87352-963-4 (cloth)   ISBN 0-87352-964-2 (pbk.)
    1. Criticism—Bibliography.   I. Title.
Z6514.C97M37   1993
[PN81]
016.801'95—dc20   92-33515

Published by The Modern Language Association of America
10 Astor Place, New York, New York 10003-6981

Printed on recycled paper

Contents

Guide for the User

This bibliography is intended for advanced undergraduates, graduate students, and those who are not specialists in critical theory. But it may be useful as well to theorists who concentrate in a particular subfield and want an overview of adjoining subfields or of contemporary critical theory as a whole. Users may discover books of interest to them in areas they had overlooked; the listings may help them prepare a general or specialized reading plan for themselves, or they may help teachers select books to use as texts or as secondary reading in a course.

Criteria for Inclusion

The listing is selective and users should assume there exists further work in any special subfield and by any individual author, particularly the major theorists singled out for separate mention. Only books are listed. Theorists whose work consists mainly or exclusively of essays are likely to be represented in anthologies or collections, and I have included a list of prominent journals in theory. Nevertheless, users should be aware that important current work and early indications of emerging trends will be found in professional journals rather than in books. Current bibliographies such as the *MLA International Bibliography* or the *Arts and Humanities Citation Index* give some entrée to this area, but any published bibliography of an ongoing field of study is to some degree out of date by the time it appears. Books listed should be available in medium- to large-size academic libraries, but only the largest libraries are likely to have nearly all of them.

With some reluctance, I have excluded works in foreign languages. Theory above all has been an international area of literary study. But most of the major European theorists have been translated, at least in part. And this bibliography aims to give a picture of theory particularly as it has affected American literary study. Footnotes and bibliographies in the books themselves will lead students to important untranslated work.

I have established no fixed cutoff date to define *contemporary*: sometimes an older book continues to have wide influence. But, generally, the older the book, the lower the probability of its inclusion. Movements such as Russian formalism or figures like Bakhtin are included, because they entered American literary study only through recent translations. Some earlier movements, such as the Chicago school around R. S. Crane, and some earlier critics, such as Yvor Winters, have been excluded, because I find no evidence of a wide continuing interest in them. The exception is Anglo-American New Criticism. It became so dominant in criticism and teaching in the period from World War II to the Vietnam War that it remains the assumed background in relation to which many contemporary theories position themselves—sometimes in opposition, sometimes as highly complex extensions. Students reading contemporary theory will often encounter comments, at times elliptical, on New Criticism, and therefore it seemed useful to provide some guidance to its main texts.

Scope of Topic

It has been even more difficult to draw boundaries that keep the listing to a manageable size. Vast intellectual labor could be expended attempting to define *criticism* and *theory* and distinguishing between them or separating *critical theory* as the theory of criticism from *literary theory* as the theory of literature itself. Such efforts are themselves part of theory. I have settled for a loose usage.

Criticism I take to be the body of interpretive and evaluative commentary on literary works, whether treated individually, under various groupings, or as a whole. But critics who are sufficiently self-conscious may look like theorists. By critical theory I mean a self-consciously reflective awareness of the methods and premises of critical commentary and of its relation to other academic disciplines and to culture more generally. *Literary theory*, one could say, is aimed more directly at reflection on the nature of literary works and may ignore the body of commentary on them. But it is obviously close to *critical theory*, and I have excluded it only when it is directed to a specific class of literary works or devices, as are, for example, narrative theory and theories about metaphor. Even that exclusion is not rigidly maintained, though the probability decreases for a work in that category to be listed. Where, for instance, a book primarily on narrative seemed also to raise broad theoretical issues, I have gladly sacrificed a foolish consistency and included it. Nevertheless, I have tried always to keep in mind as a guide a clear case: a book self-consciously addressed to philosophical reflection on the general issues of how we ought to think and speak about literary works in particular and in general.

No definite border marks off critical theory from philosophy. Continental philosophical movements have often engaged issues of literary theory. In the English-speaking world, recent revived interest in moral philosophy has frequently led philosophers to observations about literature. Even the more austere analytic philosophers have been interested in logical questions such as whether literary works "refer" and, if so, how and to what, or in epistemological questions such as whether literature gives knowledge and how fictional stories and characters could evoke real emotions. Moreover, theory has been steadily interdisciplinary, and I have had in mind the needs of students when I listed, very selectively, works by Freud, Jung, Marx, and others who are common reference points for contemporary theorists. But I have left it to a student's reading to discover that theorists do not draw strict lines around literary study and that not only are philosophers from Plato and Kant to Hegel, Nietzsche, and Heidegger part of theory but so are major figures in other disciplines, such as the linguists Ferdinand de Saussure and Noam Chomsky, the anthropologists Clifford Geertz and Victor Turner, the sociologist and philosopher Jürgen Habermas, the historians Hayden White and Hans Blumenberg, and so on through scholars in the whole range of academic fields. The difficulty of drawing logical distinctions and the indefensibility of drawing arbitrary ones make the bibliographer's task sometimes thankless. But they reflect the reality of the field and indeed one of its chief intellectual merits.

Categorical Organization of Listings

The listings divide contemporary critical theory into a number of branches or approaches. Within each division, the works of leading individual theorists are given separately. I begin with a section of introductory general anthologies and surveys, followed by a list of collections and books that do not fit other categories easily or well. Subsequent topical sections move, roughly speaking, from a focus on analyzing literary works themselves to approaches that set works in a psychological or cultural context. A reader should glance at the table of contents for orientation to the entire bibliography.

These categories have a mainly pragmatic justification. They attempt to group books so that a user seeking a particular work will find it surrounded by works closely related in topic and approach. Obviously, the classifications may overlap in the case of particular individuals or books, and other compilers might classify the works differently. Readers should use caution in this respect and be aware that for a given subject, relevant books may be distributed under several categories. Cross-listings try to compensate for the limitations of any classification scheme, and I restate the author and title to help readers see the relevance of the work and decide whether to seek further information about it.

The headnotes and annotations are intended to provide additional guidance to users in selecting books for particular purposes. They occasionally state a judgment, but sparingly. There is some repetition among headnotes, since I assume a reader is likely to read only the note nearest for information about an author or subject. The notes do not claim to be original, comprehensive, or penetrating and should not be taken as a serious survey of theory and theorists (a number of such surveys are listed in the opening section).

In categories with numerous listings, I provide separate sections for introductory books and for collections surveying a subfield. Wherever I found them, I list bibliographies on individual authors and on various specific approaches.

Format

Listings follow the format of *The MLA Style Manual*. I have tried to provide reliable information about editions, though with contemporary works strict bibliographic standards are unattainable. Each edition listed exists, though many works are issued by different publishers and with different dates in the United Kingdom and the United States. I have actually seen most of the works listed, but a bibliography that aims to be as current as possible cannot verify every listing, since no library or bookstore would ever have all these works available within the time period spent compiling them. I have taken more pains where I felt it might be important to know when a particular work was published or became available in translation, since that information may permit inferences about influence or about emergent interest in an author or topic. But, again, a reader should treat this information with caution.

Acknowledgments

I want to thank George Valassi, who first proposed I compile this list and who, together with David Klemm, encouraged me to pursue its publication. Thanks are also due to the Modern Language Association and its Committee on Research Activities and its Publications Committee; to Walter S. Achtert, director of Book Publications and Research Programs;

and to Joseph Gibaldi, director of Acquisitions and Development, for making its appearance possible. Several anonymous readers for the MLA offered many helpful suggestions. The Argus-eye of the copyeditor Karla Reganold saved me and the reader from many errors and infelicities.

The bibliography was completed in 1992.

Introduction

In the past twenty-five years, the professional study of literature in colleges and universities has undergone a dramatic change. Traditionally, literature was approached in one of two ways. The older originated in nineteenth-century German historicism (with long roots reaching back to Renaissance antiquarianism, classicism, and biblical studies). Institutionalized in universities as a research program under the name *philology*, it was adopted by American and British academics before the turn of the century. The philologist undertakes a wide variety of studies. The first aim is to establish a reliable text for a literary work, drawing on the evidence of manuscripts and printed editions, in order to discern the author's "final intentions." An author's correct *canon*, or list of writings, needs to be determined also, including problems of assigning responsibility in cases of joint authorship (common in the Renaissance). Once an author's writings have been established, they must be inserted into the context of his or her life, whose factual details are uncovered by historical research. Influences on the author are found by studying what he or she read and pinpointing close parallels in thought or wording. Obscure words in a text need explanation, which may require examining vanished customs, historical events, the vocabularies of special trades, fields of knowledge like science or religion, and social spheres like politics. More broadly, the philologist tries to define literary traditions, the historical development of literary forms, or the influence of earlier authors on later ones. An author's words must be set into the general history of a language and the evolution of its grammar, vocabulary, and special forms like proverbs and idioms. Key ideas and the words that express them are considered in their historical context. Finally, literature needs to be inserted into the general history of various epochs and of humankind.

This vast program of work inspired generations of scholars to heroic labors. But during the 1920s and 1930s, a number of distinguished academics, thoroughly trained in philology, began to express dissatisfaction with it as an exclusive approach to literature. The emphasis on rigorous historical evidence seemed to them to neglect an attention to works of literature as artistic creations and diverted critics from examining actual works, redirecting them instead into discussions of historical facts outside the works. Criticism and evaluation were left to drift into impressionistic comment and unsupported judgments, often the mere reflections of current prejudices. Some new way needed to be found to focus attention on individual literary works and to provide a sound basis for critical interpretation, commentary, and evaluation.

There was no single-minded agreement on what the new approach should be, though the general watchword was to learn how to read individual works. At the University of Chicago, Ronald S. Crane denounced the historical approach of which he was an acknowledged master. He led a group of scholars who came to be called the Chicago school, and together they worked to adapt the spirit of Aristotle's *Poetics* to a method adequate to deal with the wide range of modern literature. They tried to define various kinds of literary works, seeing each work as a whole structured to produce a certain intellectual and emotional response from a reader.

In England, I. A. Richards began to attend closely to the complex language of poetry, and his example was important for the American *New Critics*, from Cleanth Brooks to W. K. Wimsatt. They elaborated techniques for close analysis of poetic language, especially of devices like irony, metaphor, imagery, and the dramatic sequence of emotional tones and attitudes expressed by the posited speaker of a poem. While their critical language was more traditional and nontechnical, these American formalists exhibited many parallels to the autonomous contemporary movements of Russian formalism and Prague structuralism, which were more systematic and based more closely on contemporary structural linguistics. New Critical methods brought great subtlety to critical reading and provided more explicit grounds for critical judgment. But despite the self-consciousness of their method and its philosophical foundations, the New Critics remained convinced that critical theory was subservient to the criticism of individual literary works. The New Critics waged fierce battle with the older philological school within universities and colleges, and gradually the new approach won out. Philology continues, but the bulk of academic teaching and criticism remains within the orbit of formalism.

Formalism and the tension, sometimes fruitful, sometimes acrimonious, between formalism and philological historicism dominated into the 1960s, even though there were in the same period Marxist, politically and socially oriented, psychoanalytic, and other kinds of criticism, along with sometimes idiosyncratic but widely read critics like Northrop Frye and Kenneth Burke. But the general social upheavals of the 1960s did not leave criticism unaffected. To many younger scholars, formalism had come to represent a stifling orthodoxy, locking them into a narrow aesthetic sphere cut off from broader concerns with politics, culture, and human psychology. Into this fluid situation there suddenly poured fresh intellectual currents from Europe that seemed to break open the critical orthodoxy. The most significant of these, called *structuralism*, took inspiration from structural linguistics but carried new ideas into widely dispersed cultural areas, from anthropology to psychoanalysis to Marxism to philosophy and history. In the late 1960s and early 1970s, these imported movements spread rapidly, especially among younger academics, and changed the entire nature of professional literary study. Instead of an almost exclusive focus on the close reading of literary classics, whose study was served by critical theory, there emerged a vast debate over critical theory itself, a debate that, some critics feared, threatened to displace almost entirely the study of literature itself.

Theorists often turn to philosophers to help them articulate their ideas, but critical theory is also open to ideas and influences from the theorists of other fields—politics, psychology, history, and so on. As a consequence, the formalist isolation of literary study has receded. Teachers of literature may now be found writing about mass culture, psychoanalysis, or the leading figures of philosophy and its history and not exclusively about works that strike a nonacademic as more obviously "literary." Theorists tend to assume a knowledge not just of the range of literature but also of the latest and most intricate ideas from many fields, and their writings are often couched in a highly specialized and technical jargon. Their speculations may be directed to particular works of literature, but they may also argue about theoretical issues with virtually no reference to specific literary works. They may even, in a somewhat involuted move, apply critical theories to the analysis of critical theory itself. Indeed, the whole field of critical theory and of the literary criticism most deeply indebted to it presents occasionally stiff challenges for the ordinary educated reader. Yet, at the same time, this approach to literary study is full of energy and intelligence and an unblushing ambition to pursue the largest and most important cultural issues. Consequently, it is worth some effort, and making that effort will rapidly lead to familiarity with central ideas and terms and to an understanding and appreciation of critical theory's concerns.

1. Contemporary Critical Theory: General

This section begins with bibliographies, reference guides, and dictionaries (entries 1–9); lists journals that emphasize critical theory; continues with introductory anthologies surveying contemporary theory (entries 10–30), followed by introductory books and collections surveying the field (entries 31–58); goes on to theoretical works on both general and specific topics that do not readily fit other categories in this bibliography (entries 59–260); and concludes with books on the institutions of literary study, including discussions of universities and their history and considerations of the curricular and pedagogical implications of contemporary theory (entries 261–305).

Bibliographies, Reference Guides, and Dictionaries

1. Borkland, Elmer. *Contemporary Literary Critics*. 2nd ed. Detroit: Gale, 1982. Short essays and complete bibliographies on 124 British and American critics.

2. Fowler, Roger, ed. *Dictionary of Modern Critical Terms*. Rev. ed. London: Routledge, 1987. Includes terms from recent theories.

3. Jay, Gregory S., ed. *Modern American Critics, 1920–1955*. Vol. 63 of *Dictionary of Literary Biography*. Detroit: Gale, 1988. Essays by various

scholars with bibliographies of books and articles by and on twenty-five critics.

4. ———, ed. *Modern American Critics since 1955*. Detroit: Gale, 1988. Essays with bibliographies of books and articles by and on twenty-seven critics; appendix, "Modern Critical Terms, Schools, and Movements."

5. Lentricchia, Frank, and Thomas McLaughlin, eds. *Critical Terms for Literary Study*. Chicago: U of Chicago P, 1990. Twenty-three theorists each examine the history and uses of a key term.

6. Magill, Frank N., ed. *Critical Survey of Literary Theory*. 4 vols. Pasadena: Salem, 1988. Short essays with bibliographies on 257 theorists from antiquity to the present. Concludes with short chapters surveying the history of literary theory, contemporary theory, the history of theory in China and Japan, a glossary of terms, and indexes.

7. Orr, Leonard, comp. *A Dictionary of Critical Theory*. Westport: Greenwood, 1991. Entries include source information.

8. ———, comp. *Research in Critical Theory since 1965: A Classified Bibliography*. Westport: Greenwood, 1989.

9. Peck, Jeffrey M., ed. *International Bibliography of Literary Theory and Criticism*. Baltimore: Johns Hopkins UP, 1988. Compiled by twenty-nine international bibliographers, covers twenty-one languages; an annual bibliography sponsored by the eminent journal of theory *New Literary History*, edited by Ralph Cohen.

Journals

Many journals now include essays with a theoretical orientation. Listed here are a few journals that emphasize theory. Some journals frequently feature attacks on particular theories and on theory in general.

The list shows the specific topics, issues, or approaches the journal emphasizes. If a standard abbreviation is established, it precedes the title.

American Journal of Semiotics.

American Scholar. Has regularly included articles critical of many trends in contemporary theory.

Boundary 2. Mainly poststructuralist.

BJA   *British Journal of Aesthetics.*

Common Knowledge. Aims to establish common ground among the various and opposed contemporary intellectual movements.

Comparative Criticism. An annual sponsored by the British Comparative Literature Association. Each volume, on a specific topic, includes book reviews and a survey of recent work in comparative literature in the British

Isles. Particular volumes and their topics are listed in the "General" section below under the name of the editor, E. S. Shaffer. See entry 193.

CI   *Critical Inquiry.* A leading journal with essays representing various approaches.

Critical Studies. Cross-disciplinary work in critical theory.

Critical Texts. Essays, translations, and interviews in critical theory, with full-length reviews of current books.

Cultural Critique. Interdisciplinary cultural interpretation, particularly in relation to political economy.

Cultural Studies. Essays on social practices, texts, and cultural domains, media communications and cultural studies, with an emphasis on popular culture.

Diacritics. Review essays on current books; generally poststructuralist orientation.

Differences: A Journal of Feminist Cultural Studies.

Discourse: Journal for Theoretical Studies in Media and Culture.

Ellipsis. Focuses on "displacement of the subject" in fields from critical and cultural theory to psychoanalysis and feminism.

Genders. Essays in art, literature, history, and film that connect gender to politics, economics, and style.

Glyph. Deconstruction and poststructuralism. No longer published.

JAAC   *Journal of Aesthetics and Art Criticism.*

Journal of Comparative Literature and Aesthetics. Published in India.

LIT: Literature Interpretation Theory.

MLN   *Modern Language Notes.* Frequently publishes theoretical essays.

New Criterion. Often critical of recent theory, especially poststructuralism and cultural criticism.

New Formations. Focuses on issues of meaning and power, sexual and cultural differences, psychoanalytic and poststructuralist approaches.

New German Critique. Mainly Marxist, includes translations of recent and older essays.

NLH   *New Literary History: A Journal of Theory and Interpretation.* A leading journal with essays representing various approaches; each issue features a particular topic.

Paragraph: The Journal of the Modern Critical Theory Group. A British journal.

Philosophy and Literature. Essays representing various approaches.

PTL   *Poetics Theory Literature.* Predecessor of *Poetics Today.*

Poetics Today. Various approaches.

Representations. Emphasizes new historicism.

Signs. Leading feminist journal.

Stony Brook Bulletin for Theory and Criticism.

SubStance. Emphasizes current French theory.

Textual Practice. Modern critical theory and practice, adopting a broad understanding of "text" and "textuality."

Works and Days. Theoretically informed essays on literature and literary institutions and their cultural relations.

Yale French Studies. Annual, each issue on a special topic; emphasizes French literature and theory.

Yale Journal of Criticism.

Anthologies

Virtually all the issues central to contemporary literary theory have been debated from antiquity to the present, and contemporary theorists frequently refer to the history of the subject. A number of the anthologies listed are historically comprehensive, and students will often find it helpful to explore the history of the subjects that interest them.

10.   Adams, Hazard, ed. *Critical Theory since Plato.* 2nd ed. Fort Worth: Harcourt, 1992.

11.   Adams, Hazard, and Leroy Searle, eds. *Critical Theory since 1965.* Tallahassee: UP of Florida, 1986. A companion to the preceding, with selections by fifty-four authors, an overview by Searle, and a selective list of books.

12.   Allen, Gay W., and Harry Hayden Clark, eds. *Literary Criticism: Pope to Croce.* 1941. Detroit: Wayne State UP, 1962. Strong on German Romanticism. See companion volume, entry 17.

13.   Bate, Walter Jackson, ed. *Criticism: The Major Texts.* Enl. ed. New York: Harcourt, 1970. Historically comprehensive, with emphasis on English tradition.

14.   Davis, Robert Con, and Laurie Finke, eds. *Literary Criticism and Theory: The Greeks to the Present.* New York: Longman, 1989. Includes short guides: "Women, Gender, and Criticism," "History, Literature, and Criticism," "Semiotics and Criticism," and "Psychology, the Subject, and Criticism."

15.   Davis, Robert Con, and Ronald Schleifer, eds. *Contemporary Literary Criticism: Literary and Cultural Studies.* 2nd ed. London: Longman, 1989. Sections on formalism; reader-response criticism; structuralism and semiotics; deconstruction; psychology and psychoanalysis; Marxism and new historicism; feminism; and ethics, profession, and the canon.

16.   De Beaugrande, Robert. *Critical Discourse: A Survey of Literary Theorists.* Norwood: Ablex, 1988. Surveys a range of theorists, excerpting key statements.

17.   Gilbert, Allan H., ed. *Literary Criticism: Plato to Dryden.* 1940. Detroit: Wayne State UP, 1962. Includes good selection from Italian Renaissance critics, translated for this volume. See companion volume, entry 12.

18.   Hofstadter, Albert, and Richard Kuhns, eds. *Philosophies of Art and Beauty: Selected Readings in Aesthetics from Plato to Heidegger.* Chicago: U of Chicago P, 1964. Lengthy excerpts, especially strong on Neoplatonism; includes revised translation of Heidegger's "Origin of the Work of Art."

19.   Kaplan, Charles, ed. *Criticism: The Major Statements.* 2nd ed. New York: St. Martin's, 1986. From Plato to contemporaries.

20.   Lambropoulos, Vassilis, and David Neal Miller, eds. *Twentieth Century Literary Theory: An Introductory Anthology.* Albany: State U of New York P, 1987. Selections from 1909 to 1983, arranged under topics: theory, literature, author, tradition, conventions, style, narrative, interpretation, reception, evaluation.

21.   Latimer, Dan, ed. *Contemporary Critical Theory.* San Diego: Harcourt, 1988. Selections showing structuralism, deconstruction, Marxism, hermeneutics and reception theory, psychoanalysis and myth criticism, feminism.

22.   Lodge, David, ed. *Modern Criticism and Theory.* London: Longman, 1988.

23.   Newton, K. M., ed. *Twentieth-Century Literary Theory: A Reader.* New York: St. Martin's, 1988.

24.   Rice, Philip, and Patricia Waugh, eds. *Modern Literary Theory: A Reader.* London: Arnold, 1989.

25.   Richter, David H., ed. *The Critical Tradition: Classic Texts and Contemporary Trends.* New York: St. Martin's, 1989. Contemporary selections are classified under Marxist, psychological, formalist, structuralist and semiotic, poststructuralist, feminist, and reader-response criticism, with sections on debates over the canon and the concept of authorial intention.

26.   Rylance, Rick, ed. *Debating Texts: Readings in Twentieth-Century Literary Theory and Method.* Toronto: U of Toronto P, 1987. Selections showing traditional humanist, formalist, structuralist, poststructuralist, reader-response, Marxist, and feminist approaches.

27.   Selden, Raman, ed. *The Theory of Criticism from Plato to the Present: A Reader.* London: Longman, 1988. Arranges authors under broad topics.

28.   Smith, James Harry, and Edd Winfield Parks, eds. *Great Critics.* 3rd ed. New York: Norton, 1977. Plato to Eliot and John Crowe Ransom.

29.   Staton, Shirley F., ed. *Literary Theories in Praxis.* Philadelphia: U of Pennsylvania P, 1987. Applied essays representing various approaches: New Criticism; phenomenology; archetype and genre; and structuralist-semiotic, sociological (historical, Marxist, feminist), psychoanalytic, reader-response, deconstructionist, and humanist criticism, with selective bibliography.

30.   Walder, Dennis, ed. *Literature in the Modern World: Critical Essays and Documents*. New York: Oxford UP, 1990. Selections from a wide range of modern critics addressing in particular questions of the canon, interpretation, ideology, ethnic and Third World perspectives, and language and gender.

Surveys and Introductions

31.   Atkins, G. Douglas, and Laura Morrow, eds. *Contemporary Literary Theory*. Amherst: U of Massachusetts P, 1989. Twelve essays survey various approaches, with annotated bibliographies.

32.   Barricelli, Jean-Pierre, and Joseph Gibaldi. *Interrelations of Literature*. New York: MLA, 1982. Thirteen essays on literature in relation to fields from linguistics, philosophy, and religion to politics, law, and science.

33.   Birch, David. *Language, Literature and Critical Practice: Ways of Analysis Text*. London: Routledge, 1989. Surveys the full range of language theories and illustrates how each analyzes a literary text.

34.   Caws, Mary Ann, ed. *Textual Analysis: Some Readers Reading*. New York: MLA, 1986. A range of approaches at work: historical, psychoanalytic, thematic, semiotic, rhetorical, deconstructive, political, feminist.

35.   Cohen, Ralph, ed. *The Future of Literary Theory*. New York: Routledge, 1988. Twenty-five commissioned essays survey various approaches.

36.   Collier, Peter, and Helga Geyer-Ryan, eds. *Literary Theory Today*. Ithaca: Cornell UP, 1990. Essays on new historicism, feminist and psychoanalytic literary theory, relevance of race and imperialism to literary study.

37.   Davis, Robert Con, and Ronald Schleifer. *Criticism and Culture: The Role of Critique in Modern Literary Theory*. White Plains: Longman, 1992. Reviews varieties of literary criticism, stressing the concept of critique and interpreting criticism as an intellectual and cultural activity.

38.   Doležel, Lubomír. *Occidental Poetics: Tradition and Progress*. Lincoln: U of Nebraska P, 1990. History of poetics places Russian formalism and Prague structuralism in tradition dating from Aristotle.

39.   Durant, Alan, and Nigel Fabb. *Literary Studies in Action*. New York: Routledge, 1990. Integrates theory with an introduction to literary study; bibliography.

40.   Eagleton, Terry. *Literary Theory: An Introduction*. Minneapolis: U of Minnesota P, 1983. Surveys various approaches from a Marxist point of view.

41.   Fokkema, D. W., and Elrud Kunne-Ibsch. *Theories of Literature in the Twentieth Century: Structuralism, Marxism, Aesthetics of Reception, Semiotics*. New York: St. Martin's, 1977. Clear exposition, especially good on structuralism and semiotics.

42.   Fry, Paul. *The Reach of Criticism: Method and Perception in Literary*

Theory. New Haven: Yale UP, 1983. Discusses Aristotle, Longinus, Dryden, and Shelley from the perspective of deconstruction, with final chapter on Benjamin.

43.   Harari, Josue V., ed. *Textual Strategies: Perspectives in Post-structuralist Criticism*. Ithaca: Cornell UP, 1979. Essays by critics including Barthes, Derrida, de Man, Foucault, Said, Girard, Serres, and others, with bibliography of works in English and French.

44.   Hawthorn, Jeremy, ed. *Criticism and Critical Theory*. London: Arnold, 1984. Essays on various approaches.

45.   Hicks, Malcolm, and Bill Hutchings. *Literary Criticism: A Practical Guide for Students*. London: Arnold, 1989. Guide to literary theory with extensive illustrative examples and answers to questions students frequently ask.

46.   Jefferson, Ann, and David Robey, eds. *Modern Literary Theory: A Comparative Introduction*. 2nd ed. London: Batsford, 1986. Essays survey the major varieties, including formalist, structuralist, Marxist, psychoanalytic, and others.

47.   Koelb, Clayton, and Virgil Lokke, eds. *The Current in Criticism: Essays on the Present and Future of Literary Theory*. West Lafayette: Purdue UP, 1987. Fifteen essays by Culler, Fish, Girard, Jameson, Spivak, and others.

48.   Konigsberg, Ira, ed. *American Criticism in the Poststructuralist Age*. Ann Arbor: U of Michigan P, 1981. Essays by Fish, Graff, Spivak, Girard, Culler, Krieger, Barbara Herrnstein Smith, J. Hillis Miller, and others.

49.   Kramer, Victor A., ed. *American Critics at Work: Examinations of Contemporary Literary Theories*. Troy: Whitston, 1984. Good collection of prominent theorists, concentrating on deconstruction, reader-response theories, and cultural criticism.

50.   Leitch, Vincent B. *American Literary Criticism from the Thirties to the Eighties*. New York: Columbia UP, 1988. Broad survey of theories and theorists.

51.   Natoli, Joseph, ed. *Tracing Literary Theory*. Urbana: U of Illinois P, 1987. Twelve essays surveying a full range of approaches and their history.

52.   Pope, Randolph D., ed. *The Analysis of Literary Texts: Current Trends in Methodology*. Ypsilanti: Bilingual, 1980. Essays showing a wide range of contemporary approaches.

53.   Selden, Raman. *Practicing Theory and Reading Literature: An Introduction*. Lexington: UP of Kentucky, 1989. Surveys formalist, structuralist, deconstructive, reader-response, Marxist, feminist, and psychoanalytic approaches and shows how each can be applied to a wide range of literary texts.

54.   ———. *A Reader's Guide to Contemporary Literary Theory*. Lexington: UP of Kentucky, 1985.

55.   Stamiris, Yiannis. *Twentieth Century Literary Criticism: A Critical Presentation of the Main Currents of the Twentieth Century*. Troy: Whitston, 1985.

56.   Webster, Roger. *Studying Literary Theory: An Introduction.* New York: Arnold, 1989.

57.   Wellek, René. *A History of Modern Criticism: 1750–1950.* 7 vols. New Haven: Yale UP, 1955–91. Vol. 1: *The Later Eighteenth Century* (1955); vol. 2: *The Romantic Age* (1955); vol. 3: *The Age of Transition* (1965); vol. 4: *The Late Nineteenth Century* (1965); vol. 5: *English Criticism, 1900–1950* (1986); vol. 6: *American Criticism, 1900–1950* (1986); vol. 7: *German, Russian, and East European Criticism, 1900–1950* (1991).

58.   Wimsatt, William K., and Cleanth Brooks. *Literary Criticism: A Short History.* New York: Knopf, 1957. Excellent historical survey up to New Criticism.

Books and Collections

General

59.   Abrams, M. H. *Doing Things with Texts: Essays: in Criticism and Literary Theory.* Ed. Michael Fischer. New York: Norton, 1989.

60.   Adams, Hazard. *Philosophy of the Literary Symbolic.* Tallahassee: UP of Florida, 1983.

61.   Andrews, James R. *The Practice of Rhetorical Criticism.* White Plains: Longman, 1990. Introduces students to the study of discourse, theory, and criticism.

62.   Appignanesi, Lisa, ed. *Ideas from France: The Legacy of French Theory.* London: Inst. of Contemporary Arts, 1985. Essays on Foucault, the "structural Marxism" of Althusser, historical study, Barthes, and the general influence of French ideas in literary theory.

63.   Arac, Jonathan, and Barbara Johnson, eds. *Consequences of Theory.* Selected Papers from the English Institute, 1987–88, ns 14. Baltimore: Johns Hopkins UP, 1991. Essays by three literary critics, three philosophers, one historian, and one legal scholar on themes of professionalism, politics, history, feminism, and postcolonialism.

64.   Armstrong, Paul B. *Conflicting Readings: Variety and Validity in Interpretation.* Chapel Hill: U of North Carolina P, 1990. Argues that though interpretations vary, interpreters can demonstrate that some are wrong.

65.   Aschenbrenner, Karl. *The Concepts of Criticism.* Dordrecht: Reidel, 1974.

66.   Avni, Ora. *The Resistance of Reference: Linguistics, Philosophy, and the Literary Text.* Baltimore: Johns Hopkins UP, 1990. Critiques the philosopher Frege and the linguist Saussure and discusses the referential and representational properties of literature.

67.   Barnes, Annette. *On Interpretation: A Critical Analysis.* Oxford: Blackwell, 1988.

68. Battersby, James L. *Paradigms Regained: Pluralism and the Practice of Criticism.* Philadelphia: U of Pennsylvania P, 1991. Criticizes poststructuralist theory and argues for concepts like intention, determinate meaning, and objective value judgments; draws on Anglo-American analytic philosophy.

69. Bersani, Leo. *The Culture of Redemption.* Cambridge: Harvard UP, 1990. Draws on psychoanalysis, Benjamin, Bataille, and others.

70. Berthoff, Werner. *Literature and the Continuances of Virtue: A Theory of Literary Meaning.* Princeton: Princeton UP, 1987. Focuses on a broadened concept of virtue to argue against metacritical skepticism while avoiding naive humanism.

71. Birch, David. *Language, Literature and Critical Practice: Ways of Analysing Text.* London: Routledge, 1989. Presents a wide range of language theories and their relevance to literary criticism.

72. Bové, Paul. *In the Wake of Theory.* Middletown: Wesleyan UP, 1992. Includes essays on Said, on Foucault, and on intellectuals in France and America and their social role.

73. Bruss, Elizabeth W. *Beautiful Theories: The Spectacle of Discourse in Contemporary Criticism.* Baltimore: Johns Hopkins UP, 1982. Discusses Gass, Sontag, Bloom, and Barthes.

74. Budick, Sanford, and Wolfgang Iser, eds. *Languages of the Unsayable: The Play of Negativity in Literature and Literary Theory.* New York: Columbia UP, 1989. Fifteen essays by Derrida, Kermode, Culler, Hartman, Iser, Cavell, and others.

75. Burks, Don M., ed. *Rhetoric, Philosophy, and Literature: An Exploration.* West Lafayette: Purdue UP, 1978.

76. Butler, Christopher. *Interpretation, Deconstruction, and Ideology: An Introduction to Some Current Issues in Literary Theory.* Oxford: Clarendon–Oxford UP, 1984. Tests deconstruction and Marxist approaches against the conception that literary interpretation aims to perceive implications.

77. Buttigieg, Joseph A., ed. *Criticism without Boundaries: Directions and Crosscurrents in Postmodern Critical Theory.* Notre Dame: U of Notre Dame P, 1987.

78. Cain, William E., ed. *Philosophical Approaches to Literature: New Essays on Nineteenth- and Twentieth-Century Texts.* Lewisburg: Bucknell UP, 1984. Includes essays by O'Hara on Ricoeur, Altieri on Wittgenstein, and Spivak on Marx and Derrida.

79. Carroll, David, ed. *The States of "Theory": History, Art, and Critical Discourse.* New York: Columbia UP, 1989. Twelve essays by Derrida, Jameson, Iser, Krieger, J. Hillis Miller, Lyotard, and others.

80. Cascardi, Anthony J., ed. *Literature and the Question of Philosophy.* Baltimore: Johns Hopkins UP, 1987. Essays by literary theorists and philosophers on subjects from Plato to postmodernism.

81. Cassedy, Steven. *Flight from Eden: The Origins of Modern Literary Criti-

cism and Theory. Berkeley: U of California P, 1991. Finds origin of modern approaches to literary criticism in late nineteenth- and early twentieth-century poetry.

82. Catano, James V. *Language, History, Style: Leo Spitzer and the Critical Tradition.* Urbana: U of Illinois P, 1988. On a major Austrian philologist of the first half of the century.

83. Chatman, Seymour, ed. *Approaches to Poetics.* Selected Papers from the English Institute. New York: Columbia UP, 1973. Essays by Kermode, Ohmann, Fish, and Todorov on Barthes, Jakobson, and others.

84. Clayton, Jay, and Eric Rothstein, eds. *Influence and Intertextuality in Literary History.* Madison: U of Wisconsin P, 1991. Thirteen essays span English and American literary history.

85. Cohen, Ralph, ed. *New Directions in Literary History.* Baltimore: Johns Hopkins UP, 1974. Thirteen essays by leading critics.

86. Collins, Christopher. *Reading the Written Image: Verbal Play, Interpretation, and the Roots of Iconophobia.* University Park: Pennsylvania State UP, 1991. Argues that written texts transform an oral-dramatic situation onto an inner, imaginary stage and should be read as performances; shows how the verbal cues of literature prompt imagination.

87. Craige, Betty Jean. *Reconnection: Dualism to Holism in Literary Study.* Athens: U of Georgia P, 1988.

88. Crant, Phillip, ed. *French Literary Criticism.* French Literature Ser. 4. Columbia: Dept. of Foreign Languages and Literatures, U of South Carolina, 1977. Wide historical range with several essays on contemporary theorists and a bibliography.

89. Crews, Frederick. *Skeptical Engagements.* New York: Oxford UP, 1988. Essays skeptical of many recent developments in critical theory.

90. Cunningham, Valentine. *In the Reading Gaol.* Oxford: Blackwell, 1990. Criticizes poststructuralism for closing texts on themselves and reinstates concepts of reference and presence.

91. Currie, Gregory. *The Nature of Fiction.* Cambridge: Cambridge UP, 1990. Philosophical analysis of fictional truth, characters, and fictionality in terms of communicative relations among author, reader, and text.

92. Davis, Robert Con, and Ronald Schleifer. *Criticism and Culture: The Role of Critique in Modern Literary Theory.* White Plains: Longman, 1992. Traces eighteenth-century idea of critique in later literary theory.

93. Davis, Walter A. *The Act of Interpretation: A Critique of Literary Reason.* Chicago: U of Chicago P, 1978. Argues that literary works may validly be approached from diverse and even conflicting critical theories.

94. Ditta, Joseph M. *Natural and Conceptual Design: Radical Confusion in Critical Theory.* New York: Lang, 1984. Criticizes psychoanalytic, structuralist, deconstructive, and Marxist approaches and argues for reinstating the concept of intention.

95.   Docherty, Thomas. *On Modern Authority: The Theory and Condition of Writing, 1500 to the Present Day.* Sussex, Eng.: Harvester, 1987. Wide-ranging, with special attention to issues of gender.

96.   Eaton, Trevor. *Semantics of Literature.* The Hague: Mouton, 1966. Takes Richards's work as starting point.

97.   ———. *Theoretical Semics.* The Hague: Mouton, 1972. Broadens the theory of his *Semantics of Literature.*

98.   Eldridge, Richard. *On Moral Personhood: Philosophy, Literature, Criticism, and Self-Understanding.* Chicago: U of Chicago P, 1989.

99.   Ellis, John M. *The Theory of Literary Criticism: A Logical Analysis.* Berkeley: U of California P, 1974.

100.   Epstein, William H., ed. *Contesting the Subject: Essays in the Postmodern Theory and Practice of Biography and Biographical Criticism.* West Lafayette: Purdue UP, 1992. Includes issues such as identity, intention, and authorship.

101.   Ferguson, Frances. *Solitude and the Sublime: The Romantic Aesthetics of Individuation.* New York: Routledge, 1992. Discusses Kant, Burke, Adorno, Eagleton, Derrida, de Man, and new historicism in relation to topics in Romantic literature.

102.   Fischer, Michael. *Stanley Cavell and Literary Skepticism.* Chicago: U of Chicago P, 1989. Draws on a prominent contemporary philosopher to challenge deconstruction as well as the ideas of Fish.

103.   Fowler, Roger. *Linguistic Criticism.* Oxford: Oxford UP, 1986. Introduction to literary criticism using modern linguistics; with bibliography.

104.   ———. *Literature as Social Discourse: The Practice of Linguistic Criticism.* Bloomington: Indiana UP, 1981. Essays on language, literary styles, and their social contexts and functions.

105.   Freadman, Richard, and Seumas Miller. *Re-thinking Theory: A Critique of Contemporary Literary Theory and an Alternative Account.* Cambridge: Cambridge UP, 1992. Discusses Althusser, Derrida, Foucault, new historicism.

106.   Garvin, Harry R., and Steven Mailloux, eds. *Rhetoric, Literature, and Interpretation.* Lewisburg: Bucknell UP, 1983. Essays on hermeneutics, psychology, feminism, Marxism, and other approaches in relation to rhetoric.

107.   Goodheart, Eugene. *The Failure of Criticism.* Cambridge: Harvard UP, 1978. On the loss of the moral and evaluative function of criticism as "modernism" spreads from literature into criticism itself.

108.   Graham, Joseph F. *Onomatopoetics: Theory of Language and Literature.* Cambridge: Cambridge UP, 1992.

109.   Griffiths, A. Phillips, ed. *Philosophy and Literature.* Cambridge: Cambridge UP, 1984. Thirteen essays on topics ancient to modern.

110.   Gunn, Giles. *The Culture of Criticism and the Criticism of Culture.* New

York: Oxford UP, 1987. On the purpose and place of moral reflection in the analysis of discursive and other symbolic forms; includes discussion of Burke, Bakhtin, and the anthropologist Geertz.

111.   Harpham, Geoffrey Galt. *The Ascetic Imperative in Culture and Criticism.* Chicago: U of Chicago P, 1988.

112.   Harris, Wendell V. *Interpretive Acts: In Search of Meaning.* Oxford: Clarendon–Oxford UP, 1988. Argues that interpretation reconstructs intended meaning by finding the contexts in which the author assumed the audience would place the text; criticizes deconstruction.

113.   Harrison, Bernard. *Inconvenient Fictions: Literature and the Limits of Theory.* New Haven: Yale UP, 1991. Argues that literature produces knowledge by challenging values readers take for granted.

114.   Hassan, Ihab. *Paracriticisms: Seven Speculations of the Times.* Urbana: U of Illinois P, 1975. Criticism absorbing modernist trends in literature.

115.   Hawthorn, Jeremy. *Unlocking the Text: Fundamental Issues in Literary Theory.* London: Arnold, 1987.

116.   Heller, Agnes, and Ferenc Feher, eds. *Reconstructing Aesthetics: Writings of the Budapest School.* Oxford: Blackwell, 1986. Essays on art and music as well as on literary works and theory.

117.   Henderson, John B. *Scripture, Canon, and Commentary: A Comparison of Confucian and Western Exegesis.* Princeton: Princeton UP, 1991.

118.   Hermand, Jost, and Evelyn Torton Beck. *Interpretive Synthesis: The Task of Literary Scholarship.* New York: Ungar, 1976. Surveys theories from formalist to Marxist and urges an interdisciplinary approach to literary study.

119.   Hernadi, Paul, ed. *The Horizon of Literature.* Lincoln: U of Nebraska P, 1982. Essays by a range of eminent critics, including a symposium with Hans-Georg Gadamer.

120.   ———, ed. *The Rhetoric of Interpretation and the Interpretation of Rhetoric.* Durham: Duke UP, 1989.

121.   ———, ed. *What Is Criticism?* Bloomington: Indiana UP, 1981.

122.   ———, ed. *What Is Literature?* Bloomington: Indiana UP, 1978.

123.   Hobsbaum, Philip. *Theory of Criticism.* Bloomington: Indiana UP, 1970. In the tradition of Richards and Leavis.

124.   Jay, Gregory S., and David Miller, eds. *After Strange Texts: The Role of Theory in the Study of Literature.* University: U of Alabama P, 1985. Argues that the choice of theory alters the practice of reading, which in turn calls forth new theories.

125.   Jayne, Edward. *Negative Poetics.* Iowa City: U of Iowa P, 1992. Argues that lying is fundamental in fictional narration and that this fact requires changes in current critical theories; examines career of Barthes.

126.   Kamuf, Peggy. *Signature Pieces: On the Institutions of Authorship.* Ithaca: Cornell UP, 1989. On authority, writing, and authorial identity.

127.   Kaplan, E. Ann, ed. *Postmodernism and Its Discontents.* London: Verso, 1988.

128.   Kavanagh, Thomas M., ed. *The Limits of Theory.* Stanford: Stanford UP, 1989.

129.   Kermode, Frank. *Forms of Attention.* Chicago: U of Chicago P, 1985. Account and critique of recent critical theory.

130.   ———. *The Genesis of Secrecy: On the Interpretation of Narrative.* Cambridge: Harvard UP, 1979. Wide-ranging discussion of interpretation through reading of the Gospels, especially Mark.

131.   Kermode (book on). Gorak, Jan. *Critic of Crisis: A Study of Frank Kermode.* Columbia: U of Missouri P, 1987.

132.   Kermode (book on). Tudeau-Clayton, Margaret, and Martin Warner, eds. *Addressing Frank Kermode: Essays in Criticism and Interpretation.* Urbana: U of Illinois P, 1991.

133.   Kirwan, James. *Literature, Rhetoric, Metaphysics: Literary Theory and Literary Aesthetics.* London: Routledge, 1990. Surveys theorists from Plato to Derrida to ask whether criticism can ever be consistent with its own subject, literary texts.

134.   Koelb, Clayton, and Susan Noakes, eds. *The Comparative Perspective on Literature: Approaches to Theory and Practice.* Ithaca: Cornell UP, 1988.

135.   Krieger, Murray, ed. *The Aims of Representation: Subject/Text/History.* New York: Columbia UP, 1987. Essays on the criticism of consciousness, deconstruction, and the theory of social power.

136.   Kurrik, Maire. *Literature and Negation.* New York: Columbia UP, 1979. Studies the presence and role of negation in literary and philosophical texts.

137.   Lefevere, André. *Literary Knowledge: A Polemical and Programmatic Essay on Its Nature and Growth, Relevance and Transmission.* Assen, Neth.: Van Gorcum, 1977.

138.   Lerner, Laurence, ed. *Reconstructing Literature.* Oxford: Blackwell, 1983. Eight essays critically assess the influence of Marxism, feminism, deconstruction, and structuralism.

139.   Liu, James J. Y. *Chinese Theories of Literature.* Chicago: U of Chicago P, 1975. Presents Chinese theories with references to contemporary Western theories.

140.   ———. *Language—Paradox—Poetics: A Chinese Perspective.* Ed. Richard John Lynn. Princeton: Princeton UP, 1988. Argues that Chinese poetry takes a deictic ("pointing"), not mimetic, view of language.

141.   Livingston, Paisley. *Literary Knowledge: Humanistic Inquiry and the Philosophy of Science.* Ithaca: Cornell UP, 1988. Argues against theorists who have used one school of the philosophy of science to support skeptical

epistemological claims; uses Wittgenstein and philosophy of science to argue that reliable knowledge of reality is possible.

142.   ———. *Literature and Rationality: Ideas of Agency in Theory and Fiction*. Cambridge: Cambridge UP, 1991. Challenges poststructuralist notions of science and their relation to criticism and theory.

143.   MacCabe, Colin. *Tracking the Signifier: Theoretical Essays on Film, Linguistics, and Literature*. Minneapolis: U of Minnesota P, 1985.

144.   Macksey, Richard, ed. *Velocities of Change: Critical Essays from* MIN. Baltimore: Johns Hopkins UP, 1974. Substantial collection by major critics from an important journal.

145.   Malone, David H., ed. *The Frontiers of Criticism*. Los Angeles: Hennessy, 1974. Essays by Wellek, Hassan, Girard, and others.

146.   Marshall, Donald G., ed. *Literature as Philosophy, Philosophy as Literature*. Iowa City: U of Iowa P, 1987. Twenty-one essays on theory, philosophical issues, and philosophical and literary texts from Plato to Derrida.

147.   McCallum, Pamela. *Literature and Method: Towards a Critique of I. A. Richards, T. S. Eliot and F. R. Leavis*. London: Gill, 1983.

148.   McCormick, Peter J. *Fictions, Philosophies, and the Problems of Poetics*. Ithaca: Cornell UP, 1988. Draws on analytic and hermeneutic philosophy to argue that fiction can give us "truth" and ethical insights.

149.   McGann, Jerome J. *A Critique of Modern Textual Criticism*. Chicago: U of Chicago P, 1983. Shows how procedures of textual editing connect with contemporary theory, particularly on issues of authorial intention and authority.

150.   ———. *The Textual Condition*. Princeton: Princeton UP, 1991. Argues that texts are unstable because they enter a social process in which they develop and change.

151.   ———, ed. *Textual Criticism and Literary Interpretation*. Chicago: U of Chicago P, 1985. Eight essays on literary texts from Chaucer to contemporary drama, two general essays.

152.   Michaels, Walter Benn, and Steven Knapp. *Against Theory 2: Sentence Meaning, Hermeneutics*. Berkeley: Center for Hermeneutic Studies in Hellenistic and Modern Culture, 1986. Continues the debate started by the authors' essay "Against Theory."

153.   Mileur, Jean-Pierre. *The Critical Romance: The Critic as Reader, Writer, Hero*. Madison: U of Wisconsin P, 1990. Argues that criticism is a late Romantic literary genre related to quest adventure.

154.   Miner, Earl. *Comparative Poetics: An Intercultural Essay on Theories of Literature*. Princeton: Princeton UP, 1990. Compares European and Asian— mainly Japanese—approaches.

155.   Mitchell, W. J. T., ed. *Against Theory: Literary Studies and the New Pragmatism*. Chicago: U of Chicago P, 1985. Replies to Knapp and Michaels's controversial essay "Against Theory."

156. Moore, Arthur K. *Contestable Concepts of Literary Theory.* Baton Rouge: Louisiana State UP, 1973. Wide-ranging topics.

157. Morris, Wesley. *Friday's Footprint: Structuralism and the Articulated Text.* Columbus: Ohio State UP, 1979. On myth, theory of literary language, psychoanalysis, and hermeneutics.

158. ———. *Towards a New Historicism.* Princeton: Princeton UP, 1972.

159. Morson, Gary Saul. *Literature and History: Theoretical Problems and Russian Case Studies.* Stanford: Stanford UP, 1986. Takes up broad theoretical issues.

160. Natoli, Joseph, ed. *Literary Theory's Future(s).* Urbana: U of Illinois P, 1989. Seven essays on Lacan, de Man, Girard, science, new historicism, feminism.

161. Newton, K. M. *In Defence of Literary Interpretation: Theory and Practice.* London: Macmillan, 1986. Defends interpretation as a pluralistic and "agonistic" activity against both skeptical relativists and those who demand a "true" interpretation, or one determined by institutional or social concerns.

162. Newton-De Molina, David, ed. *On Literary Intention.* Edinburgh: Edinburgh UP, 1976. Essays on the issue of authorial intention and literary interpretation by Wimsatt, Hirsch, and others.

163. Nicholson, Colin E., and Ranjit Chatterjee, eds. *Tropic Crucible: Self and Theory in Language and Literature.* Columbus: Ohio UP, 1984. Includes essays on regional literary studies as well as on other theoretical issues.

164. Noakes, Susan. *Timely Reading: Between Exegesis and Interpretation.* Ithaca: Cornell UP, 1988. Discusses views of reading and interpretation from Dante to Baudelaire.

165. Norris, Christopher. *Spinoza and the Origins of Modern Critical Theory.* Oxford: Blackwell, 1991.

166. O'Hara, Daniel T. *The Romance of Interpretation: Visionary Criticism from Pater to de Man.* New York: Columbia UP, 1985. Also chapters on Bloom, Hartman, Frye.

167. ———, ed. *Why Nietzsche Now?* Bloomington: Indiana UP, 1985. A good introduction to the intense current interest in Nietzsche found in many varieties of contemporary theory.

168. Olsen, Stein. *The End of Literary Theory.* Cambridge: Cambridge UP, 1987. Essays on theoretical topics; skeptical toward possibility of any general theory of literature.

169. ———. *The Structure of Literary Understanding.* Cambridge: Cambridge UP, 1978. Approaches critical problems from perspective of analytic philosophy.

170. O'Neill, John. *Critical Conventions: Interpretation in the Literary Arts and Sciences.* Norman: U of Oklahoma P, 1992. Examines literary and scientific writing in the light of Thomas Kuhn's theory of scientific change.

171.   Parrinder, Patrick. *Authors and Authority: English and American Criticism, 1750–1990*. New York: Columbia UP, 1991.

172.   Paulson, William R. *The Noise of Culture: Literary Texts in a World of Information*. Ithaca: Cornell UP, 1988. Discusses the relevance of information theory to modern literature and culture.

173.   Pavel, Thomas. *Fictional Worlds*. Cambridge: Harvard UP, 1986. On the semantics of fiction; draws on analytic philosophy to get beyond structuralist and poststructuralist critiques of referentiality.

174.   Peckham, Morse. *Man's Rage for Chaos: Biology, Behavior, and the Arts*. Philadelphia: Chilton, 1965. Work of art provide experiences that increase the audience's capacity to survive in real environments.

175.   Perkins, David. *Is Literary History Possible?* Baltimore: Johns Hopkins UP, 1992.

176.   ———, ed. *Theoretical Issues in Literary History*. Cambridge: Harvard UP, 1991.

177.   Petrey, Sandy. *Speech Acts and Literary Theory*. New York: Routledge, 1990. Discusses speech-act theory developed by the philosophers Austin and Searle as used by de Man, Derrida, Fish, and others.

178.   Radford, Colin, and Sally Minogue. *The Nature of Criticism*. Brighton, Eng.: Harvester, 1981. Looks at controversies between critics and at actual critical studies to analyze critical argument and evaluation.

179.   Raval, Suresh. *Metacriticism*. Athens: U of Georgia P, 1984. Broad survey of theorists and schools.

180.   Reichert, John. *Making Sense of Literature*. Chicago: U of Chicago P, 1977. Sees understanding and evaluation as efforts to assess how an author intends a reader to respond to a work.

181.   Reiss, Timothy. *The Meaning of Literature*. Ithaca: Cornell UP, 1992. Traces development, from seventeenth century on, of concept that literature embodies universal values.

182.   ———. *The Uncertainty of Analysis: Problems in Truth, Meaning, and Culture*. Ithaca: Cornell UP, 1988. Wide-ranging essays on semiotics, Bakhtin, Sartre, Derrida, Kristeva, and other theorists and issues.

183.   Rooney, Ellen. *Seductive Reasoning: Pluralism as the Problematic of Contemporary Literary Theory*. Ithaca: Cornell UP, 1989. Questions the premises of pluralism; examines the work of Hirsch, Booth, Fish, de Man, and Jameson, using Marxist, feminist, and poststructuralist theory.

184.   Ruthven, K. K. *Critical Assumptions*. Cambridge: Cambridge UP, 1979. Discusses a number of major concepts and issues.

185.   Salusinszky, Imre, ed. *Criticism in Society: Interviews with Jacques Derrida, Northrop Frye, Harold Bloom, Geoffrey Hartman, Frank Kermode, Edward Said, Barbara Johnson, Frank Lentricchia and J. Hillis Miller*. London: Routledge, 1987.

186.   Schauber, Ellen, and Ellen Spolsky. *The Bounds of Interpretation: Linguis-tic Theory and Literary Text.* Stanford: Stanford UP, 1986. Adopts the "preference model" of the linguist Jackendoff and argues its merits with references to a wide range of contemporary theories and issues.

187.   Schleifer, Ronald. *Rhetoric and Death: The Language of Modernism and Postmodern Discourse Theory.* Urbana: U of Illinois P, 1990. Focusing on the concept of death, pairs theorists with creative writers, including Jakob-son and Yeats, Barthes and Lawrence, Lacan and Conrad, Derrida and Stevens.

188.   Scholes, Robert. *Protocols of Reading.* New Haven: Yale UP, 1989. Dis-cusses interpretation and the ethics of reading in response to deconstruc-tion, feminism, and mass culture.

189.   Schulze, Leonard, and Walter Wetzels, eds. *Literature and History.* Lan-ham: UP of America, 1983.

190.   Schwarz, Daniel R. *The Case for a Humanistic Poetics.* Philadelphia: U of Pennsylvania P, 1991. Argues for dialogue between traditional humanistic and recent theories of literature; discusses reading, de Man, interpretive communities, ethics.

191.   Serres, Michel. *Hermes: Literature, Science, Philosophy.* Trans. and ed. Josue V. Harari and David F. Bell. Baltimore: Johns Hopkins UP, 1983. Collection showing the unique range and ideas of a leading French thinker.

192.   ———. *The Parasite.* Trans. R. Lawrence. Baltimore: Johns Hopkins UP, 1982. Unique perspective and stimulating speculations.

193.   Shaffer, E. S., ed. *Comparative Criticism: A Yearbook.* Cambridge: Cam-bridge UP, 1980– . Annual with section of essays on theoretical topics, selection of translations of literature and criticism, review essays on critical topics, and bibliography of translations and of comparative literature in Britain and Ireland. Vol. 2 (1980) is on reader-response criticism; vol. 3 (1981) on rhetoric and history, with bibliography on rhetorical studies, 1970–80; vol. 5 (1983) on hermeneutic criticism, with essays on Fish and Gadamer, and a bibliography on literary and biblical interpretation; vol. 7 (1985) on "boundaries of literary theory," with essays on Derrida, Marxism, structuralism and semiotics, and Bakhtin; vol. 9 (1987) on cultural percep-tions and literary values; vol. 11 (1989) on the future of the disciplines.

194.   Sharratt, Bernard. *The Literary Labyrinth: Contemporary Critical Dis-course.* Brighton, Eng.: Harvester, 1984.

195.   Shaw, Peter. *The War against the Intellect: Episodes in the Decline of Discourse.* Iowa City: U of Iowa P, 1989. Critique of current literary theory, feminist criticism, and literary study generally.

196.   Shawcross, John T. *Intentionality and the New Traditionalism: Some Limi-nal Means to Literary Revisionism.* University Park: Pennsylvania State UP, 1992. Defends concept of authorial intention in the critical interpretation of literary texts.

197.   Shusterman, Richard. *The Object of Literary Criticism.* Amsterdam: Ro-

dopi, 1984. On the nature of the literary work of art and on interpretation and evaluation of it; draws mainly on Leavis and the New Critics.

198. ———. *T. S. Eliot and the Philosophy of Criticism.* New York: Columbia UP, 1988.

199. Siebers, Tobin. *The Ethics of Criticism.* Ithaca: Cornell UP, 1988. Elicits an implicit moral strain in contemporary theory from deconstruction to feminism while arguing against debilitating forms of skepticism or ethical demands.

200. ———. *Morals and Stories.* New York: Columbia UP, 1992. Discusses philosophers and novelists to argue that literature develops knowledge about moral character.

201. Silverman, David, and Brian Torode. *The Material Word: Some Theories of Language and Its Limits.* London: Routledge, 1980. A survey of theories from Althusser and Wittgenstein to Husserl, Barthes, and the poststructuralists.

202. Slattery, Mary Francis. *The Theory and Aesthetic Evaluation of Literature.* Selinsgrove: Susquehanna UP; London: Associated UP, 1989. Argues for a theory of evaluation and opposes deconstruction.

203. Smith, Barbara Herrnstein. *Contingencies of Values: Alternative Perspectives for Critical Theory.* Cambridge: Harvard UP, 1988.

204. ———. *On the Margins of Discourse: The Relation of Literature to Language.* Chicago: U of Chicago P, 1979. Collection of essays on contemporary theory.

205. Smith, Paul. *Discerning the Subject.* Minneapolis: U of Minnesota P, 1988.

206. Spanos, William V., Paul A. Bové, and Daniel O'Hara, eds. *The Question of Textuality: Strategies of Reading in Contemporary American Criticism.* Bloomington: Indiana UP, 1982.

207. Spariosu, Mihai, ed. *Mimesis in Contemporary Theory: An Interdisciplinary Approach.* Vol. 1: *The Literary and the Philosophical Debate.* Philadelphia: Benjamins, 1984. Only volume 1 has been published.

208. Strelka, Joseph P., ed. *Anagogic Qualities of Literature.* Yearbook of Comparative Criticism 4. University Park: Pennsylvania State UP, 1971. Relations of literature to mystic and esoteric traditions.

209. ———, ed. *Literary Criticism and Philosophy.* Yearbook of Comparative Criticism 10. University Park: Pennsylvania State UP, 1983.

210. ———, ed. *The Personality of the Critic.* Yearbook of Comparative Criticism 6. University Park: Pennsylvania State UP, 1973.

211. ———, ed. *Problems of Literary Evaluation.* Yearbook of Comparative Criticism 2. University Park: Pennsylvania State UP, 1969.

212. Sussman, Henry. *The Hegelian Aftermath: Readings in Hegel, Kierkegaard, Freud, Proust, and James.* Baltimore: Johns Hopkins UP, 1982.

213. Sussman, Herbert L., ed. *At the Boundaries.* Boston: Dept. of English,

Northeastern U, 1983. Essays on Barthes and Derrida by Culler, on cultural criticism by Graff, and on defining a literary text by Joseph Margolis.

214. ———, ed. *Literary History: Theory and Practice*. Boston: Northeastern UP, 1984. Three essays on feminism, deconstruction, and literary history.

215. Sychrava, Juliet. *Schiller to Derrida: Idealism in Aesthetics*. Cambridge: Cambridge UP, 1989.

216. Szondi, Peter. *On Textual Understanding*. Trans. Harvey Mendelsohn. Minneapolis: U of Minnesota P, 1986. Discusses German Romanticism, Diderot, Benjamin, the poetry of Celan.

217. Tallis, Raymond. *In Defence of Realism*. London: Arnold, 1988. Attacks current critical trends as inimical to the development of fiction.

218. Thurley, Geoffrey. *Counter-Modernism in Current Critical Theory*. London: Macmillan, 1983. Argues against the formalist, structuralist, poststructuralist, and Marxist theories and rethinks the traditional theory that poetry presents and expresses human experiences and feelings.

Todorov, Tzvetan. *Literature and Its Theorists: A Personal View of Twentieth-Century Criticism*. See entry 548.

219. Turner, Mark. *Reading Minds: The Study of English in the Age of Cognitive Science*. Princeton: Princeton UP, 1991. Develops concept of literary study based on a cognitive view of language and literature.

220. Valdés, Mario J., and Owen J. Miller, eds. *Identity of the Literary Text*. Toronto: U of Toronto P, 1985. Wide-ranging collection emphasizing structuralism, deconstruction, hermeneutics, and ideological criticism.

221. Valesio, Paolo. *Novantiqua: Rhetorics as a Contemporary Theory*. Bloomington: Indiana UP, 1980. Reflects the current revival of interest in traditional rhetoric as an approach to contemporary theoretical issues in many fields.

222. Vickers, Brian. *In Defense of Rhetoric*. New York: Oxford UP, 1988. Broad historical survey and defense of rhetoric's importance in understanding all human culture.

223. Watson, George. *The Certainty of Literature: Essays in Polemic*. London: Harvester, 1989. Agrees that theory has a long tradition but attacks skepticism in recent theories.

224. ———. *The Discipline of English: A Guide to Critical Theory and Practice*. London: Macmillan, 1978.

225. Weber, Samuel. *Institution and Interpretation*. Minneapolis: U of Minnesota P, 1987. Essays on Derrida, Fish, Marxism, psychoanalysis, and other topics.

226. Weinstein, Fred. *History and Theory after the Fall: An Essay on Interpretation*. Chicago: U of Chicago P, 1990.

227. Wilden, Anthony. *The Rules Are No Game: The Strategy of Communication*. London: Routledge, 1986. Wide-ranging and interdisciplinary.

228.   ———. *System and Structure: Essays in Communication and Exchange*. 2nd ed. New York: Tavistock, 1980. Far-ranging work bringing together systems and communication theory with literature and culture.

229.   Worton, Michael, and Judith Still, eds. *Intertextuality: Theories and Practices*. Manchester: Manchester UP, 1990. Essays discuss interrelations among texts from diverse theoretical perspectives.

230.   Yarbrough, Stephen R. *Deliberate Criticism: Toward a Postmodern Humanism*. Athens: U of Georgia P, 1992.

Law and Literary Theory

Fish, Stanley. *Doing What Comes Naturally: Change, Rhetoric, and the Practice of Theory in Literature and Legal Studies*. See entry 835.

231.   Levinson, Sanford, and Steven Mailloux. *Interpreting Law and Literature: A Hermeneutic Reader*. Evanston: Northwestern UP, 1988. Contributors include Fish, Graff, and others, writing on legal and literary theory, Constitutional interpretation and the legislators' intention, and applications of deconstruction to legal interpretation.

232.   Posner, Richard A. *Law and Literature: A Misunderstood Relation*. Cambridge: Harvard UP, 1988. Essays on law and literature and critiques of recent applications of literary theory to the law and to legal interpretation.

233.   Weisberg, Richard H. *Poethics and Other Strategies of Law and Literature*. New York: Columbia UP, 1992. Discusses legal themes in works from Shakespeare to Toni Morrison; studies the debasement of legal rhetoric in Nazi-occupied France; criticizes Posner.

234.   White, James Boyd. *Heracles' Bow: Essays on the Rhetoric and Poetics of the Law*. Madison: U of Wisconsin P, 1986. By a leading student of the relation of law and literature.

235.   ———. *Justice as Translation: An Essay in Cultural and Legal Criticism*. Chicago: U of Chicago P, 1990. Explores possibility of cultural criticism, nature of conceptual language, other topics.

236.   ———. *The Legal Imagination*. 2nd ed. Chicago: U of Chicago P, 1985.

237.   ———. *When Words Lose Their Meaning: Constitutions and Reconstitutions of Language, Character, and Community*. Chicago: U of Chicago P, 1984. Examines a wide range of literary and legal texts, ancient and modern.

Religion, Biblical Interpretation, and Literary Theory

Bloom, Harold. *Kabbalah and Criticism*. See entry 1002.

———. *Ruin the Sacred Truths: Poetry and Belief from the Bible to the Present*. See entry 1004.

238.   Boyarin, Daniel. *Intertextuality and the Reading of Midrash*. Bloomington:

Indiana UP, 1990. Rabbinic scriptural interpretation in the light of contemporary theoretical concepts.

239.   Edwards, Michael. *Towards a Christian Poetics*. London: Macmillan, 1984.

240.   Faur, José. *Golden Doves with Silver Dots: Semiotics and Textuality in Rabbinic Tradition*. Bloomington: Indiana UP, 1986. Connects contemporary theory with ancient rabbinic biblical interpretation.

241.   Fiddes, Paul S. *Freedom and Limit: A Dialogue between Literature and Christian Doctrine*. New York: St. Martin's, 1991. Argues that theological ideas can aid in interpreting literary texts.

242.   Fisch, Harold. *Poetry with a Purpose: Biblical Poetics and Interpretation*. Bloomington: Indiana UP, 1988.

Frieden, Ken. *Freud's Dream of Interpretation*. See entry 896.

Frye, Northrop. *The Great Code: The Bible and Literature*. See entry 1426.

————. *Words with Power: Being a Second Study of* The Bible and Literature. See entry 1435.

243.   Handelman, Susan A. *Fragments of Redemption: Jewish Thought and Literary Theory in Benjamin, Scholem, and Levinas*. Bloomington: Indiana UP, 1991.

244.   ————. *The Slayers of Moses: The Emergence of Rabbinic Interpretation in Modern Literary Theory*. Albany: State U of New York P, 1982. Relates ancient and rabbinic interpretive practices to deconstruction and other contemporary theories.

245.   Hartman, Geoffrey H., and Sanford Budick, eds. *Midrash and Literature*. New Haven: Yale UP, 1986. Essays on rabbinic methods of biblical interpretation and their relevance to literary study; includes Derrida's "Shibboleth."

246.   Prickett, Stephen. *Reading the Text: Biblical Interpretation and Literary Theory*. Oxford: Blackwell, 1990. Discusses the history of, and present relations between, the two fields.

247.   ————. *Words and* The Word: *Language, Poetics and Biblical Interpretation*. Cambridge: Cambridge UP, 1986.

248.   Schneidau, Herbert N. *Sacred Discontent: The Bible and Western Tradition*. Baton Rouge: Louisiana State UP, 1976. Argues that the Bible provides the key model in Western tradition for the concept of the book.

249.   Schwartz, Regina, ed. *The Book and the Text: The Bible and Literary Theory*. Oxford: Blackwell, 1990. Twelve essays relate literary theory to the Bible.

250.   Seerveld, Calvin. *A Christian Critique of Art and Literature*. Toronto: Assn. for the Advancement of Christian Scholarship, 1968.

Translation and Theory

251.   Benjamin, Andrew. *Translation and the Nature of Philosophy: A New Theory of Words*. London: Routledge, 1989. Examines conceptions of transla-

tion in Plato, Seneca, Heidegger, Donald Davidson, Benjamin, and Freud and sets out a theory of words based on the interplay between philosophy and translation.

252.   Biguenet, John, and Rainer Schulte, eds. *Theories of Translation: An Anthology of Essays from Dryden to Derrida.* Chicago: U of Chicago P, 1992.

253.   Graham, Joseph F., ed. *Difference in Translation.* Ithaca: Cornell UP, 1985. Essays by Derrida and others.

254.   Hermans, Theo, ed. *The Manipulation of Literature: Studies in Literary Translation.* London: Croom Helm, 1985. Twelve essays by a working group trying to establish a theoretical model for translation.

255.   Larson, Mildred L., ed. *Translation: Theory and Practice: Tension and Interdependence.* Binghamton: Center for Research in Translation, 1991.

256.   Robinson, Douglas. *The Translator's Turn.* Baltimore: Johns Hopkins UP, 1991. Uses Bakhtin, Burke, and other theorists to criticize the theory that translators should find equivalent structures between languages.

257.   Rose, Marilyn Gaddis, ed. *Translation Spectrum: Essays in Theory and Practice.* Albany: State U of New York P, 1981.

258.   Schmidt, Dennis J., ed. *Hermeneutics and the Poetic Motion.* Binghamton: Center for Research in Translation, 1990. Twelve essays on culture and language, the "untranslatability" of poetry, and the theory of translation.

259.   Toury, Gideon. *In Search of a Theory of Translation.* Tel Aviv: Porter Inst. for Poetics and Semiotics, Tel Aviv U, 1980.

260.   Will, Frederic. *The Knife in the Stone: Essays in Literary Theory.* The Hague: Mouton, 1973. Theoretical reflections beginning from the issues raised by translation.

Institutions of Criticism: Pedagogy, Universities, Disciplines, Curriculum, the Canon Controversy

261.   Adams, Hazard. *Antithetical Essays in Literary Criticism and Liberal Education.* Gainesville: UP of Florida, 1990.

262.   Altieri, Charles. *Canons and Consequences: Reflections on the Ethical Force of Imaginative Ideals.* Evanston: Northwestern UP, 1990. The debate over the canon as a test of how literary theories approach values.

Atkins, G. Douglas, and Michael L. Johnson, eds. *Writing and Reading Differently: Deconstruction and the Teaching of Composition and Literature.* See entry 563.

263.   Bergonzi, Bernard. *Exploding English: Criticism, Theory, Culture.* New York: Oxford UP, 1990. On contemporary English studies in Britain and the United States; discusses influence of poststructuralism, psychoanalysis, Marxism, and feminism.

Bleich, David. *The Double Perspective: Language, Literacy, and Social Relations.* See entry 847.

Bourdieu, Pierre, and Jean-Claude Passeron. *Reproduction: In Education, Society and Culture.* See entry 1032.

264.　Bové, Paul. *Intellectuals in Power: A Genealogy of Critical Humanism.* New York: Columbia UP, 1986. Draws on Foucault to discuss the institution of criticism and a range of critics from Kant to contemporaries.

265.　Brooker, Peter, and Peter Humm, eds. *Dialogue and Difference: English into the Nineties.* London: Routledge, 1989. Fifteen essays dealing with the effect of literary and cultural theory on the content and practice of teaching.

266.　Burt, E. S., and Janie Vanpée, eds. *Reading the Archive: On Texts and Institutions. Yale French Studies* 77. New Haven: Yale UP, 1990.

267.　Cain, William E. *The Crisis in Criticism: Theory, Literature, and Reform in English Studies.* Baltimore: Johns Hopkins UP, 1984.

268.　Culler, Jonathan. *Framing the Sign: Criticism and Its Institutions.* Norman: U of Oklahoma P, 1988.

Davis, Lennard J., and M. Bella Mirabella, eds. *Left Politics and the Literary Profession.* See entry 1040.

269.　Elbow, Peter. *What Is English?* New York: MLA; Urbana: NCTE, 1990.

270.　Engell, James, and David Perkins. *Teaching Literature: What Is Needed Now.* Cambridge: Harvard UP, 1988. Thirteen essays by leading critics and theorists.

271.　Fiedler, Leslie A., and Houston A. Baker, Jr., eds. *English Literature: Opening Up the Canon.* Selected Papers from the English Institute, 1979, ns 4. Baltimore: Johns Hopkins UP, 1981. Essays on opening the canon and the institution of literary study.

272.　Foulkes, A. P. *The Search for Literary Meaning: A Semiotic Approach to the Problem of Interpretation in Education.* Bern: Lang, 1975.

273.　Fromm, Harold. *Academic Capitalism and Literary Value.* Athens: U of Georgia P, 1991. Criticizes recent trends in literary study.

274.　Gabriel, Susan L., and Isaiah Smithson, eds. *Gender in the Classroom: Power and Pedagogy.* Urbana: U of Illinois P, 1990.

275.　Gates, Henry Louis, Jr. *Loose Canons: Notes on the Culture Wars.* New York: Oxford UP, 1992.

276.　Gorak, Jan. *The Making of the Modern Canon: Charismatic Critics: Frye, Gombrich, Kermode and Said.* London: Athlone, 1991. Studies critics to see how the literary canon is actually formed historically.

277.　Graff, Gerald. *Professing Literature: An Institutional History.* Chicago: U of Chicago P, 1987. Sets debates over literary study in the historical context of academic literary study.

278.   Graff, Gerald, and Michael Warner, ed. *The Origins of Literary Studies in America: A Documentary Anthology.* New York: Routledge, 1988.

279.   Graff, Gerald, and Reginald Gibbons, eds. *Criticism in the University.* Evanston: Northwestern UP, 1985. Essays on the academicization of literary study, curricular reform, and related topics.

280.   Gribble, James. *Literary Education: A Revaluation.* Cambridge: Cambridge UP, 1983. Considers relevance of various theoretical issues in education, particularly structuralism and deconstruction, in relation to the education of the emotions.

281.   Henricksen, Bruce, and Thaïs Morgan, eds. *Reorientations: Critical Theories and Pedagogies.* Urbana: U of Illinois P, 1990.

        Hirsch, E. D., Jr. *Cultural Literacy: What Every American Needs to Know.* See entry 779.

        ———. *The Philosophy of Composition.* See entry 780.

282.   Hogan, Patrick Colm. *The Politics of Interpretation: Ideology, Professionalism, and the Study of Literature.* New York: Oxford UP, 1990.

283.   Johnson, Barbara, ed. *The Pedagogical Imperative: Teaching as a Literary Genre. Yale French Studies* 63. New Haven: Yale UP, 1982. Essays by de Man, Derrida, and others, mostly concerning literary theory's relation to teaching.

284.   Kaplan, Carey, and Ellen Cronan Rose. *The Canon and the Common Reader.* Knoxville: U of Tennessee P, 1991. Discusses controversy over the canon, using Samuel Johnson's concept of the common reader.

        Kauffman, Linda, ed. *Feminism and Institutions: Dialogues on Feminist Theory.* See entry 1617.

285.   Kecht, Maria-Regina, ed. *Pedagogy Is Politics: Literary Theory and Critical Teaching.* Urbana: U of Illinois P, 1992.

286.   Kernan, Alvin. *The Death of Literature.* New Haven: Yale UP, 1990. Examines current state of literary study, addressing topics from censorship to literacy, print, and mass-produced art.

287.   Kreiswirth, Martin, and Mark Cheetham, eds. *Theory between the Disciplines: Authority/Vision/Politics.* Ann Arbor: U of Michigan P, 1990.

288.   Lanham, Richard. *Literacy and the Survival of Humanism.* New Haven: Yale UP, 1983.

289.   Lauter, Paul. *Canons and Context.* New York: Oxford UP, 1991. Essays in two sections: "Canon and the Literary Profession" and "The University and the Republic."

290.   Lindenberger, Herbert. *The History in Literature: On Value, Genre, Institutions.* New York: Columbia UP, 1990. Examines recent turn to history in literary study; discusses canon, values, literary institutions, historicity of texts.

291.   Lloyd-Jones, Richard, and Andrea A. Lunsford, eds. *The English Coalition*

Conference: Democracy through Language. Urbana: NCTE and MLA, 1989. Report of a conference on the present and future of English studies.

292.   Morton, Donald, and Mas'ud Zavarzadeh, eds. *Theory/Pedagogy/Politics: Texts for Change.* Urbana: U of Illinois P, 1991.

293.   Nelson, Cary, ed. *Theory in the Classroom.* Urbana: U of Illinois P, 1987. Essays on feminism, deconstruction, psychoanalysis, and various political and social approaches to teaching literature and writing.

294.   Ohmann, Richard. *English in America: A Radical View of the Profession.* New York: Oxford UP, 1976.

295.   ———. *The Politics of Letters.* Middletown: Wesleyan UP, 1987.

296.   Olson, Gary A., and Irene Gale, ed. *(Inter)Views: Cross-Disciplinary Perspectives on Rhetoric and Literacy.* Carbondale: Southern Illinois UP, 1991. Interviews with philosophers and theorists, including Chomsky, Derrida, Freire, Geertz, Rorty, and Spivak, with response essays for each figure on teaching rhetoric to freshmen.

Pagano, Jo Anne. *Exiles and Communities: Teaching in the Patriarchal Wilderness.* See entry 1645.

297.   Peterfreund, Stuart, ed. *Critical Theory and the Teaching of Literature.* Boston: Northeastern UP, 1985.

298.   Robbins, Bruce, ed. *Intellectuals: Aesthetics, Politics, Academics.* Minneapolis: U of Minnesota P, 1990. Fifteen essays by Spivak, Said, and others on topics and figures from Foucault and Gramsci to de Man.

299.   Scholes, Robert. *Textual Power: Literary Theory and the Teaching of English.* New Haven: Yale UP, 1985.

300.   Small, Ian. *Conditions for Criticism: Authority, Knowledge, and Literature in the Late Nineteenth Century.* New York: Oxford UP, 1991. Examines changes in the practice of literary criticism and its later institutionalization in the university, along with the effect on criticism of changes in various other disciplines.

Sussman, Henry S. *High Resolution: Critical Theory and the Problem of Literacy.* See entry 1382.

301.   Thompson, Ann, and Helen Wilcox, eds. *Teaching Women: Feminism and English Studies.* Manchester: Manchester UP, 1989.

Ulmer, Gregory L. *Applied Grammatology: Post(e)-Pedagogy from Jacques Derrida to Joseph Beuys.* See entry 609.

302.   Von Hallberg, Robert, ed. *Canons.* Chicago: U of Chicago P, 1984. Collection of essays on canons—including formal and informal lists of the "best" or "most important" books—and on the theoretical problems they raise.

303.   Watkins, Evan. *Work Time: English Departments and the Circulation of Social Value.* Stanford: Stanford UP, 1989.

304.   Weber, Samuel, ed. *Demarcating the Disciplines: Philosophy, Literature,*

Art. Minneapolis: U of Minnesota P, 1986. Addresses institutional and pedagogical issues emerging from contemporary theory.

305.   Widdowson, Peter, ed. *Re-reading English: Essays in Literature and Criticism in Higher Education.* London: Methuen, 1982. Essays examine alternative approaches to teaching English, including Marxist, political, feminist, and popular culture perspectives.

Winders, James A. *Gender, Theory, and the Canon: From Intellectual History to Cultural Criticism.* See entry 1689.

2. Russian Formalism and Prague Structuralism

The dominant schools in contemporary critical theory participate in the general turn of twentieth-century philosophy toward language. The *Russian formalists* focused on the linguistic devices by which poets arrest our clichéd and automatized response to words and experience and thereby make both new again. The formalists rapidly turned to linguistics to elaborate analytic models of language, plot, and larger textual structures. The linguist and "poetician" Roman Jakobson was an important mediator between the formalist critics and structural linguistics. The latter was invented at the turn of the century by the Swiss linguist Ferdinand de Saussure; his *Course in General Linguistics* (1915) was compiled by students from their lecture notes after his death and has profoundly influenced fields beyond linguistics, including anthropology, folklore, and literary criticism. Saussure distinguished between *langue* and *parole language* and *speech*. Language could be described in a system of rules, which each specific utterance (parole) followed. Distinguishing between the "synchronic," the language system as it existed at a particular moment, and the "diachronic," the evolution of a language system, Saussure turned linguists' attention away from the historical concerns that had underpinned the philological study of literature and toward the ahistorical analysis of a linguistic system. A number of Russian critics steadily extended this sort of formal analytic technique to all the elements of literature—language, character, plot, and theme—finally conceiving the literary work as an integrated structure of subsystems. For example, Vladimir Propp studied plot in folktales. Instead of examining the interconnection of character, event, and theme in individual stories, he described a rule-governed system that lay behind a group of tales. *Functions*, each connecting an agent and a single act, followed each other in a determinate sequence, much as grammar governed the sequence of words in an acceptable sentence.

Russian formalism was found by the Communist authorities to conflict with Marxism and was consequently cut off short in Russia. But Jakobson had earlier moved to Prague, where the original ideas were elaborated by a group of theorists (among them René Wellek, who, like Jakobson, eventually settled in the United States). Russian formalism and Prague structuralism later emerged in France, partly mediated by a young Bulgarian, Tzvetan Todorov. French critics themselves rediscovered Saussure, largely stimulated by Claude Lévi-Strauss's application of the *structural method* to problems in anthropology, from kinship systems to the analysis of myths, and by the psychoanalyst Jacques Lacan's reconstruction of Freudian theory on the basis of structural linguistics. French structuralism and semiotics (the study of systems of signs and signifying activities in all areas of culture) reached the United States in the late 1960s, where it linked up in complex ways with a second and autonomous stream of formalist thinking, which is described in chapter 3, "New Criticism."

Introductory Books

306.   Bennett, Tony. *Formalism and Marxism*. London: Methuen, 1979. Examines Russian formalists and recent Marxist critics.

307.   Erlich, Victor. *Russian Formalism: History-Doctrine*. 3rd ed. New Haven: Yale UP, 1981. The standard survey and history.

308.   Galan, F. W. *Historic Structures: The Prague School Project, 1928–1946*. Austin: U of Texas P, 1985.

309.   Steiner, Peter. *Russian Formalism: A Metapoetics*. Ithaca: Cornell UP, 1984.

310.   Striedter, Jurij. *Literary Structure, Evolution, and Value: Russian Formalism and Czech Structuralism Reconsidered*. Cambridge: Harvard UP, 1989.

    Thompson, Ewa M. *Russian Formalism and Anglo-American New Criticism: A Comparative Study*. See entry 369.

Books and Collections
by Representatives of the Approach

311.   Bailey, Richard W., Ladislav Matejka, and Peter Steiner, eds. *The Sign: Semiotics around the World*. Ann Arbor: Michigan Slavic, 1978.

312.   Bann, Stephen, and John E. Bowlt, eds. *Russian Formalism: A Collection of Articles and Texts in Translation*. New York: Barnes, 1973. Ranges from early formalism to contemporary essays on formalism by Kristeva, Eco, Todorov, and others.

313.   Garvin, Paul L., comp. and trans. *A Prague School Reader on Esthetics, Literary Structure, and Style*. Washington: Georgetown UP, 1964. Includes a critical bibliography of the group that carried on Russian formalism.

314.   Lemon, Lee T., and Marion J. Reis, eds. and trans. *Russian Formalism*. Lincoln: U of Nebraska P, 1965. Basic essays by the leading theorists Shklovsky, Tomashevsky, and Eikhenbaum.

315.   Matejka, Ladislav, and Irwin R. Titunik, eds. *Semiotics of Art: Prague School Contributions*. Cambridge: MIT P, 1976. Includes several essays on drama and on poetry.

316.   Matejka, Ladislav, and Krystyna Pomorska, eds. *Readings in Russian Poetics: Formalist and Structuralist Views*. Cambridge: MIT P, 1971. Excellent anthology with concluding essays by the editors reviewing Russian formalism.

317.   Mukařovský, Jan. *Aesthetic Function: Norm and Value as Social Facts*. Trans. Mark E. Suino. Ann Arbor: Dept. of Slavic Languages and Literatures, U of Michigan, 1970.

318.   ———. *On Poetic Language*. Trans. and ed. John Burbank and Peter Steiner. Lisse, Neth.: Ridder, 1976.

319.   ———. *Structure, Sign, and Function: Selected Essays*. Trans. John Burbank and Peter Steiner. New Haven: Yale UP, 1978.

320.   ———. *The Word and Verbal Art: Selected Essays by Jan Mukařovský*. Trans. Peter Steiner. New Haven: Yale UP, 1977.

321.   O'Toole, L. M., and Ann Shukman, eds. *Formalism: History, Comparison, Genre*. Oxford: Holdan, 1978. Essays by formalists.

322.   ———, eds. and trans. *Formalist Theory*. Oxford: Holdan, 1977. With bibliography of translations of formalist writings.

323.   Propp, Vladimir. *Morphology of the Folktale*. Trans. Laurence Scott. Ed. Louis A. Wagner. Austin: U of Texas P, 1968. Analyzes the narrative structure of folktales.

324.   ———. *Theory and History of Folklore*. Trans. Ariadna Y. Martin and Richard P. Martin. Ed. Anatoly Liberman. Minneapolis: U of Minnesota P, 1984.

325.   Shklovsky, Viktor. *Theory of Prose*. Trans. Benjamin Sher. 1929. Elmwood Park: Dalkey Archive, 1990.

326.   Steiner, Peter, ed. *The Prague School: Selected Writings, 1929–1946*. Trans. John Burbank and Olga Hasty. Austin: U of Texas P, 1982.

Individual Authors

ROMAN JAKOBSON (1896–1982)

Born in Moscow, Roman Jakobson eventually emigrated to Prague and thence to the United States. His long life, wide-ranging erudition, and prolific writing have made him an influential figure in many disciplines, including linguistics, folklore, and literary theory. Together with the Russian formalists, he sought to identify the linguistic feature that universally distinguishes poetic language. This he found in special patterns of language—such as rhyme and meter—that went beyond the minimum requirements of grammar and gave a defined structure and identity to a verbal utterance. In a series of essays on poems in many languages, usually written in collaboration with a native speaker, Jakobson analyzed poetic structures in purely linguistic and usually binary terms. This concentration on the linguistic to the exclusion of social and moral matters has been questioned, and some critics (notably Michael Riffaterre) have argued that linguistic analysis, even within its own terms, elicits patterns too subtle and complex to have any effect on an actual reader. But many of Jakobson's terms and concepts not only have influenced linguistics and literary study but have been found fruitful in anthropology and other fields, and they played a key role in the transition from Russian formalism to French structuralism.

327.   *Language in Literature*. Ed. Krystyna Pomorska and Stephen Rudy. Cambridge: Belknap–Harvard UP, 1987. Excellent and comprehensive collection on literary theory and analysis.

328.   *On Language*. Ed. Linda R. Waugh and Monique Monville-Burston. Cambridge: Harvard UP, 1990. Includes previously untranslated and unpublished writings.

329.   *Pushkin and His Sculptural Myth*. Trans. and ed. John Burbank. The Hague: Mouton, 1975. A stylistic analysis of poems by Pushkin.

330.   *Selected Writings*. 8 vols. The Hague: Mouton, 1962– . Particularly relevant are vol. 3, *The Grammar of Poetry and the Poetry of Grammar*, ed. Stephen Rudy (1981); vol. 5, *Verse, Its Masters, and Explorers*, ed. Stephen Rudy and Martha Taylor (1979); and vol. 7, *Contributions to Comparative Mythology. Studies in Linguistics and Philology, 1972–1982*, ed. Stephen Rudy (1985).

331.   *Six Lectures on Sound and Meaning*. Trans. John Mepham. Cambridge: MIT P, 1978.

332.   *Verbal Art, Verbal Sign, Verbal Time*. Ed. Krystyna Pomorska and Stephen Rudy. Minneapolis: U of Minnesota P, 1984. Eleven essays selected by Jakobson to introduce his linguistic theories and work in poetics.

333.   Jakobson, Roman, and Krystyna Pomorska. *Dialogues*. Cambridge: MIT P, 1982.

334. Jakobson, Roman and Lawrence G. Jones. *Shakespeare's Verbal Art in Th'Expence of Spirit.* The Hague: Mouton, 1970.

Book on Jakobson

335. Holenstein, Elmar. *Roman Jakobson's Approach to Language: Phenomeno-logical Structuralism.* Trans. Catherine Schelbert and Tarcisius Schelbert. Bloomington: Indiana UP, 1976.

MIKHAIL M. BAKHTIN (1895–1975)

Though Mikhail Bakhtin's work has gained prominence only recently, it has evoked a strongly sympathetic response in a surprising variety of contemporary theorists, from Todorov and Wayne Booth to feminist and cultural critics. Given the special interest of cultural theorists in his work, it is not clear that he should be included among the Russian formalists. But his own thinking concentrated closely on the nature of literary language and genres. Against the formalist view of the literary text as a self-contained system, Bakhtin argued that virtually every utterance stands against a background of other utterances as reply, parody, allusion, polemic, or the like. Language is thus fundamentally "dialogical." The literary form that best reflects this reality is the novel, in which the most various voices resound without any simple unification or resolution. The novel is, in his terms, "polyphonic" or "heteroglossic."

Bakhtin traced the history of the dialogic form from Plato to modern novels with extraordinary erudition and energy. In his study of Rabelais, he tried to show how Rabelais's *Gargantua and Pantagruel* in its spirit and form reflected the contemporary world of "carnival," and he suggested that this atmosphere of temporary misrule was fundamental to many kinds of literature. Bakhtin's emphasis on dialogue and on a heterogeneous multiplicity of voices has appealed to cultural critics who wish to avoid the apparent dogmatism and potential totalitarianism of Marxist thought but who also seek a way of speaking about the social dimension of language and literature. Nevertheless, Bakhtin's focus on literary texts and on the nature of language, however broadened or social his view of it, gives him a strong affinity with the formalist tradition.

Bakhtin's bibliography is somewhat uncertain. There is evidence that he wrote or at least had a considerable role in books by students or colleagues on Freud, on formalism, and on Marxist theory of language.

336. *Art and Answerability: Early Philosophical Essays.* Ed. Michael Holquist and Vadim Liapunov. Trans. Liapunov. Austin: U of Texas P, 1990. Three early essays, with introduction by Holquist.

337. *The Dialogic Imagination: Four Essays.* Trans. Caryl Emerson and Michael

Holquist. Ed. Holquist. Austin: U of Texas P, 1981. Important essays on time, language, and the novel.

338.   *Problems of Dostoevsky's Poetics.* Trans. and ed. Caryl Emerson. Minneapolis: U of Minnesota P, 1984.

339.   *Rabelais and His World.* Trans. Helene Iswolsky. Bloomington: Indiana UP, 1984. Describes the oral and popular traditions of "carnival" as a context for Rabelais, with implications for culture and the novel.

340.   *Speech Genres and Other Late Essays.* Trans. Vern W. McGee. Ed. Caryl Emerson and Michael Holquist. Austin: U of Texas P, 1986.

341.   Bakhtin, Mikhail, and P. N. Medvedev. *The Formal Method in Literary Scholarship: A Critical Introduction to Sociological Poetics.* 1928. Trans. Albert J. Wehrle. Cambridge: Harvard UP, 1985. Connects formalism with Marxist and sociological approaches to language and literature.

342.   Vološinov, V. N. *Freudianism: A Marxist Critique.* 1927. Trans. I. R. Titunik. New York: Academic, 1976. Actually by Bakhtin, a Marxist critique of Freud and modern psychology, focusing on language, culture, and ideology.

343.   ———. *Marxism and the Philosophy of Language.* 1929. Trans. Ladislav Matejka and I. R. Titunik. New York: Seminar, 1973. Actually by Bakhtin, brings formalism and Marxism together.

Books on Bakhtin

344.   Bauer, Dale M., and Susan Jaret McKinstry, eds. *Feminism, Bakhtin, and the Dialogic.* Albany: State U of New York P, 1991.

345.   Berrong, Richard M. *Rabelais and Bakhtin: Popular Culture in Gargantua and Pantagruel.* Lincoln: U of Nebraska P, 1986. Critical of Bakhtin's *Rabelais and His World.*

346.   Clark, Katerina, and Michael Holquist. *Mikhail Bakhtin.* Cambridge: Belknap–Harvard UP, 1984. Excellent biography and introduction, with bibliography.

347.   Hirschkop, Ken, and David Shepherd, eds. *Bakhtin and Cultural Theory.* New York: St. Martin's, 1989.

348.   Holquist, Michael. *Dialogism: Bakhtin and His World.* New York: Routledge, 1991.

349.   Lodge, David. *After Bakhtin: Essays on Fiction and Criticism.* London: Routledge, 1990. Expounds and applies Bakhtin's ideas to modern novels from Austen to contemporary fiction.

350.   Morson, Gary Saul, and Caryl Emerson. *Mikhail Bakhtin: Creation of a Prosaics.* Stanford: Stanford UP, 1991.

351.   ———, eds. *Rethinking Bakhtin: Extensions and Challenges.* Evanston: Northwestern UP, 1989. Includes two previously untranslated texts by Bakhtin; with essays on his work.

352.   Patterson, David. *Literature and Spirit: Essays on Bakhtin and His Contemporaries*. Lexington: UP of Kentucky, 1988. Discusses Foucault, Lacan, Levinas, and Heidegger.

353.   Shukman, Ann, ed. *Bakhtin School Papers*. Oxford: Russian Poetics in Translation, in ass. with the Dept. of Literature, U of Essex, 1983.

        Todorov, Tzvetan. *Mikhail Bakhtin: The Dialogical Principle*. See entry 549.

RENÉ WELLEK (1903–)

A participant in the Prague structuralist circle that continued the work of the Russian formalists, René Wellek emigrated to the United States at the outbreak of World War II. During the 1930s, he came to feel the limitations of the historicist study of literature and with Austin Warren wrote *The Theory of Literature* (1949), in which the traditions of Russian formalism and Anglo-American New Criticism fuse. Reviewing the variety of existing approaches to literature, Wellek and Warren drew on Roman Ingarden (see chapter 6, "Hermeneutics and Phenomenology") to argue that literary works should be regarded as autonomous multilayered systems of signs, whose integrated structure should be described and analyzed by critics. In the 1930s, in a famous exchange with F. R. Leavis, the British critic and follower of I. A. Richards, Wellek defended the importance of literary theory and philosophical ideas in literary study, but in the 1980s, he argued against contemporary theories that he felt displaced the primacy of literature itself. In many essays, he has contributed analyses of key terms in literary history and criticism.

354.   *The Attack on Literature and Other Essays*. Chapel Hill: U of North Carolina P, 1982. Takes a dim view of recent developments in theory.

355.   *Concepts of Criticism*. Ed. Stephen G. Nichols, Jr. New Haven: Yale UP, 1963.

356.   *Confrontations: Studies in the Intellectual Relations between Germany, England, and the United States during the Nineteenth Century*. Princeton: Princeton UP, 1965.

357.   *Discriminations: Further Concepts of Criticism*. New Haven: Yale UP, 1970.

358.   *Four Critics: Croce, Valéry, Lukács, and Ingarden*. Seattle: U of Washington P, 1981.

        A History of Modern Criticism: 1750–1950. See entry 57.

359.   Wellek, René, and Austin Warren. *Theory of Literature*. 3rd ed. New York: Harcourt, 1956. Probably the most influential introduction to literary theory; surveys varieties of criticism and recommends formalist approach.

Books on Wellek

360.   Bucco, Martin. *René Wellek*. Boston: Twayne, 1981.

361.   Strelka, Joseph P., ed. *Literary Theory and Criticism: Festschrift Presented to René Wellek in Honor of His Eightieth Birthday*. 2 vols. Bern: Lang, 1984. Vast collection, first volume on theory, second on criticism.

3. New Criticism, English and American

An interest in the nature of language and meaning led the Englishman I. A. Richards to some historic experiments in criticism with Cambridge undergraduates: he asked them to write comments on poems whose authors and titles were withheld. In his book *Practical Criticism*, Richards subjected these "protocols" to devastating analysis, showing the generally slovenly and sentimental responses and preference for bad poems expressed by these presumably educated individuals. Richards proposed a general theory that poetry is a complex verbal artifact whose function is to order and regulate equally complex mental impulses. His work inspired a group of American critics, most importantly Cleanth Brooks and W. K. Wimsatt, to develop specific techniques for analyzing the complexities of poetic language. More obviously than the European formalists who were responding directly to the work of Ferdinand de Saussure, the founder of modern structural linguistics, the Anglo-American formalists, or *New Critics* as they came to be called, revived an older style of grammatical and rhetorical analysis that went back to antiquity and preceded the historical linguistics known as philology. They combined their analytic technique with a Coleridgean conception of a poem as a complex unity reconciling opposed ideas and feelings.

This native tradition of *close reading* came gradually to dominate the teaching of literature in America. Its theoretical structure was elaborated in brilliant essays by Brooks and Wimsatt and in their survey of the history of critical ideas and also in René Wellek and Austin Warren's influential *Theory of Literature*. Taught by the early pioneers of Russian formalism and Prague structuralism (see chapter 2), Wellek had emigrated from Prague to the United States and finally joined the faculty at Yale, where he became a colleague of Brooks, Wimsatt, and Robert Penn Warren. With them, he formed the first *Yale school* of formalism. Like Brooks, Wellek had been trained in the philological tradition, but in widely influential essays in the 1930s he had abandoned historicism for formal analysis. His and Warren's book reviewed the various approaches to literature—biographical, psychological, sociological, historical, and so on—and concluded that while each had some merit, all had ultimately to answer to the formal analysis of the work as an autonomous entity. Wellek turned to Roman Ingarden, the phenomenologist and student of Edmund Husserl (see chapter 6, "Hermeneutics and Phenomenology"), to support his case, though Ingarden later insisted his views had been misrepresented.

European formalism (Russian formalism and Prague structuralism) developed independently of Anglo-American formalism, and there are important differences between the two schools. But there are also important parallels, so that when European formalism entered the United States in the 1960s, it sometimes conflicted and sometimes fused with the dominant New Critical approach. European poststructuralism (including deconstruction) emerged through a critique of formalism's and structuralism's fundamental premises. But since that critique proceeds by working through those premises to reveal unavoidable contradictions, poststructuralism remains deeply involved with the very premises it examines. This relation became even more complex in the United States, where poststructuralism confronted the already intricate interaction between American and European varieties of formalism.

Books and Collections

362.   Bagwell, J. Timothy. *American Formalism and the Problem of Interpretation*. Houston: Rice UP, 1986.

363.   Cowan, Louise. *The Southern Critics: An Introduction to the Criticism of John Crowe Ransom, Allen Tate, Donald Davidson, Robert Penn Warren, Cleanth Brooks, and Andrew Lytle*. Irving: U of Dallas P, 1971. On the poets and critics who largely created New Criticism.

364.   Foster, Richard. *The New Romantics: A Reappraisal of the New Criticism*. Bloomington: Indiana UP, 1962.

365.   Graff, Gerald. *Poetic Statement and Critical Dogma*. Chicago: U of Chicago P, 1970. Critique of New Critical conceptions of language and poetry.

366.   Handy, William J. *Kant and the Southern New Critics*. Austin: U of Texas P, 1963.

367.   ———, ed. *Symposium on Formalist Criticism: Proceedings.* Austin: U of Texas Humanities Research Center, 1965.

368.   Pratt, Mary Louise. *Toward a Speech Act Theory of Literary Discourse.* Bloomington: Indiana UP, 1977. Uses speech-act philosophy to criticize formalist theory.

369.   Thompson, Ewa M. *Russian Formalism and Anglo-American New Criticism: A Comparative Study.* The Hague: Mouton, 1971.

370.   Wetherell, P. M. *The Literary Text: An Examination of Critical Methods.* Oxford: Blackwell, 1974. Presents a formalist theory and argues against alternatives.

371.   Young, Thomas D., ed. *The New Critics and After.* Charlottesville: UP of Virginia, 1976.

Individual Authors

I. A. RICHARDS (1893–1979)

I. A. Richards's influence is oddly narrower than his actual work. In *Principles of Literary Criticism*, he proposed a broad psychological and social conception of the nature and function of poetry. For the most part, he argued, we react to our experience (of life as well as of poems) in stereotypical ways. Bad poems simply embody and reinforce these "stock responses." But, at our best, our minds are open to the full range of our experiences and impulses and bring this often contradictory range into some coherent synthesis. Good poetry both records and accomplishes for sensitive readers just this synthesis of diverse impulses. Most literary criticism, however, consists of historical chitchat, impressionism, isolated insights, and purple patches. During the 1920s, in Cambridge, Richards invited his students to write comments on poems whose titles and authors were withheld. *Practical Criticism* prints selections from these "protocols" with his sometimes acid comments. He has no trouble showing the varieties of misreading—the failure often simply to grasp what a poem says—to say nothing of the inability to distinguish great from terrible poetry.

It may be difficult to realize today how devastating this demonstration was, for it applied not just to undergraduates but to presumably skilled scholars and critics, who showed not much more ability to read closely, accurately, and sensitively. But the technical skill was not what most attracted Richards, that was left to the American New Critics to elaborate. For Richards the lesson was much broader: the very fate of civilization depended on the human ability to reconcile the widest range of impulses in the absence of any authoritative systems of dogma or belief. In *Science and Poetry*, he distinguished the referential, propositional statements of science from the emotive "pseudostatements" of poetry. Unhappily missing the pejorative suggestion of his term, Richards meant to suggest that only poetry could serve the cause of civilization by bringing the whole of human personality into orderly play. He spent the remainder of his life pursuing the effort to bring these civilizing potentials into reality through elementary education, writing only occasional essays in which he continued to exhibit a remarkable power of analyzing poetry. Not much to their credit, most contemporary critics showed little interest in this evolution of Richards's concerns toward educational issues. His psychology and his view of the civilized individual as a balanced synthesis of diverse impulses seem to some a quaint relic of literary humanism. Yet his attention to the reading process and to the development of analytic techniques to undergird critical commentary remain decisive contributions to contemporary theory.

372.   *Beyond.* New York: Harcourt, 1974. Essays on the *Iliad,* Job, and the *Divine Comedy.*

373.   *Complementarities: I. A. Richards' Uncollected Essays.* Ed. John P. Russo. Cambridge: Harvard UP, 1976.

374.   *How to Read a Page: A Course in Effective Reading, with an Introduction to a Hundred Great Words.* New York: Norton, 1942.

375.   *Interpretation in Teaching.* New York: Harcourt, 1938. Where *Practical Criticism* analyzed student responses to poems, this work analyzes responses to passages of prose.

376.   *The Philosophy of Rhetoric.* Oxford: Oxford UP, 1936.

377.   *Poetries: Their Media and Ends.* The Hague: Mouton, 1974. Essays on general topics and particular poems.

378.   *Practical Criticism: A Study of Literary Judgment.* London: Kegan, 1929. Influential manifesto advocating close reading over impressionistic criticism.

379.   *Principles of Literary Criticism.* London: Kegan, 1924. The influential founding book for Anglo-American formalism.

380.   *Richards on Rhetoric: Selected Essays (1929–1974).* Ed. Ann E. Berthoff. New York: Oxford UP, 1990.

381.   *Science and Poetry.* 1926. 2nd ed. Rev. and enl. London: Kegan, 1935. Rpt. with notes and revisions as *Poetries and Sciences.* New York: Norton, 1970.

382.   *So Much Nearer: Essays toward a World English.* New York: Harcourt, 1968. Essays on language, technology, education, and literature from 1934 to 1968.

383.   *Speculative Instruments.* Chicago: U of Chicago P, 1955. Essays on topics in theory and education.

384.   Ogden, Charles K., I. A. Richards, and James Wood. *The Foundation of Aesthetics.* London: Allen, 1921.

385.   Richards, I. A., and Charles K. Ogden. *The Meaning of Meaning*. London: Kegan, 1923.

Books on Richards

386.   Brower, Reuben, Helen Vendler, and John Hollander, eds. *I. A. Richards: Essays in His Honor*. New York: Oxford UP, 1973. Poems for Richards, an interview, nineteen essays on his work, and a bibliography.

387.   Needham, John. *The Completest Mode: I. A. Richards and the Continuity of English Literary Criticism*. Edinburgh: Needham, 1982.

388.   Russo, John Paul. *I. A. Richards: His Life and Work*. Baltimore: Johns Hopkins UP, 1989.

389.   Schiller, Jerome P. *I. A. Richards' Theory of Literature*. New Haven: Yale UP, 1969.

CLEANTH BROOKS (1906–   )

Along with John Crowe Ransom, Robert Penn Warren, and Alan Tate, Cleanth Brooks was one of the *southern New Critics* whose influence on American criticism has been dominant in this century. Brooks was trained in the traditional philological approach, but, drawn by I. A. Richards and by the modern poetry of T. S. Eliot and his own fellow southerners, Brooks began to formulate critical principles that could explain the excellence of this poetry and its relation to the English poetic tradition.

His fundamental idea was the concept of irony, by which he meant the qualification its poetic context gives to everything said in a poem. The complex interactions among the meanings and tones dramatized in a poem make it, as he says, a "heresy" to reduce a poem to a paraphrase. Scientific or ordinary language is abstract, approximate, and susceptible to paraphrase. Poetic language is intricate, contextual, and so specific that it cannot be encompassed by conscious conceptualization. Its language thus makes the poem not a vehicle for an experience but the actual experience itself. This experience is fundamentally a mature acknowledgment that life is never simple, but not therefore incoherent. Through devices like irony, paradox, and metaphors, poetry renders this complexity directly apprehensible.

Modern poetry's dedication to these devices connects it with the older poetry of the metaphysicals, Donne, Herbert, and their contemporaries. Brooks tended to downgrade the poetry of the English Romantics and their heirs, an estimate he later regretted. The method of careful reading with close attention to tone, to imagery and metaphors, and to dramatic changes or developments of tone and attitude in poems was brought to generations of students in Brooks and Robert Penn Warren's *Understanding Poetry*, perhaps the most influential critical textbook ever written. Now widely and strenuously challenged in contemporary critical theory, this method and its assumptions nevertheless remain the ordinary heritage of virtually every academic student of literature.

390.   *Modern Poetry and the Tradition.* Chapel Hill: U of North Carolina P, 1939. Essays applying close attention to language and imagery in Elizabethan and modern poems.

391.   *The Well-Wrought Urn: Studies in the Structure of Poetry.* New York: Renal, 1947. Presents and applies a method of close reading to a variety of English poems.

392.   Brooks, Cleanth, and Robert Penn Warren. *Understanding Poetry.* 1939. 4th ed. New York: Holt, 1976. One of the most influential textbooks of the century, teaches the New Critical method of close reading.

Brooks Bibliography

393.   Walsh, John Michael. *Cleanth Brooks: An Annotated Bibliography.* New York: Garland, 1990.

Book on Brooks

394.   Simpson, Lewis P., ed. *The Possibilities of Order: Cleanth Brooks and His Work.* Baton Rouge: Louisiana State UP, 1976.

W. K. WIMSATT (1907–75)

With the philosopher Monroe Beardsley, W. K. Wimsatt formulated two key positions of New Critical theory. In "The Intentional Fallacy" (1946) they argued that the author's stated intention, even when information about it is available, cannot decide the meaning of a work of literature, which remains a public utterance. And in "The Affective Fallacy" (1949) they argued that meaning is not the same as any reader's actual emotive response. Instead of directly judging a work on the basis of its content, the critic should "explicate" it, analyzing its verbal structure, describing it in multiple ways, and showing its coherence and unity, so that a reader can respond more precisely and fully to it as a symbolic presentation and recreation of human experience. Literary works can thus be analyzed and evaluated rationally and objectively on their own terms as autonomous objects, without reference to external moral, religious, or political dogmas.

These ideas are most penetratingly expressed in the essays in *The Verbal Icon.* Wimsatt's other collections continue to defend his basic position against other critical schools and, as he saw it, errors. With Cleanth Brooks, he wrote an excellent short history of literary criticism, which took its organizing concerns from New Critical principles.

395.   *Day of the Leopards: Essays in Defense of Poems.* New Haven: Yale UP, 1976.

396.   *Hateful Contraries: Studies in Literature and Criticism.* Lexington: U of Kentucky P, 1966.

397.   *The Verbal Icon: Studies in the Meaning of Poetry.* Lexington: UP of Kentucky, 1954.

       Wimsatt, William K., and Cleanth Brooks. *Literary Criticism: A Short History.* See entry 58.

MURRAY KRIEGER (1923–   )

       The most persistent defender of New Critical theory in the contemporary context, Murray Krieger tries to engage seriously the positions of structuralists and deconstructionists and to reply to what he sees as a dehumanizing abstraction introduced by reliance on speculative conceptions of language. He remains virtually the only critic who directly addresses poststructuralist thought while holding steadily to the doctrine of formalism.

398.   *Arts on the Level: The Fall of the Elite Object.* Knoxville: U of Tennessee P, 1981.

399.   *Ekphrasis: The Illusion of the Natural Sign.* Baltimore: Johns Hopkins UP, 1991.

400.   *The New Apologists for Poetry.* Minneapolis: U of Minnesota P, 1956. On I. A. Richards and the New Critics.

401.   *The Play and Place of Criticism.* Baltimore: Johns Hopkins UP, 1967. Sixteen essays on theory and works of literature.

402.   *Poetic Presence and Illusion: Essays in Critical History and Theory.* Baltimore: Johns Hopkins UP, 1980.

403.   *A Reopening of Closure: Organicism against Itself.* New York: Columbia UP, 1989. Defends the Romantic and New Critical idea of organicism against critiques by poststructuralist and cultural theorists.

404.   *Theory of Criticism: A Tradition and Its System.* Baltimore: John Hopkins UP, 1976. On the humanistic tradition of literary theory, with a critique of poststructuralism.

405.   *Words about Words about Words: Theory, Criticism, and the Literary Text.* Baltimore: Johns Hopkins UP, 1988.

Book on Krieger

406.   Henricksen, Bruce, ed. *Murray Krieger and Contemporary Critical Theory.* New York: Columbia UP, 1986.

4. Structuralism and Semiotics

In the confluence of New Criticism and Russian formalism and Prague structuralism, Yale University was a leading center: Cleanth Brooks, W. K. Wimsatt, and René Wellek were colleagues, along with Victor Erlich, the leading historian of the Russian formalists. But while this approach was coming to dominance in England and America after World War II, a group of thinkers, mainly French, were discovering *structural linguistics*. This approach to the study of language, which had been created by Ferdinand de Saussure (1857–1913), revolutionized linguistics by emphasizing systematic description of the structure of a given language instead of the then standard examination of its history and development. Structural linguistics, it appeared, provided a rigorous model that could be applied to all the *signifying processes* that made up human culture. These varied fields came to be called the *human sciences*, and the approach that applied this common model was called *structuralism*.

In his early phase, Roland Barthes was an energetic spokesman for structuralism. The movement also spread into psychoanalysis with Jacques Lacan's reinterpretations of Freud's texts and ideas (see chapter 8, "Psychological and Psychoanalytic Critical Theory"), into Marxism with Louis Althusser's rereadings of Marx (see chapter 10, "Marxist Critical Theory"), and into anthropology with Claude Lévi-Strauss's studies of kinship, myths, and social structure. In literary studies, it was elaborated not only by Barthes but by theorists like A. J. Greimas, Gérard Genette, Julia Kristeva, Tzvetan Todorov, and the Italians Umberto Eco and Cesare Segre. Some theorists began to speak of a general science of all human sign systems and gave it the name *semiotics*, taken from Saussure and from the American philosopher Charles S. Peirce.

This new French structuralism first achieved significance in the United States at a celebrated conference in 1966 at Johns Hopkins University, whose proceedings were published as *The Structuralist Controversy* (see Macksey and Donato below). Relations between New Criticism and structuralism were often uneasy. The rigorous spirit of system and the alien technical vocabulary the French borrowed from linguistics or invented on the model of that discipline offended the Americans' sense that literary analysis, however technical, was addressed to a general audience and was intended to foster intelligent appreciation, not analytic technicalities seemingly for their own sake. The French structuralists were ambitious to extend their approach to all cultural fields, whereas American formalism had been founded on separating the discussion of literature from other disciplines and making it a field in its own right. Yet much of what the structuralists said had an uncannily familiar ring, and many younger critics found an easy transition from their New Critical educations to the new wave of structuralism.

Meanwhile, the formalist heritage was reviving in the Soviet Union, particularly among a group centered at Tartu University and under the leadership of Jurij Lotman. This group emphasized the broader field of sign-using activity within which literature is located. It became known as the *Soviet semiotic school*. Difficulties of communication have prevented its free interaction with Western European theorists, but its work is becoming increasingly known.

Despite these developments in Russia, France, and the United States, as early as the late 1970s structuralism was already undergoing a critique and challenge from Jacques Derrida's deconstruction (see chapter 5, "Poststructuralism and Deconstruction"). This critique was largely responsible for displacing structuralism and semiotics from center stage, and many of its major representatives, including Kristeva, Todorov, and Barthes, went on to very different approaches. Yet structuralism and semiotics continue to have many adherents, particularly in Europe, and their general premises are not so much superseded in later work as taken for granted as a starting point.

Bibliography and Dictionary

407.   Miller, Joan M. *French Structuralism: A Multidisciplinary Bibliography with a Checklist of Sources for Louis Althusser, Roland Barthes, Jacques Derrida, Michel Foucault, Lucien Goldmann, Jacques Lacan, and an Update of Works on Claude Lévi-Strauss.* New York: Garland, 1981.

408.   Ducrot, Oswald, and Tzvetan Todorov. *Encyclopedic Dictionary of the Sciences of Language.* Trans. Catherine Porter. Baltimore: Johns Hopkins

UP, 1979. Defines terms basic to semiotics, with a concluding essay on recent critiques of the concept of sign.

Introductory Anthologies and Surveys

409.   Caws, Peter. *Structuralism: The Art of the Intelligible.* Atlantic Highlands: Humanities Intl., 1990.

410.   Champagne, Roland A. *French Structuralism.* Boston: Hall, 1990.

411.   Clarke, D. S., Jr. *Sources of Semiotic: Readings with Commentary from Antiquity to the Present.* Carbondale: Southern Illinois UP, 1989.

412.   Corti, Maria. *An Introduction to Literary Semiotics.* Trans. Margherita Bogat and Allen Mandelbaum. Bloomington: Indiana UP, 1978.

413.   Culler, Jonathan. *Structuralist Poetics: Structuralism, Linguistics, and the Study of Literature.* London: Routledge, 1975. Perhaps the most widely read introductory survey.

414.   Deely, John. *Introducing Semiotic: Its History and Doctrine.* Bloomington: Indiana UP, 1982.

415.   De George, Richard T., and Fernande M. De George, eds. *The Structuralists: From Marx to Lévi-Strauss.* Garden City: Doubleday, 1972. Includes Freud, Saussure, Jakobson, Barthes, Lévi-Strauss, Althusser, Foucault, and Lacan.

Gras, Vernon W., ed. *European Literary Theory and Practice: From Existential Phenomenology to Structuralism.* See entry 672.

416.   Hawkes, Terence. *Structuralism and Semiotics.* Berkeley: U of California P, 1977. Introductory text with good bibliography.

417.   Innis, Robert E., ed. *Semiotics: An Introductory Anthology.* Bloomington: Indiana UP, 1985. Classic statements by Jakobson, Eco, Lévi-Strauss, and others in literary criticism, anthropology, philosophy, and linguistics.

Jameson, Fredric. *The Prison-House of Language: A Critical Account of Structuralism and Russian Formalism.* See entry 1267.

418.   Kurzweil, Edith. *The Age of Structuralism: Lévi-Strauss to Foucault.* New York: Columbia UP, 1980. Surveys various disciplines.

419.   Lane, Michael, ed. *Introduction to Structuralism.* New York: Basic, 1970. From Saussure to Barthes, including some fields outside literature.

420.   Macksey, Richard A., and Eugenio Donato, eds. *The Structuralist Controversy: The Languages of Criticism and the Sciences of Man.* Baltimore: Johns Hopkins UP, 1972. Originally published as *The Languages of Criticism and the Sciences of Man: The Structuralist Controversy.* Baltimore: Johns Hopkins UP, 1970. This key collection introduced varieties of Continental structuralism to America.

421.   Matejka, Ladislav, and I. Titunik, eds. *Semiotics of Art: Prague School*

Contributions. Cambridge: MIT P, 1976. Essays by Jakobson, Mukařovský, and others on folk art, theater, poetry; with postscript reviewing the Prague school's work.

422.   Orr, Leonard. *Semiotic and Structuralist Analyses of Fiction: An Introduction and a Bibliographic Survey.* Troy: Whitston, 1987.

423.   Robey, David, ed. *Structuralism: An Introduction.* Oxford: Clarendon–Oxford UP, 1973. Includes essays by Culler, Eco, Todorov, and others on structuralism in linguistics, anthropology, literature, and mathematics.

424.   Scholes, Robert. *Structuralism in Literature: An Introduction.* New Haven: Yale UP, 1974. Good introductory survey.

425.   Sturrock, John. *Structuralism.* London: Paladin, 1986. Comprehensive introductory survey of linguistics, social sciences, semiotics, literature, and poststructuralism.

426.   Todorov, Tzvetan, ed. *French Literary Theory Today: A Reader.* Trans. R. Carter. Cambridge: Cambridge UP, 1982. Selections representing the structuralist approach.

Books on and Representing Structuralism and Semiotics

427.   Benoist, Jean-Marie. *The Structural Revolution.* New York: St. Martin's, 1978.

428.   Blanchard, Marc E. *Description: Sign, Self, Desire: Critical Theory in the Wake of Semiotics.* The Hague: Mouton, 1979.

429.   Bojár, Endre. *Slavic Structuralism.* Amsterdam: Benjamins, 1985. Concentrates on Jan Mukařovský and Roman Ingarden.

430.   Boon, James A. *From Symbolism to Structuralism: Lévi-Strauss in a Literary Tradition.* New York: Harper, 1972. Sets French structuralism in its cultural tradition.

431.   Borbé, Tasso, ed. *Semiotics Unfolding.* 3 vols. Berlin: Mouton, 1984. Volume 2 is *Semiotics in Text and Literature. Linguistics and Semiotics.*

432.   Carter, Ronald, and Paul Simpson, eds. *Language, Discourse and Literature: An Introductory Reader in Discourse Stylistics.* London: Allen, 1988.

433.   Chambers, Ross. *Meaning and Meaningfulness: Studies in the Analysis and Interpretation of Texts.* Lexington: French Forum, 1979.

434.   Champagne, Roland A. *Beyond the Structuralist Myth of Ecriture.* The Hague: Mouton, 1977.

435.   Champigny, Robert. *Sense, Nonsense, Antisense.* Gainesville: UP of Florida, 1986.

436.   Chatman, Seymour. *Story and Discourse: Narrative Structure in Fiction and Film*. Ithaca: Cornell UP, 1978.

437.   Ching, Marvin K. L., Michael C. Haley, and Ronald F. Lunsford, eds. *Linguistic Perspectives on Literature*. London: Routledge, 1980. Eighteen essays on figurative language and stylistics, with an introduction surveying linguistics and literary studies.

438.   Clarke, D. S., Jr. *Principles of Semiotic*. London: Routledge, 1987. Includes discussion of medieval sign theory.

439.   Culler, Jonathan. *Ferdinand de Saussure*. Rev. ed. Ithaca: Cornell UP, 1986. Excellent presentation of Saussure, the turn-of-the-century founder of structural linguistics and the source of structuralism.

440.   ———. *The Pursuit of Signs: Semiotics, Literature, Deconstruction*. Ithaca: Cornell UP, 1981.

441.   De George, Richard T., ed. *Semiotic Themes*. Lawrence: U of Kansas P, 1981. Essays by Culler, Sebeok, Todorov (on Bakhtin), and others on semiotics.

442.   Di Girolamo, Costanzo. *A Critical Theory of Literature*. Madison: U of Wisconsin P, 1981. Formalist development of Louis Hjelmslev's linguistic theories called "glossematics."

443.   Doubrovsky, Serge. *The New Criticism in France*. Trans. Derek Coltman. Chicago: U of Chicago P, 1973. Good introduction to structuralism.

444.   Dubois, J., F. Edeline, J.-M. Klinkenberg, P. Minguet, F. Pire, H. Trinon (Group mu). *A General Rhetoric*. Trans. Paul B. Burrell and Edgar M. Slotkin. Baltimore: Johns Hopkins UP, 1981. Systematic outline of semiotic analysis.

445.   Gadet, Françoise. *Saussure and Contemporary Culture*. Trans. Gregory Elliott. London: Century, 1989.

446.   Garvin, Harry R., and Patrick Brady, eds. *Phenomenology, Structuralism, Semiology*. Lewisburg: Bucknell UP, 1975. Thirteen essays, theoretical and applied, in the human and social sciences.

447.   Genette, Gérard. *The Architext: An Introduction*. Trans. Jane E. Lewin. Berkeley: U of California P, 1992.

448.   ———. *Figures of Literary Discourse*. Trans. Alan Sheridan. New York: Columbia UP, 1984. Essays on poetic language and on narrative.

449.   ———. *Narrative Discourse: An Essay in Method*. Trans. Jane E. Lewin. Ithaca: Cornell UP, 1979.

450.   ———. *Narrative Discourse Revisited*. Trans. Jane E. Lewin. Ithaca: Cornell UP, 1988. Responds to his commentators and critics.

451.   Greimas, Algirdas Julien. *On Meaning: Selected Writings in Semiotic Theory*. Trans. Paul J. Perron and Frank H. Collins. Minneapolis: U of Minnesota P, 1987.

452.   ———. *Structural Semantics: An Attempt at a Method.* Trans. Danielle McDowell, Ronald Schleifer, and Alan Velie. Lincoln: U of Nebraska P, 1983.

453.   Greimas, A. J., et al., eds. *Sign Language Culture.* The Hague: Mouton, 1970.

454.   Greimas (book on). Schleifer, Ronald. *A. J. Greimas and the Nature of Meaning: Linguistics, Semiotics, and Discourse Theory.* Lincoln: U of Nebraska P, 1987. Sets Greimas's work in context with Lacan, Lévi-Strauss, Derrida, and de Man.

455.   Hendricks, William O. *Essays on Semiolinguistics and Verbal Art.* The Hague: Mouton, 1973.

456.   Hussey, Eugene H. *Structure Theory: Language, Science, and Aesthetics.* Laureldale: Demecon, 1978.

457.   Jackson, Leonard. *The Poverty of Structuralism: Literature and Structuralist Theory.* White Plains: Longman, 1991. Traces and criticizes the transformation of structural linguistics in French theorists of the 1950s and 1960s, including Barthes and Derrida.

458.   Krieger, Murray, and Larry S. Dembo, eds. *Directions for Criticism: Structuralism and Its Alternatives.* Madison: U of Wisconsin P, 1977. Includes essays by Krieger, Said, Hayden White, Girard, and others.

        Lewis, Thomas E. *Fiction and Reference.* See entry 1150.

459.   Lodge, David. *Working with Structuralism: Essays and Reviews on Nineteenth- and Twentieth-Century Literature.* London: Routledge, 1981.

460.   Lotman, Jurij. *Analysis of the Poetic Text.* Ed. and trans. D. Barton Johnson. Ann Arbor: Ardis, 1976. Russian structuralist approach; with bibliography of English translations of Lotman's work.

461.   ———. *The Structure of the Artistic Text.* Trans. Ronald Vroon and Gail Vroon. Ann Arbor: Dept. of Slavic Languages and Literatures, U of Michigan, 1977.

462.   Lotman (book on). Shukman, Ann. *Literature and Semiotics: A Study of the Writings of Yu. M. Lotman.* Amsterdam: North-Holland, 1977.

463.   Lucid, Daniel P., ed. and trans. *Soviet Semiotics: An Anthology.* Baltimore: Johns Hopkins UP, 1978. Overview of Soviet semiotics from 1960s to mid-1970s.

464.   MacCannell, Dean, and Juliet Flower MacCannell. *The Time of the Sign: A Semiotic Interpretation of Modern Culture.* Bloomington: Indiana UP, 1982.

465.   MacDonnell, Diane. *Theories of Discourse: An Introduction.* Oxford: Blackwell, 1986.

466.   Merrell, Floyd. *Semiotic Foundations: Steps toward an Epistemology of Written Texts.* Bloomington: Indiana UP, 1982.

467.   ———. *A Semiotic Theory of Texts.* Berlin: Mouton, 1985. Highly technical;

includes analysis of Fuentes's novel *The Death of Artemio Cruz* and of a story by Borges.

468.   Morris, Wesley. *Friday's Footprint: Structuralism and the Articulated Text.* Columbus: Ohio State UP, 1979.

Ngara, Emmanuel. *Stylistic Criticism and the African Novel: A Study of the Language, Art and Content of African Fiction.* See entry 1513.

469.   Odmark, John, ed. *Language, Literature and Meaning.* 2 vols. Amsterdam: Benjamins, 1979–80. Vol. 1: *Problems of Literary Theory*; vol. 2: *Current Trends in Literary Research.* Surveys current East European approaches, structuralist and Marxist, including essays on Lukács and Ingarden.

470.   O'Toole, L. M., and Ann Shukman, eds. *General Semiotics.* Oxford: Holdan, 1976.

471.   Pagnini, Marcello. *The Pragmatics of Literature.* Trans. Nancy Jones-Henry. Bloomington: Indiana UP, 1987. Semiotic approach to the transmission and reception of the literary message, especially in drama.

472.   Pavel, Thomas. *The Feud of Language: A History of Structuralist Thought.* Oxford: Blackwell, 1989. Analyzes tension between the structuralist linguistic model and poststructuralism.

473.   Peckham, Morse. *Explanation and Power: The Control of Human Behavior.* 1979. Minneapolis: U of Minnesota P, 1988. Argues that the meaning of a sign is the response to it.

474.   Peirce, C. S. *Peirce on Signs: Writing on Semiotic by Charles Sanders Peirce.* Ed. James Hoopes. Chapel Hill: U of North Carolina P, 1991. Though the American philosopher Peirce died in 1914, his key contributions to semiotics have only recently become widely influential.

475.   Pettit, Philip. *The Concept of Structuralism: A Critical Analysis.* Berkeley: U of California P, 1975.

476.   Prince, Gerald. *A Grammar of Stories: An Introduction.* The Hague: Mouton, 1974. Structuralist approach.

477.   ———. *Narratology: The Form and Functioning of Narrative.* The Hague: Mouton, 1982.

478.   Riffaterre, Michael. *Semiotics of Poetry.* Bloomington: Indiana UP, 1978.

479.   ———. *Text Production.* Trans. Terese Lyons. New York: Columbia UP, 1983. Essays applying structuralist analysis to poems and narratives.

480.   Saussure (book on). Starobinski, Jean. *Words upon Words: The Anagrams of Ferdinand de Saussure.* Trans. Olivia Emmett. New Haven: Yale UP, 1979. Excerpts and discusses work by Saussure from 1906 to 1909 in which he speculated that in Latin poems were concealed the letters of the gods' names.

481.   Scholes, Robert. *Semiotics and Interpretation.* New Haven: Yale UP, 1982.

482.   Sebeok, Thomas A., ed. *The Tell-Tale Sign: A Survey of Semiotics.* Lisse,

Neth.: Ridder, 1975. Nine essays by Eco, Kristeva, Lotman, Todorov, and other leading critics.

483. Segre, Cesare. *Semiotics and Literary Criticism*. The Hague: Mouton, 1973.

484. ———. *Structures and Time: Narration, Poetry, Models*. Trans. John Meddemmen. Chicago: U of Chicago P, 1979.

485. Segre, Cesare, with Tomaso Kemeny. *Introduction to the Analysis of the Literary Text*. Trans. John Meddemmen. Bloomington: Indiana UP, 1988. Presents the structuralist method.

486. Seyffert, Peter. *Soviet Literary Structuralism: Background, Debate, Issues*. Columbus: Slavica, 1989. Reviews the work of the Soviet semiotic school at Tartu University, including that of Lotman.

487. Shapiro, Michael, and Marianne Shapiro. *Figuration in Verbal Art*. Princeton: Princeton UP, 1988. Theory and illustrations of figuration in literary works.

488. Sheriff, John K. *The Fate of Meaning: Charles Peirce, Structuralism, and Literature*. Princeton: Princeton UP, 1989. Part 1 reviews Culler, Todorov, Fish, Barthes, Derrida, and others; part 2 develops a theory based on the semiotics of the nineteenth-century American Peirce.

489. Sørensen, Dolf. *Theory Formation and the Study of Literature*. Amsterdam: Rodopi, 1987. Draws on Karl Popper to develop a theory of scientific theory and then tests Greimas's and Lotman's structuralist approaches against it.

490. Strickland, Geoffrey. *Structuralism or Criticism? Thoughts on How We Read*. Cambridge: Cambridge UP, 1981. Critique of structuralism, with a concluding chapter on Leavis.

491. Tallis, Raymond. *Not Saussure: A Critique of Post-Saussurean Literary Theory*. London: Macmillan, 1988.

492. Thibault, Paul J. *Social Semiotics: Text, Meaning, and Nabokov's Ada*. Minneapolis: U of Minnesota P, 1990. Aims to develop new theoretical and methodological resources for studying the processes of meaning in the wake of poststructuralist critiques.

493. Uspensky, Boris. *A Poetics of Composition: The Structure of the Artistic Text and Typology of a Compositional Form*. Trans. Valentina Zavarin and Susan Wittig. Berkeley: U of California P, 1983. Russian structuralist approach.

494. Van der Eng, Jan, and Mojmir Grygar, eds. *Structure of Texts and Semiotics of Culture*. The Hague: Mouton, 1973. East European structuralism.

495. Van Dijk, Teun A., ed. *Discourse and Literature*. Amsterdam: Benjamins, 1985. Analysis of literary forms of discourse (poems, songs, letters, myths, and so on) and their relation to other forms of discourse; thirteen essays, each with a bibliography.

496. Zholkovsky, Alexander. *Themes and Texts: Toward a Poetics of Expressive-*

ness. Trans. Zholkovsky. Ed. Kathleen Parthe. Ithaca: Cornell UP, 1984. Russian postformalist approach.

497.   Zima, Peter V., ed. *Semiotics and Dialectics: Ideology and the Text*. Amsterdam: Benjamins, 1981. Essays in English, French, and German on the relations between formalism and Marxism and the work of Lotman and Bakhtin.

Individual Authors

ROLAND BARTHES (1915–80)

Educated in French literature and the classics, Roland Barthes taught in Romania and Egypt before returning to Paris. He was an active participant in every cultural development in France after World War II and first gained prominence through *Writing Degree Zero*, an implicit reply to Jean-Paul Sartre's *What Is Literature?* Barthes defended literary innovations, such as the "new novel" developed by Alain Robbe-Grillet and others, as well as the first performances in France of Brecht's plays in the 1950s. He also applied his elegant analyses to fashion writing in *The Fashion System* and to cultural artifacts ranging from the Eiffel Tower to the traditional French dish of steak and french fries. His *Elements of Semiology* is a rigorous outline of semiotic analysis, yet his own practice is far more supple, guided by the sensibility and stylistic brilliance that make him a major addition to the tradition of the French essay. *S/Z* combines semiotic analysis of a novella by Balzac with brilliant excursions into cultural and literary topics. In works like *The Pleasure of the Text*, Barthes moved steadily beyond semiotics to formulate an erotics of reading and literature. Well-versed in all the structuralist and poststructuralist ideas, Barthes converted everything he absorbed into an expression of his own individuality, powerfully influential but finally inimitable and escaping reduction to any narrow application of his thought.

498.   *A Barthes Reader*. Ed. Susan Sontag. New York: Hill, 1982.

499.   *Camera Lucida: Reflections on Photography*. Trans. Richard Howard. New York: Hill, 1981.

500.   *Critical Essays*. Trans. Richard Howard. Evanston: Northwestern UP, 1972.

501.   *Criticism and Truth*. Trans. Katrine Pilcher Keuneman. Minneapolis: U of Minnesota P, 1987. Reply to a sharp critique by Raymond Picard (see entry 529).

502.   *The Eiffel Tower and Other Mythologies*. Trans. Richard Howard. New York: Hill, 1979. Essays on various aspects of literature and French culture.

503. *Elements of Semiology*. Trans. Annette Lavers and Colin Smith. New York: Hill, 1968. A rigorous introduction to structuralist analysis.

504. *The Empire of Signs*. Trans. Richard Howard. New York: Hill, 1982. On Japanese culture.

505. *The Fashion System*. Trans. Matthew Ward and Richard Howard. New York: Hill, 1983. Analysis of writing about women's fashions.

506. *The Grain of the Voice: Interviews, 1962–1980*. Trans. Linda Coverdale. New York: Hill, 1985.

507. *Image-Music-Text*. Trans. Stephen Heath. New York: Hill, 1978.

508. *A Lover's Discourse: Fragments*. Trans. Richard Howard. New York: Hill, 1978.

509. *Mythologies*. Trans. Annette Lavers. New York: Hill, 1972.

510. *New Critical Essays*. Trans. Richard Howard. New York: Hill, 1980.

511. *On Racine*. Trans. Richard Miller. New York: Hill, 1964.

512. *The Pleasure of the Text*. Trans. Richard Miller. New York: Hill, 1975.

513. *The Responsibility of Forms: New Critical Essays on Music, Art, and Representation*. Trans. Richard Howard. New York: Hill, 1985.

514. *Roland Barthes*. Trans. Richard Howard. New York: Hill, 1977. Barthes on himself.

515. *The Rustle of Language*. Trans. Richard Howard. New York: Hill, 1986. Forty-five essays written from 1967 to 1980.

516. *S/Z*. Trans. Richard Miller. New York: Hill, 1974. A close reading of Balzac's novella "Sarrasine" interspersed with short, dazzling speculative statements on literature and theory.

517. *Sade-Fourier-Loyola*. Trans. Richard Miller. New York: Hill, 1976.

518. *The Semiotic Challenge*. Trans. Richard Howard. New York: Hill, 1988.

519. *Writer Sollers*. Trans. Philip Thody. Minneapolis: U of Minnesota P, 1987. On the contemporary French novelist and critic.

520. *Writing Degree Zero*. Trans. Annette Lavers and Colin Smith. New York: Hill, 1968. Partly a response to Sartre's *What Is Literature?*, a brilliant essay on literature, language, and society.

Barthes Bibliography

521. Freedman, Sanford, and Carole Anne Taylor. *Roland Barthes: A Bibliographical Reader's Guide*. New York: Garland, 1983.

Books on Barthes

522. Bensmaia, Réda. *The Barthes Effect: The Essay as Reflective Text*. Trans. Pat Fedkiew. Minneapolis: U of Minnesota P, 1987. On the nature of the essay and four late works by Barthes.

523.   Champagne, Roland A. *Literary History in the Wake of Roland Barthes: Re-defining the Myths of Reading*. Birmingham: Summa, 1984.

524.   Culler, Jonathan. *Roland Barthes*. New York: Oxford UP, 1983.

525.   Klinkowitz, Jerome. *Rosenberg/Barthes/Hassan: The Postmodern Habit of Thought*. Athens: U of Georgia P, 1988.

526.   Lavers, Annette. *Roland Barthes: Structuralism and After*. Cambridge: Harvard UP, 1982.

527.   Moriarty, Michael. *Roland Barthes*. Stanford: Stanford UP, 1992.

528.   Mortimer, Armine Kotin. *The Gentlest Law: Roland Barthes's* The Pleasure of the Text. New York: Lang, 1989.

529.   Picard, Raymond. *New Criticism or New Fraud?* Trans. Frank Towne. Pullman: Washington State UP, 1969. A traditional historical scholar sharply attacks Barthes's *On Racine*.

530.   Thody, Philip. *Roland Barthes: A Conservative Estimate*. Atlantic Highlands: Humanities, 1977.

531.   Ungar, Steven. *Roland Barthes: The Professor of Desire*. Lincoln: U of Nebraska P, 1984.

532.   Ungar, Steven, and Betty R. McGraw, eds. *Signs in Culture: Roland Barthes Today*. Iowa City: U of Iowa P, 1989. Nine essays on Barthes's career.

533.   Wasserman, George. *Roland Barthes*. Boston: Twayne, 1981.

534.   Wiseman, Mary Bittner. *The Ecstasies of Roland Barthes*. London: Routledge, 1989.

UMBERTO ECO (1932–   )

After early work on medieval aesthetics and a study of "open form" in modern literature (especially Joyce), Umberto Eco embraced semiotics as a general theory of the human use of signs. He has expounded this theory in many works and applied it to subjects from high art to pop culture. But his greatest renown came from his novel *The Name of the Rose*, which the knowledgeable reader will find teeming with allusions to, and jokes based on, semiotics and its history from antiquity to the present.

535.   *The Limits of Interpretation*. Bloomington: Indiana UP, 1990. Sees rights of interpreter as overstressed in some contemporary theory.

536.   *The Open Work*. Trans. Anna Cancogni. 1962. Cambridge: Harvard UP, 1989. Discusses works that resist formal closure.

537.   *The Role of the Reader: Explorations in the Semiotics of Texts*. Bloomington: Indiana UP, 1979. Semiotic approach to reader-response criticism.

538.   *Semiotics and the Philosophy of Language*. Bloomington: Indiana UP, 1984.

539.   A *Theory of Semiotics*. Bloomington: Indiana UP, 1984.

540.   Eco, Umberto, and Thomas A. Sebeok, eds. *The Sign of Three: Dupin, Holmes, Peirce*. Bloomington: Indiana UP, 1984. A witty exposition of semiotics using detective fiction.

JULIA KRISTEVA (1941–)

The early phase of Julia Kristeva's work was structuralist, and books with that orientation are listed here. But she has increasingly turned to psychoanalysis, and fuller discussion will be found in chapter 7, under "Psychological and Psychoanalytic Critical Theory."

541.   *Desire in Language: A Semiotic Approach to Literature and Art*. Trans. Alice Jardine and Thomas Gora. New York: Columbia UP, 1980. An anthology of her early structuralist writing.

542.   *Language: The Unknown: An Initiation into Linguistics*. Trans. Anne M. Menke. New York: Columbia UP, 1989. Traces linguistic theory to its ancient roots and shows advantages and disadvantages of using linguistics to gain insight into all human activities.

543.   *Revolution in Poetic Language*. Trans. Margaret Waller. New York: Columbia UP, 1984. The change in poetic language brought about by Mallarmé and its cultural consequences.

TZVETAN TODOROV (1939–)

After emigrating from Bulgaria to France in 1963, Tzvetan Todorov published a series of books that translated and reintroduced the Russian formalists and outlined and applied the core ideas of structuralism. But in a trilogy comprising *Theories of the Symbol, Symbolism and Interpretation*, and *Literature and Its Theorists*, Todorov moved to a different view: literature should not be analyzed by neutral operations, because it is a kind of discourse oriented to truth and morality, and criticism too must be a search for truth and values. Truth, however, is not dogma but emerges out of genuine dialogue. In this new orientation, Todorov's response to the work of Mikhail Bakhtin (see chapter 2, "Russian Formalism and Prague Structuralism") has been decisive.

544.   *The Conquest of America*. Trans. Richard Howard. New York: Harper, 1984. Todorov in his recent phase as a cultural critic discusses representations of the discovery and conquest of the New World.

545.   *The Fantastic: A Structural Approach to a Literary Genre*. Trans. Richard Howard. Ithaca: Cornell UP, 1973.

546.   *Genres in Discourse*. Cambridge: Cambridge UP, 1990.

547. *An Introduction to Poetics.* Trans. Richard Howard. Minneapolis: U of Minnesota P, 1981. A classic statement of structuralism.

548. *Literature and Its Theorists: A Personal View of Twentieth-Century Criticism.* Trans. Catherine Porter. Ithaca: Cornell UP, 1987. Discusses four traditions: Russian formalism and Bakhtin; the German writers Döblin and Brecht; French writers, including Sartre, Blanchot, and Barthes; and Frye and Watt.

549. *Mikhail Bakhtin: The Dialogical Principle.* Trans. Wlad Godzich. Minneapolis: U of Minnesota P, 1984. With this work, Todorov announced his conversion from structuralism to a non-Marxist cultural criticism based on Bakhtin.

550. *The Poetics of Prose.* Trans. Richard Howard. Ithaca: Cornell UP, 1977. Applied essays in structuralist analysis.

551. *Symbolism and Interpretation.* Trans. Catherine Porter. Ithaca: Cornell UP, 1982.

552. *Theories of the Symbol.* Trans. Catherine Porter. Ithaca: Cornell UP, 1982. History of semiotics; sign theory in modern criticism.

5. Poststructuralism and Deconstruction

At the very moment when American academics were beginning to absorb structuralism, that movement fell victim to a further intellectual development in France: *deconstruction*. The philosopher Jacques Derrida created deconstruction from the tradition of phenomenology, especially the work of Edmund Husserl and his student Martin Heidegger. But in his attention to literature, Derrida drew heavily on a native French tradition, especially writers like Maurice Blanchot and Georges Bataille. (For Heidegger and Blanchot, see chapter 6, "Hermeneutics and Phenomenology.") Like the structuralists, Derrida focused on language, but instead of finding a unified system as the basis of communication, he found dispersive energies that pulled structure apart and that writers and readers held in check only by willed and arbitrary impositions. Derrida's central claim may be grasped in his formula that we always say more and other than we mean or intend to say. Derrida traces throughout Western history the attempt to suppress the explosive energies of language, which he characterizes as an attempt to make voice sovereign over writing. In recent work, he has turned to the social processes that use and underwrite structures of meaning but that are simultaneously undermined by the disseminating energies of those structures.

Independently of Derrida, the Belgian Paul de Man was gradually evolving a parallel line of thought in literary criticism. His essays in the 1950s show his debt to Jean-Paul Sartre's existentialism. Then, in the early 1960s, de Man came to the United States and studied and taught at Harvard, working with Reuben Brower, one of the most accomplished adapters of

New Criticism to teaching. De Man always retained profound respect for New Criticism, but his own investigations of radical strains in Romantic literary theory, of Rousseau, and of Nietzsche led him to a conception of language very different from the New Critics' and quite similar to Derrida's. The coming together of de Man and Derrida and the spread of deconstruction in literary criticism was the strongest single movement in critical theory in the decade from the mid-1970s to the mid-1980s. An institutional center of the movement emerged with the second Yale school (see that heading in this chapter). The term *poststructuralism* is sometimes used as a synonym for deconstruction. But, somewhat confusingly, it is also used to name an array of contemporary approaches from cultural criticism (see chapters 9 and 11) to some Marxist movements (see the section "Marxism: Poststructuralist and Contemporary" in chapter 10) to Lacanian psychoanalytic theory (see the listings under Lacan in chapter 8) and even to some kinds of ethnic and postcolonialist (see chapter 14) and feminist (see chapter 15) theories. The claim that some or all of these movements or the individuals identified with them share certain ideas or aims is itself controversial, particularly since leading figures in various movements have sometimes been sharply critical of one another: Derrida has criticized Lacan and Foucault, for instance, and Foucault has replied vigorously. Nevertheless, for many, Derrida's ideas and way of reading texts are exemplary for any line of thought they would label poststructuralist.

In recent years, cultural and historical criticism have come to dominate literary study. Deconstruction, along with structuralism, has been criticized as ahistorical and as at best uncertain, at worst suspect in its political and social implications. Fresh and often acrimonious controversy broke out after de Man's death, when it was discovered that as a young man he had contributed to collaborationist newspapers in Nazi-occupied Belgium. At least one of his articles seems undeniably anti-Semitic, and the parallel with Heidegger, whose writings have also come under fresh scrutiny recently (see chapter 6, "Hermeneutics and Phenomenology"), has led to accusations that deconstruction is politically tainted. In its extreme form, the charge seems patently unjust, but not even Derrida's deconstruction, despite his explicit engagement in leftist politics, has escaped suspicion. In any case, the controversy only fueled already existing criticism of deconstruction on political grounds. Advocates of the approach have increasingly addressed these criticisms directly, and, notwithstanding the controversy, deconstruction remains an important and pervasive presence in contemporary theory.

And yet, in spite of the resurgence of cultural study, the professional and academic study of literature remains strongly influenced by one or another variety of formalism, evolving continuously and in connected ways from the Russians to poststructuralism. Even political and cultural approaches are frequently challenged to demonstrate their fruitfulness for the close analysis of specific texts. And it is natural enough that literary critics should give priority to careful attention to the language of literature, if not in their theories, at least in their practice. The techniques of close analysis are the greatest and most distinctive achievement of twentieth-century criticism, and no critical theory will flourish that fails to come to terms with them.

Introductory Anthologies and Surveys

553. Blonsky, Marshall, ed. *On Signs*. Baltimore: Johns Hopkins UP, 1985. Essays by Barthes, Derrida, Eco, Foucault, Greimas, Hartman, Jameson, Kristeva, Lacan, Scholes, and others.

554. Crowley, Sharon. *A Teacher's Introduction to Deconstruction*. Urbana: NCTE, 1989. Discusses implications of deconstruction for teaching, especially teaching writing.

555. Culler, Jonathan. *On Deconstruction: Theory and Criticism after Structuralism*. Ithaca: Cornell UP, 1984. Good introduction to deconstruction.

556. Leitch, Vincent B. *Deconstructive Criticism: An Advanced Introduction and Survey*. New York: Columbia UP, 1982.

557. Norris, Christopher. *Deconstruction: Theory and Practice*. London: Methuen, 1982. Good introduction to the background and ideas of deconstruction.

558. Sarup, Madan. *An Introductory Guide to Post-structuralism and Postmodernism*. Athens: U of Georgia P, 1989. Discusses Lacan, Derrida, and Foucault.

559. Sturrock, John, ed. *Structuralism and Since: From Lévi-Strauss to Derrida*. Oxford: Oxford UP, 1979. Leading experts offer chapters on Lévi-Strauss, Barthes, Foucault, Lacan, and Derrida.

560. Taylor, Mark C., ed. *Deconstruction in Context: Literature and Philosophy*. Chicago: U of Chicago P, 1986. Selections from the philosophical tradition from Kant through Derrida provide a context for deconstruction.

Books and Collections

561. Argyros, Alexander J. *A Blessed Rage for Order: Deconstruction, Evolution, and Chaos*. Ann Arbor: U of Michigan P, 1992. Criticizes deconstructionist ideas of nature and human culture, using concepts from chaos theory and evolution.

562. Atkins, G. Douglas. *Reading Deconstruction—Deconstructive Reading*. Lexington: UP of Kentucky, 1983. On Derrida, Hartman, J. Hillis Miller, with essays applying deconstruction to Restoration and eighteenth-century literature.

563. Atkins, G. Douglas, and Michael L. Johnson, eds. *Writing and Reading*

Differently: Deconstruction and the Teaching of Composition and Literature. Lawrence: U of Kansas P, 1985. Essays by a variety of leading theorists on teaching at all levels.

564.   Bannet, Eve Tavor. *Structuralism and the Logic of Dissent: Barthes, Derrida, Foucault, Lacan.* Urbana: U of Illinois P, 1988.

565.   Beitchman, Philip. *I Am a Process with No Subject.* Tallahassee: UP of Florida, 1988. Deconstruction in modern literature and literature's resistance to philosophical and social order.

566.   Berman, Art. *From the New Criticism to Deconstruction: The Reception of Structuralism and Post-structuralism.* Urbana: U of Illinois P, 1988. Describes structuralism and poststructuralism (Foucault, Lacan, Althusser, Derrida) and shows how New Criticism and American culture prepared for the particular form these movements took here.

567.   Bloom, Clive. *The "Occult" Experience and the New Criticism: Daemonism, Sexuality, and the Hidden in Literature.* Savage: Barnes, 1987. Discusses Freud, Lacan, Foucault, Derrida, Barthes, and others to explore relations of textuality, sexuality, and psyche in poststructuralism.

Butler, Christopher. *Interpretation, Deconstruction, and Ideology: An Introduction to Some Current Issues in Literary Theory.* See entry 76.

568.   Carroll, David. *The Subject in Question: The Languages of Theory and the Strategies of Fiction.* Chicago: U of Chicago P, 1982.

569.   Chase, Cynthia. *Decomposing Figures: Rhetorical Readings in the Romantic Tradition.* Baltimore: Johns Hopkins UP, 1986. On "disfiguration" in a range of literary and philosophical texts.

570.   Cornis-Popoe, Marcel. *Hermeneutic Desire and Critical Rewriting: Narrative Interpretation in the Wake of Poststructuralism.* New York: St. Martin's, 1991. Develops interactive model of literary interpretation.

571.   Dasenbrock, Reed Way, ed. *Redrawing the Lines: Analytic Philosophy, Deconstruction, and Literary Theory.* Minneapolis: U of Minnesota P, 1989. Ten essays, several on Wittgenstein and deconstruction; with bibliography.

Dews, Peter. *Logics of Disintegration: Post-structuralist Thought and the Claims of Critical Theory.* See entry 1043.

572.   Donoghue, Denis. *Ferocious Alphabets.* New York: Columbia UP, 1984. Critical study of contemporary criticism, especially deconstruction.

573.   Easthope, Antony. *British Post-structuralism.* London: Routledge, 1988. Discerns two tendencies in poststructuralism, one formalist, the other political; discusses the failure of Derrida's philosophy to take root in Britain.

574.   Ellis, John M. *Against Deconstruction.* Princeton: Princeton UP, 1988. A sharp critique.

575.   Fabb, Nigel, Derek Attridge, Alan Durant, and Colin MacCabe, eds. *The Linguistics of Writing: Arguments between Language and Literature.* New

York: Methuen, 1988. Essays by Derrida, Fish, Jameson, Williams, and others, from a conference where Marxist, structuralist, and poststructuralist approaches confronted one another.

Fekete, John, ed. *The Structural Allegory: Reconstructive Encounters with the New French Thought.* See entry 1145.

576. Felperin, Howard. *Beyond Deconstruction: The Uses and Abuses of Literary Theory.* Oxford: Clarendon–Oxford UP, 1985. Discusses deconstruction, structuralism, and Marxist theory.

577. Fischer, Michael. *Does Deconstruction Make Any Difference? Poststructuralism and the Defense of Poetry in Modern Criticism.* Bloomington: Indiana UP, 1985. Discusses Matthew Arnold, Frye, Derrida, Fish, J. Hillis Miller, and others.

578. Frank, Manfred. *What Is Neostructuralism?* Trans. Sabine Wilke and Richard T. Gray. Minneapolis: U of Minnesota P, 1988. On Saussure, Lévi-Strauss, Derrida, Lacan, Foucault, Lyotard, and others.

579. Gallop, Jane. *Intersections: A Reading of Sade with Bataille, Blanchot, and Klossowski.* Lincoln: U of Nebraska P, 1981.

580. Goodheart, Eugene. *The Skeptic Disposition in Contemporary Criticism.* Princeton: Princeton UP, 1985. Critique of poststructuralist criticism.

581. Harland, Richard. *Superstructuralism: The Philosophy of Structuralism and Post-structuralism.* London: Methuen, 1987. On Lacan, Althusser, Barthes, Foucault, Derrida, and others; with bibliography.

582. Hirsch, David H. *The Deconstruction of Literature: Criticism after Auschwitz.* Hanover: UP of New England, 1991. Finds antihumanist and authoritarian strains in postmodern literary theories and links them to nazism.

583. Jacobs, Carol. *The Dissimulating Harmony: The Image of Interpretation in Nietzsche, Rilke, Artaud, and Benjamin.* Baltimore: Johns Hopkins UP, 1978.

584. Johnson, Barbara. *The Critical Difference: Essays in the Contemporary Rhetoric of Reading.* Baltimore: Johns Hopkins UP, 1985. Analyzes French and American literary works and contemporary theories of Barthes, Lacan, Austin, and Derrida.

585. ———. *A World of Difference.* Baltimore: Johns Hopkins UP, 1988. On deconstruction and politics, with a new preface addressing the controversy over de Man.

586. Kavanagh, Thomas M., ed. *The Limits of Theory.* Stanford: Stanford UP, 1989. Eight essays in the wake of deconstruction.

Kennedy, Alan. *Reading Resistance Value: Deconstructive Practice and the Politics of Literary Critical Encounters.* See entry 1059.

587. Krupnick, Mark, ed. *Displacement: Derrida and After.* Bloomington: Indiana UP, 1983. Seven essays on deconstruction, politics, feminism, and other topics.

588.   Lacoue-Labarthe, Philippe. *Typography: Mimesis, Philosophy, Politics*. Ed. Christopher Fynsk. Cambridge: Harvard UP, 1989. On mimesis, subjectivity, and representation; introduction by Derrida.

589.   Libertson, Joseph. *Proximity: Levinas, Blanchot, Bataille, and Communication*. The Hague: Nijhoff, 1982.

590.   Loesberg, Jonathan. *Aestheticism and Deconstruction: Pater, Derrida, and de Man*. Princeton: Princeton UP, 1991. By deepening the concept of deconstruction, defends it against dismissive charges of "aestheticism."

591.   Machin, Richard, and Christopher Norris, eds. *Post-structuralist Readings of English Poetry*. Cambridge: Cambridge UP, 1987. Essays by Bloom, Hartman, Krieger, J. Hillis Miller, Spivak, and others.

        McKenna, Andrew J. *Violence and Difference: Girard, Derrida, and Deconstruction*. See entry 1460.

592.   Melville, Stephen W. *Philosophy beside Itself: On Deconstruction and Modernism*. Minneapolis: U of Minnesota P, 1986. Argues that modernism begins with Kant's critical philosophy and discusses deconstruction's relation to Hegel, to French Hegel studies from the 1930s to the 1950s, and to psychoanalysis.

593.   Merquior, J. G. *From Prague to Paris: A Critique of Structuralism and Post-structuralist Thought*. London: Verso, 1987.

594.   Merrell, Floyd. *Deconstruction Reframed*. West Lafayette: Purdue UP, 1985. Considers deconstruction in relation to philosophers Peirce, Gödel, and Popper and to the philosophy of science.

595.   Norris, Christopher. *Deconstruction and the Interests of Theory*. London: Pinter, 1988. Collects essays on de Man, Derrida, Hartman, legal interpretation, and other topics.

596.   ———. *The Deconstructive Turn: Essays in the Rhetoric of Philosophy*. London: Methuen, 1984. Brings together deconstruction and Anglo-American analytic philosophy.

597.   Pefanis, Julian. *Heterology and the Postmodern: Bataille, Baudrillard, and Lyotard*. Durham: Duke UP, 1991.

598.   Rajnath, ed. *Deconstruction: A Critique*. London: Macmillan, 1988.

        Ray, William. *Literary Meaning: From Phenomenology to Deconstruction*. See entry 690.

599.   Richman, Michele H. *Reading Georges Bataille: Beyond the Gift*. Baltimore: Johns Hopkins UP, 1982. Discusses a philosopher and novelist whose theories influenced Derrida.

600.   Ronell, Avital. *The Telephone Book: Technology–Schizophrenia–Electric Speech*. Lincoln: U of Nebraska P, 1989. Uses unconventional typography to develop deconstructive themes from an analysis of modern communications technology.

601.   Royle, Nicholas. *Telepathy and Literature*. Oxford: Blackwell, 1990. Draws

on Freud and Derrida to discuss concept of telepathy and its implications for literature and theory.

Ryan, Michael. *Marxism and Deconstruction: A Critical Articulation.* See entry 1153.

Said, Edward. *Beginnings: Intention and Method.* See entry 1322.

602.   Schoeck, R. J. *Intertextuality and Renaissance Texts.* Bamberg, Germ.: Kaiser, 1984. Reconsiders issues of editing texts and finding an author's sources in the light of poststructuralist theory.

603.   Shaviro, Steven. *Passion and Excess: Blanchot, Bataille, and Literary Theory.* Tallahassee: Florida State UP, 1990. Discusses two major influences on Derrida's theories.

604.   Silverman, Hugh, and Gary E. Aylesworth, eds. *The Textual Sublime: Deconstruction and Its Differences.* Albany: State U of New York P, 1990. Eighteen essays mainly on Derrida and de Man, including an essay by de Man on Kant.

605.   Silverman, Kaja. *The Subject of Semiotics.* New York: Oxford UP, 1983. On Barthes, Lacan, Althusser, poststructuralism, and the concept of the human "subject."

606.   Sollers, Philippe. *Writing and the Experience of Limits.* Trans. Phillip Barnard. New York: Columbia UP, 1983. A founder of the important journal *Tel Quel*, Sollers remains a maverick in poststructuralist theory.

607.   Stoekl, Allan, ed. *On Bataille. Yale French Studies* 78. New Haven: Yale UP, 1990. Essays on a philosopher and novelist who influenced Derrida.

608.   ——. *Politics, Writing, Mutilation: The Cases of Bataille, Blanchot, Roussel, Leiris, and Ponge.* Minneapolis: U of Minnesota P, 1985. Discusses ideas of five French writers who influenced poststructuralism.

Sussman, Henry S. *High Resolution: Critical Theory and the Problem of Literacy.* See entry 1382.

609.   Ulmer, Gregory L. *Applied Grammatology: Post(e)-Pedagogy from Jacques Derrida to Joseph Beuys.* Baltimore: Johns Hopkins UP, 1985. Moves from Derrida's most recent ideas to performance art and pedagogy.

610.   Warminski, Andrzej. *Readings in Interpretation: Hölderlin, Hegel, Heidegger.* Minneapolis: U of Minnesota P, 1987. Argues that a negative moment in texts is not a prelude to a unity on the model of self-consciousness or subjectivity but requires a new reading theory and practice.

611.   Young, Robert, ed. *Untying the Text: A Post-structuralist Reader.* London: Routledge, 1981. Theoretical and applied essays by leading French and American poststructuralists, including a Marxist essay by Balibar and Macherey.

Individual Author

JACQUES DERRIDA (1930–   )

For a brief discussion of Derrida's ideas, see the headnote to this chapter.

612.   *Acts of Literature.* Ed. Derek Attridge. New York: Routledge, 1992. Collects essays and excerpts on works of Rousseau, Mallarmé, Joyce, Kafka, and Shakespeare; includes an interview with Derrida written for this volume.

613.   *The Archaeology of the Frivolous: Reading Condillac.* Trans. John P. Leavey. Pittsburgh: Duquesne UP, 1981.

614.   *Cinders.* Trans. and ed. Ned Lukacher. Lincoln: U of Nebraska P, 1991.

615.   *A Derrida Reader: Between the Blinds.* Ed. Peggy Kamuf. New York: Columbia UP, 1990. Twenty-two essays and excerpts from twenty-five years of writing, organized in five sections with introductions.

616.   *Dissemination.* Trans. Barbara Johnson. Chicago: U of Chicago P, 1981.

617.   *The Ear of the Other: Otobiography, Transference, Translation: Texts and Discussion with Jacques Derrida.* Trans. Peggy Kamuf and Avital Ronell. Ed. Christie V. McDonald. New York: Schocken, 1985. Essay by and discussions with Derrida.

618.   *Edmund Husserl's "Origin of Geometry": An Introduction.* Trans. John P. Leavey, Jr. Lincoln: U of Nebraska P, 1989. Derrida's first book, a study of an essay by the philosopher Husserl.

619.   *Glas.* Trans. John P. Leavey, Jr., and Richard Rand. Lincoln: U of Nebraska P, 1987. Printed in adjacent columns, texts by Hegel and the contemporary French novelist Genet are analyzed.

620.   *Limited Inc.: Abc* . . . Baltimore: Johns Hopkins UP, 1977. Polemics against a critic who challenged his interpretation of Austin's speech-act theory of language and meaning.

621.   *Margins of Philosophy.* Trans. Alan Bass. Chicago: U of Chicago P, 1982.

622.   *Mémoires: For Paul de Man.* Trans. Cecile Lindsay, Jonathan Culler, and Eduardo Cadava. Ed. Avital Ronell and Eduardo Cadava. Rev. ed. New York: Columbia UP, 1989. This revised paperback edition contains an epilogue in response to the controversy over de Man's wartime writings.

623.   *Of Grammatology.* Trans. Gayatri Chakravorty Spivak. Baltimore: Johns Hopkins UP, 1976.

624.   *Of Spirit: Heidegger and the Question.* Trans. Geoffrey Bennington and Rachel Bowlby. Chicago: U of Chicago P, 1989. Sets Heidegger's use of the term *spirit* in a political context.

625.   *Positions.* Trans. Alan Bass. Chicago: U of Chicago P, 1981.

626. *The Post Card: From Socrates to Freud and Beyond.* Trans. Alan Bass. Chicago: U of Chicago P, 1987.

627. *Signeponge = Signsponge.* Trans. Richard Rand. New York: Columbia UP, 1984. On the French poet Ponge.

628. *Speech and Phenomena and Other Essays on Husserl's Theory of Signs.* Trans. David B. Allison. Evanston: Northwestern UP, 1973.

629. *Spurs/Eperons.* Trans. Barbara Harlow. Chicago: U of Chicago P, 1981. On Nietzsche, "style," and the feminine.

630. *The Truth in Painting.* Trans. Geoff Bennington and Ian McLeod. Chicago: U of Chicago P, 1987.

631. *Writing and Difference.* Trans. Alan Bass. Chicago: U of Chicago P, 1978.

Derrida Bibliography

632. Nordquist, Joan. *Jacques Derrida: A Bibliography.* Santa Cruz. Reference and Research Services, 1986.

Books on Derrida

Carroll, David. *Paraesthetics: Foucault, Lyotard, Derrida.* See entry 1305.

633. Gasché, Rodolphe. *The Tain of the Mirror: Derrida and the Philosophy of Reflection.* Cambridge: Harvard UP, 1986.

634. Hartman, Geoffrey. *Saving the Text: Literature/Derrida/Philosophy.* Baltimore: Johns Hopkins UP, 1982. A sophisticated introduction to Derrida by a distinguished literary critic.

635. Leavey, John P., Jr. *Glassary.* Lincoln: U of Nebraska P, 1986. Includes Ulmer, "Sounding the Unconscious," and Derrida, "Proverb, 'He That Would Pun—.'"

636. Llewelyn, John. *Derrida on the Threshold of Sense.* New York: St. Martin's, 1986.

637. Magliola, Robert. *Derrida on the Mend.* West Lafayette: Purdue UP, 1984. Discusses deconstruction in connection with ancient Chinese philosophy.

Megill, Allan. *Prophets of Extremity: Nietzsche, Heidegger, Foucault, Derrida.* See entry 725.

Michelfelder, Diane P., and Richard E. Palmer, eds. *Dialogue and Deconstruction: The Gadamer-Derrida Encounter.* See entry 738.

Muller, John P., and William J. Richardson. *The Purloined Poe: Lacan, Derrida, and Psychoanalytic Reading.* See entry 977.

638. Neel, Jasper. *Plato, Derrida, and Writing.* Carbondale: Southern Illinois UP, 1988. Considers Derrida's discussion of Plato's critique of writing.

639. Norris, Christopher. *Derrida.* Cambridge: Harvard UP, 1988.

640. Rapaport, Herman. *Heidegger and Derrida: Reflections on Time and Language.* Lincoln: U of Nebraska P, 1989.

641.   Smith, Joseph H., and William Kerrigan, eds. *Taking Chances: Derrida, Psychoanalysis, and Literature*. Baltimore: John Hopkins UP, 1984. Includes an essay by Derrida.

642.   Staten, Henry. *Wittgenstein and Derrida*. Lincoln: U of Nebraska P, 1984. Relevance of Wittgenstein and deconstruction for literary theory.

643.   Wood, David, ed. *Derrida: A Critical Reader*. Oxford: Blackwell, 1992. Essay by Derrida, nine essays on his work, and a bibliography of his writings.

The Yale School

Just as Yale emerged as the center of New Critical theory, a second *Yale school* of deconstruction appeared in the 1970s, though *school* is too strong a term for a rather loose grouping of sympathetic colleagues. Harold Bloom (see chapter 8, "Psychological and Psychoanalytical Critical Theory") and Geoffrey Hartman (see chapter 6, "Hermeneutics and Phenomenology") have been counted as members, but their own views diverge sharply from those of deconstruction. The group's center was Paul de Man, authoritatively seconded by J. Hillis Miller, with frequent visits by Jacques Derrida. De Man's early death and Miller's departure for the University of California at Irvine brought this "school" to an end. Yet it remains true that these important critics and theorists, working with graduate students who have become outstanding younger representatives of deconstruction, have enriched one another in ways that justify speaking of them as a group.

Collections and Books

644.   Arac, Jonathan, Wallace Martin, and Wlad Godzich, eds. *The Yale Critics: Deconstruction in America*. Minneapolis: U of Minnesota P, 1983

645.   Bloom, Harold, et al. *Deconstruction and Criticism*. New York: Seabury, 1979. Essays by members of the Yale school: Bloom, Hartman, de Man, Derrida, and J. Hillis Miller.

646.   Davis, Robert Con, and Ronald Schleifer, eds. *Rhetoric and Form: Deconstruction at Yale*. Norman: U of Oklahoma P, 1985.

647.   Moynihan, Robert. *A Recent Imagining: Interviews with Harold Bloom, Geoffrey Hartman, J. Hillis Miller, Paul de Man*. Hamden: Archon, 1986.

Individual Authors

PAUL DE MAN (1919–83)

Paul de Man's critical essays of the 1950s are chiefly indebted to the existential philosophy of Jean-Paul Sartre. Yet their concern with how a text may undermine its own apparent statement forecasts his later development.

Coming from Europe to Harvard in the early 1960s, he studied and taught with Reuben Brower and a group of faculty members who ran an introductory course on the New Critical approach to literature. Virtually his last published essay recalled and in bitter terms defended close reading against its cultured and uncultured detractors, even though de Man's own ideas had evolved in directions seemingly opposed to basic New Critical doctrines.

Close analysis of texts, de Man argued, reveals that the operation of language, particularly of rhetorical tropes like metaphor and irony, subverts a text's apparent statement. He formulated the fundamental principle somewhat cryptically: "Every text is an allegory of its own unreadability." The distinctiveness—and merit, if the term is apt—of literature is its undeluded awareness of this fact. Despite the efforts of non-literary writers to fix meanings, words generate endlessly varying understandings. But literature's very point, de Man insisted, is to create exactly this endless stream of reading, rereading, and interpretation. De Man's approach and the strikingly similar one of Derrida shared the name deconstruction. Some see in it a nihilistic skepticism. Others discern a defensive reaction to every authoritarianism's foundation in sacred texts or unquestionable dogmas, whether religious or political. Still others see simply an attempt to respond with scrupulous honesty to literature as it is actually experienced and to the burgeoning criticism that surrounds it. De Man's sometimes dizzyingly intricate analyses of literary language attracted wide and respectful attention, especially from younger critics and theorists. Despite the controversy that followed his death (see the headnote to this chapter), de Man remains an important and influential theorist.

648. *Allegories of Reading: Figural Language in Rousseau, Nietzsche, Rilke, and Proust.* New Haven: Yale UP, 1979.

649. *Blindness and Insight: Essays in the Rhetoric of Contemporary Criticism.* 2nd rev. ed. Minneapolis: U of Minnesota P, 1983. Essays on American and European critics and issues.

650. *Critical Writings, 1953–1978.* Ed. Lindsay Waters. Minneapolis: U of Minnesota P, 1989. Wide-ranging and important essays and reviews written before and after the formulation of deconstruction.

651. *The Resistance to Theory.* Minneapolis: U of Minnesota P, 1986. Includes an interview with and a bibliography of de Man.

652. *The Rhetoric of Romanticism.* New York: Columbia UP, 1984. Essays on German and English literature from Wordsworth to Yeats.

653. *Wartime Journalism, 1939–43.* Ed. Werner Hamacher, Neil Hertz, and Tom Keenan. Lincoln: U of Nebraska P, 1988. Facsimile reprints of many of de Man's journalistic pieces in French, along with English translations of pieces in Flemish, all written for collaborationist newspapers during the Nazi occupation of Belgium.

Books on de Man

654. Brooks, Peter, Shoshana Felman, and J. Hillis Miller, eds. *The Lesson of Paul de Man*. New Haven: Yale UP, 1985.

Derrida, Jacques. *Mémoires: For Paul de Man*. See entry 622.

655. Hamacher, Werner, Neil Hertz, and Tom Keenan, eds. *Response: On Paul de Man's Wartime Journalism*. Lincoln: U of Nebraska P, 1988. Essays by various contributors on the issues raised by de Man's wartime journalism, and a collection of recent newspaper responses to the controversy.

656. Lehman, David. *Signs of the Times: Deconstruction and the Fall of Paul de Man*. New York: Poseidon, 1991. General review of deconstruction, with full discussion of de Man's wartime journalism and the reactions by friends and foes to its discovery.

657. Norris, Christopher. *Paul de Man: Deconstruction and the Critique of Aesthetic Ideology*. New York: Methuen, 1988.

658. Waters, Lindsay, and Wlad Godzich, eds. *Reading de Man Reading*. Minneapolis: U of Minnesota Press, 1989. Fourteen essays by Hartman, Derrida, J. Hillis Miller, Jauss, and others.

J. HILLIS MILLER (1928–   )

J. Hillis Miller's earliest books closely followed the phenomenological critical method of Georges Poulet (for these titles see chapter 6, "Hermeneutics and Phenomenology"), who was for a time a colleague of Miller's at Johns Hopkins. After moving to Yale, Miller became an adherent of deconstruction, and his work took an entirely new direction. He remains one of the most lucid and accessible of the deconstructionists, still finally more interested in attending to literary works than to elaborating theory at an abstract level.

659. *The Ethics of Reading: Kant, de Man, Eliot, Trollope, James, and Benjamin*. New York: Columbia UP, 1986.

660. *Fiction and Repetition: Seven English Novels*. Cambridge: Harvard UP, 1982.

661. *The Linguistic Moment: From Wordsworth to Stevens*. Princeton: Princeton UP, 1985. Focuses on passages where language is both medium and theme.

662. *Theory Now and Then*. Durham: Duke UP, 1991. Collects essays from 1966 to 1989, many on literary theorists and theories.

663. *Versions of Pygmalion*. Cambridge: Harvard UP, 1990. Analyzes narratives to argue that ethics is at the heart of deconstruction.

6. Hermeneutics and Phenomenology

Hermeneutics is an unfamiliar term for a straightforward critical issue. Originally, the word meant the rules or methods for interpreting the Bible. During the nineteenth century, its meaning was gradually broadened to cover every effort to understand something, whether a text or a social situation. At the end of the century, the philosopher Wilhelm Dilthey sought a foundation for understanding all historical phenomena, including institutions and cultural objects like art and literature. This extension of meaning culminated in the philosophy of Martin Heidegger, who argued that understanding was the fundamental reality of human existence.

That a philosophy concerned with all aspects of understanding and how it is achieved has importance for literary criticism is obvious enough. Only recently, however, has this largely German philosophical tradition begun to permeate critical theory, chiefly through the attention paid to Hans-Georg Gadamer and Paul Ricoeur. Hermeneutics has stirred considerable interest in the social sciences in recent years, enabling hermeneutic criticism to forge important links with political and sociological theory, particularly through basic concepts like practice, authority, tradition, and the relation of understanding and consensus building to basic political and social processes. The emphasis of hermeneutic philosophers on the role of historical tradition in underpinning our understanding also connects with important varieties of historical theory. Leading figures in these extensions of hermeneutics include Edward Shils, Fred Dallmayr, and Chaim Perelman, the last of whom has written extensively on rhetoric and legal theory.

Phenomenology is concerned with how every variety of our experience appears to our minds. In the work of its founder, Edmund Husserl, phenomenology took the form of exacting descriptions of the states and forms of consciousness, particularly perception. Ultimately, Husserl came to recognize the ways the very nature and structure of our consciousness determine how the world appears to us and also the ways our collective historical experience, recorded or "sedimented" in our language and culture, also shapes our perceptions. This extension opened the way for the *Geneva school* of critics, led by Georges Poulet. Using the whole body of an author's writings, including diaries, letters, and unpublished materials, these critics aimed to describe the precise, individual pattern the author's consciousness gave phenomena like time and space as they appeared in his or her work. The *critics of consciousness*, as they were sometimes called, shared an orientation similar to that of Gaston Bachelard, who also tried to describe how the material world appeared to consciousness through its representation in poetic images that emerged from "waking reverie," a state between consciousness and the unconscious. Meanwhile, Husserl's student Roman Ingarden applied Husserl's earlier method of rigorous description to literature and the drama.

The two critical movements overlap considerably, since Heidegger was Husserl's most prominent student and in turn influenced his teacher through his own philosophical writings. The hermeneutic emphasis is dominant in current theory, but the phenomenological critics remain important figures.

Books and Collections

664.   Altieri, Charles. *Act and Quality: A Theory of Literary Meaning and Humanistic Understanding.* Amherst: U of Massachusetts P, 1981. Draws on Wittgenstein and language analysis to link meaning to use and action; analyzes poetry by William Carlos Williams.

665.   Amacher, Richard E., and Victor Lange, eds. *New Perspectives in German Literary Criticism.* Princeton: Princeton UP, 1979. Translated essays selected from five volumes of a German series on poetics and hermeneutics.

Binswanger, Ludwig. *Being in the World: Selected Papers of Ludwig Binswanger.* See entry 877.

666.   Bleicher, Josef. *Contemporary Hermeneutics: Hermeneutics as Method, Philosophy and Critique.* London: Routledge, 1980. Discusses general issues and history of hermeneutics, with excerpts from Emilio Betti, Gadamer, Habermas, Ricoeur, and others.

667.   Blum, Alan, and Peter McHugh. *Self-Reflection in the Arts and Sciences.* Atlantic Highlands: Humanities, 1984.

668.   Bové, Paul. *Destructive Poetics: Heidegger and Modern American Poetry.* New York: Columbia UP, 1980.

669.   Bozarth-Campbell, Alla. *The World's Body: An Incarnational Aesthetic of Interpretation.* University: U of Alabama P, 1980.

670.   Bruns, Gerald L. *Inventions: Writing, Textuality, and Understanding in Literary History.* New Haven: Yale UP, 1982. Brilliant collection of essays, wide-ranging in topics and texts discussed.

671.   Frei, Hans W. *The Eclipse of Biblical Narrative: A Study in Eighteenth and Nineteenth Century Hermeneutics.* New Haven: Yale UP, 1974. Excellent historical study with broad cultural implications.

672.   Gras, Vernon W., ed. *European Literary Theory and Practice: From Existential Phenomenology to Structuralism.* New York: Delta-Dell, 1973. Excellent selections representing structuralism and hermeneutics.

         Harris, Wendell V. *Interpretive Acts: In Search of Meaning.* See entry 112.

673.   Hofstadter, Albert. *Agony and Epitaph: Man, His Art, and His Poetry.* New York: Braziller, 1970.

674.   ———. *Truth and Art.* New York: Columbia UP, 1965.

675.   Holdheim, W. Wolfgang. *The Hermeneutic Mode: Essays on Time in Literature and Literary Theory.* Ithaca: Cornell UP, 1984. Essays on general topics and interpretations of works by Gide, Hugo, Constant, Dostoevsky, and Tolstoy.

676.   Hopper, Stanley Romaine, and David L. Miller, eds. *Interpretation: The Poetry of Meaning.* New York: Harcourt, 1967.

677.   Horton, Susan R. *Interpreting Interpreting: Interpreting Dickens' Dombey.* Baltimore: Johns Hopkins UP, 1979. Raises general issues while focusing on Dickens's novel.

678.   Howard, Roy J. *Three Faces of Hermeneutics: An Introduction to Current Theories of Understanding.* Berkeley: U of California P, 1982. Describes analytic, Marxist, and phenomenological hermeneutics.

679.   Hoy, David Couzens. *The Critical Circle: Literature, History, and Philosophical Hermeneutics.* Berkeley: U of California P, 1978. Excellent introduction to hermeneutics in relation to contemporary philosophy and criticism.

680.   Juhl, Peter D. *Interpretation: An Essay in the Philosophy of Literary Criticism.* Princeton: Princeton UP, 1980. Follows Hirsch in arguing that authorial intention should guide interpretation.

681.   Lundin, Roger, Anthony C. Thiselton, and Clarence Walhout. *The Responsibility of Hermeneutics.* Grand Rapids: Eerdmans, 1985. History and application of hermeneutics to literary and biblical texts.

682.   Mazzeo, Joseph Anthony. *Varieties of Interpretation.* Notre Dame: U of Notre Dame P, 1978. Discusses what occasions interpretation, particularly allegorical interpretation.

683.   Medina, Angel. *Time, Reflection, and the Novel: Toward a Communicative*

Theory of Literature. London: Routledge, 1979. Argues that narrative provides structures for understanding our experience.

684.   Mueller-Volmer, Kurt, ed. *The Hermeneutics Reader: Texts of the German Tradition from the Enlightenment to the Present.* New York: Continuum, 1985. Anthology with substantial introduction.

685.   Murray, Michael. *Modern Critical Theory: A Phenomenological Introduction.* The Hague: Nijhoff, 1975. On Greek poetics, New Criticism, hermeneutics, Husserl, Ingarden, and Heidegger.

686.   Ormiston, Gayle L., and Alan D. Schrift, eds. *The Hermeneutic Tradition: From Ast to Ricoeur.* Albany: State U of New York P, 1989. Anthology showing a traditional line of hermeneutics from the early nineteenth century to the present.

687.   ———, eds. *Transforming the Hermeneutic Context: From Nietzsche to Nancy.* Albany: State U of New York P, 1989. Anthology showing a divergent line of hermeneutics from Nietzsche to the present.

688.   Palmer, Richard E. *Hermeneutics: Interpretation Theory in Schleiermacher, Dilthey, Heidegger, and Gadamer.* Evanston: Northwestern UP, 1969. Good introductory survey.

689.   Peck, Jeffrey M. *Hermes Disguised: Literary Hermeneutics and the Interpretation of Literature.* Bern: Lang, 1983. Broad study of hermeneutics since the late eighteenth century, with application to three German writers.

690.   Ray, William. *Literary Meaning: From Phenomenology to Deconstruction.* Oxford: Blackwell, 1984. On a wide range of critics from Poulet, Sartre, and Blanchot to Ingarden, Iser, Hirsch, Fish, Barthes, and de Man.

691.   Schrift, Alan. *Nietzsche and the Question of Interpretation.* New York: Routledge, 1990. Discusses language, philology, genealogy, and related topics in Nietzsche, showing their implications for theory of interpretation.

692.   Seung, T. K. *Semiotics and Thematics in Hermeneutics.* New York: Columbia UP, 1982.

693.   ———. *Structuralism and Hermeneutics.* New York: Columbia UP, 1982.

694.   Shapiro, Gary, and Alan Sica, eds. *Hermeneutics: Questions and Prospects.* Amherst: U of Massachusetts P, 1984. Important collection of essays by major philosophers and literary critics.

695.   Singleton, Charles S., ed. *Interpretation: Theory and Practice.* Baltimore: Johns Hopkins UP, 1969. Essays by leading critics and scholars.

696.   Valdés, Mario J. *Phenomenological Hermeneutics and the Study of Literature.* Toronto: U of Toronto P, 1987. Discusses phenomenological hermeneutics and reader-reception aesthetics, Derrida, and Ricoeur, with chapters on literary works by Octavio Paz and Borges.

697.   ———. *Shadows in the Cave: A Phenomenological Approach to Literary Criticism Based on Hispanic Texts.* Toronto: U of Toronto P, 1982.

698.   Watkins, Evan. *The Critical Act: Criticism and Community.* New Haven:

Yale UP, 1978. Discusses Hirsch, Frye, Barthes, Derrida, Williams; plays New Critical formalist and Marxist criticism against each other, arguing for a hermeneutic perspective.

699.   Webb, Eugene. *Philosophies of Consciousness: Polanyi, Lonergan, Voegelin, Ricoeur, Girard, Kierkegaard.* Seattle: U of Washington P, 1988.

700.   Weinsheimer, Joel. *Philosophical Hermeneutics and Literary Theory.* New Haven: Yale UP, 1991. Excellent and accessible essays.

701.   Wolff, Janet. *Hermeneutic Philosophy and the Sociology of Art: An Approach to Some of the Epistemological Problems of the Sociology of Knowledge and the Sociology of Art and Literature.* London: Routledge, 1975.

Hermeneutics:
Individual Philosophical Authors

WILHELM DILTHEY (1833–1911)

Wilhelm Dilthey's main philosophical effort was to establish the nature and foundations of the humanities in general and of historical knowledge in particular. His interests led him to wide-ranging investigations of epistemology, moral philosophy, and hermeneutics, as well as to extensive historical research and writing. He distinguished between the explanations, generally causal and often quantitative, which constitute scientific knowledge, and the understanding, based on sympathy and imaginative insight into particular historic events and cultural objects, which characterizes the humanities. He recognized that humanistic understanding moves in a "hermeneutic circle": to understand an author, we must understand his or her historical period, but understanding the period requires understanding the authors who wrote in and created it. The same circle applies to the relation between whole works and their parts and even between a single word and language. Yet Dilthey argued that this path is not a vicious circle but a movement that can be progressively enlarged by a shuttling of sympathetic involvement between cultural worlds, past and present. Martin Heidegger (see below) argued emphatically against Dilthey's conception that understanding is directed toward imaginative sympathy with another person's mind or personality; he asserted instead that understanding is directed toward a *what*, whatever aspect of experience is brought to light in conversing or in reading texts.

The announcement of a project to translate Dilthey's major works into English promises renewed interest in this important theorist of humanistic understanding. Only the most relevant of his many works are listed here.

702.   *Descriptive Psychology and Historical Understanding.* Trans. Richard M. Zaner and Kenneth L. Heiges. The Hague: Nijhoff, 1977.

703.   *Introduction to the Human Sciences: An Attempt to Lay a Foundation for
       the Study of Society and History.* Trans. Ramon J. Betanzos. Detroit:
       Wayne State UP, 1988.

704.   *Pattern and Meaning in History: Thoughts on History and Society.* Ed.,
       trans., and introd. H. P. Rickman. New York: Harper, 1962. Topically
       organized selections from his writings.

705.   *The Philosophy of Existence: Introduction to Weltanschauungslehre.* Trans.
       William Kluback and Martin Weinbaum. New York: Bookman, 1957.

706.   *Selected Works.* Ed. Rudolf Makkreel and Frithjof Rodi. Princeton:
       Princeton UP, 1985– . Vol. 1: *Introduction to the Human Sciences*; vol.
       5: *Poetry and Experience.* Further volumes planned.

707.   *Selected Writings.* Ed., trans., and introd. H. P Rickman. Cambridge:
       Cambridge UP, 1976.

Books on Dilthey

708.   Bulhof, Ilse N. *Wilhelm Dilthey: A Hermeneutic Approach to the Study of
       History and Culture.* The Hague: Nijhoff, 1980.

709.   Ermarth, Michael. *Wilhelm Dilthey: The Critique of Historical Reason.*
       Chicago: U of Chicago P, 1978.

710.   Hodges, Herbert A. *The Philosophy of Wilhelm Dilthey.* London:
       Routledge, 1952.

711.   ———. *Wilhelm Dilthey: An Introduction.* London: Kegan, 1944. Includes
       sixty pages of selected passages from Dilthey.

712.   Makkreel, Rudolf A. *Dilthey: Philosopher of the Human Studies.* Princeton:
       Princeton UP, 1980.

713.   Mueller-Volmer, Kurt. *Towards a Phenomenological Theory of Literature:
       A Study of Wilhelm Dilthey's Poetik.* The Hague: Mouton, 1963.

714.   Plantinga, Theodore. *Historical Understanding in the Thought of Wilhelm
       Dilthey.* Toronto: U of Toronto P, 1980.

715.   Rickman, H. P. *Wilhelm Dilthey: Pioneer of the Human Sciences.* Berkeley:
       U of California P, 1980.

MARTIN HEIDEGGER (1889–1976)

Martin Heidegger is, of course, not a literary critic, but the evolution
of his philosophy led him to give special and penetrating attention to poetry.
Regarding the greatest poetry as akin to philosophy, he turned his astounding
powers of concentrated "listening" to hear what poetry revealed about language and our existence in the world. He favored a certain kind of poet, one
in a recognizably German tradition, from the Romantic Friedrich Hölderlin
to modernists like Georg Trakl and Stefan George. Heidegger's readings are
so immediately both the reflection of his philosophy and the medium in
which he came to conduct his philosophical meditations that they are inimita-

ble and cannot be reduced to any set of propositions about poetry, criticism, and language. But his ideas and approach have been broadly influential, and his whole philosophy stands behind hermeneutics, the deconstruction of Derrida, and many other critical movements and individual critics.

It has long been known that Heidegger joined the Nazi party in the 1930s, but evidence that his collusion with the Nazis was deeper and more long-lasting than had been fully realized has led to fresh controversy. It is certainly dismaying that perhaps the outstanding philosopher of the century was unable to grasp the nature of nazism, and for some his work is irredeemably spoiled. Yet it seems difficult to achieve any serious philosophical reflection without taking his thinking into account, and he has decisively influenced literary theory. Only a few of his basic writings and those most relevant to literary theory are included here.

716.   *Basic Writings*. Ed. David F. Krell. New York: Harper, 1977. Good collection of fundamental selections.

717.   *Being and Time*. Trans. John Macquarrie and Edward Robinson. New York: Harper, 1962. His most important single work, refocusing philosophy on issues of being, time, interpretation, and language.

718.   *Existence and Being*. Chicago: Gateway, 1949. Includes essays on truth, poetry, and metaphysics.

719.   *Nietzsche*. 4 vols. New York: Harper, 1979–82. Vol. 1: *The Will to Power as Art*, trans. David F. Krell (1979); vol. 2: *The Eternal Recurrence of the Same*, trans. David F. Krell (1984); vol. 3: *Will to Power as Knowledge and as Metaphysics*, trans. Joan Stambaugh, David Farrell Krell, and Frank A. Capuzzi (1985); vol. 4: *Nihilism*, trans. Frank Capuzzi (1982).

720.   *On the Way to Language*. Trans. Peter D. Hertz. New York: Harper, 1982. On language and poetry.

721.   *Poetry, Language, Thought*. Trans. Albert Hofstadter. New York: Harper, 1975. Includes the important essay "The Origin of the Work of Art."

Books on Heidegger

722.   Bruns, Gerald. *Heidegger's Estrangements: Language, Truth, and Poetry in the Later Writings*. New Haven: Yale UP, 1989. A brilliant study that avoids Heidegger's jargon and finds an accessible language to present his difficult insights.

Derrida, Jacques. *Of Spirit: Heidegger and the Question*. See entry 624.

723.   Halliburton, David. *Poetic Thinking: An Approach to Heidegger*. Chicago: U of Chicago P, 1982.

724.   Kockelmans, Joseph J., ed. and trans. *On Heidegger and Language*. Evanston: Northwestern UP, 1972.

725.   Megill, Allan. *Prophets of Extremity: Nietzsche, Heidegger, Foucault, Der-

rida. Berkeley: U of California P, 1985. By an intellectual historian who stresses the political and social dimensions.

726.   Spanos, William V., ed. *Martin Heidegger and the Question of Literature: Toward a Postmodern Literary Hermeneutics.* Bloomington: Indiana UP, 1979.

727.   White, David A. *Heidegger and the Language of Poetry.* Lincoln: U of Nebraska P, 1978.

HANS-GEORG GADAMER (1900–   )

Hans-Georg Gadamer is arguably the most important philosopher of the humanities in this century. He was trained as a scholar of Greek philosophy, especially Plato, and was a student of Martin Heidegger. His thinking begins with Heidegger's assertion that understanding is fundamental, not just as a mental activity, but as the basic fact of human existence. Modern science, he observes, supplies us with a model of knowledge we take for granted. Yet that model seems to be inappropriate to the realm of culture or art. How then can we defend our conviction that the humanities give us genuine and irreplaceable insights? Gadamer recovers within the tradition of the humanities some characteristic humanistic concepts such as taste, *Bildung* (cultural and educational shaping of the individual person), and the probable (neither ignorance nor scientific-conceptual knowledge, yet legitimate in its own sphere). He contends that understanding in the humanities has a distinct nature, defined by these concepts. For Gadamer, language establishes the common ground on which human beings come to a shared understanding of every particular subject matter. Since the humanities focus on what is said and conveyed in the language of texts passed down through tradition, the way understanding is achieved in the humanities is exemplary for all of social life. Criticizing what he sees as a narrow and restrictive rationalism, Gadamer stresses the power of "prejudice," defined as everything we already know and are. Although prejudices may distort perception, he argues, they also perform a positive function: they are what enable us to understand at all. At the same time, he stresses that the common recognition that we have misunderstood something is both negative and positive. In the experience of seeing our error, we gain insight not just into the thing we previously misunderstood but into the fact that as mortal human beings we have limited powers of understanding. To achieve our authentic human potential, we need the challenge and aid offered by the full range of works—mainly texts—that come down to us from the past.

This bare summary does no justice to the range and power of Gadamer's thought—or its sometimes daunting difficulty. But his is perhaps the most balanced and comprehensive interpretation of humanistic understanding we possess.

728. *Dialogue and Dialectic: Eight Hermeneutical Studies on Plato.* Trans. P. Christopher Smith. New Haven: Yale UP, 1980.

729. *Hegel's Dialectic: Five Hermeneutical Studies.* Trans. P. Christopher Smith. New Haven: Yale UP, 1982.

730. *The Idea of the Good in Platonic-Aristotelian Philosophy.* Trans. P. Christopher Smith. New Haven: Yale UP, 1986.

731. *On Education, Poetry, and History: Applied Hermeneutics.* Ed. Dieter Misgeld and Graeme Nicholson. Trans. Lawrence Schmidt and Monica Reuss. Albany: State U of New York P, 1992.

732. *Philosophical Apprenticeships.* Trans. Robert R. Sullivan. Cambridge: MIT P, 1985. Memoirs of Gadamer's studies with Heidegger and others.

733. *Philosophical Hermeneutics.* Trans. and ed. David E. Linge. Berkeley: U of California P, 1977. A collection of wide-ranging essays; good as an introduction to Gadamer's thought.

734. *Plato's Dialectical Ethics: Phenomenological Interpretations Relating to the Philebus.* Trans. Robert M. Wallace. New Haven: Yale UP, 1991.

735. *Reason in the Age of Science.* Trans. Frederick G. Lawrence. Cambridge: MIT P, 1982. On hermeneutics and "practice" and the "practical."

736. *The Relevance of the Beautiful and Other Essays.* Trans. Nicholas Walker. Ed. Robert Bernasconi. Cambridge: Cambridge UP, 1986. With bibliography of English translations of Gadamer's writings.

737. *Truth and Method.* Rev. trans. Joel Weinsheimer and Donald G. Marshall. New York: Continuum, 1989. His magnum opus; one of the most important works of twentieth-century philosophy of the humanities.

Books on Gadamer

738. Michelfelder, Diane P., and Richard E. Palmer, eds. *Dialogue and Deconstruction: The Gadamer-Derrida Encounter.* Albany: State U of New York P, 1989. Essays by, and an interchange between, Derrida and Gadamer from a conference, with later essays by commentators on the relations between hermeneutics and deconstruction.

739. Silverman, Hugh J., ed. *Gadamer and Hermeneutics.* New York: Routledge, 1991. Includes essay by Gadamer and essays on his work in relation to Plato, Heidegger, Ricoeur, Barthes, Derrida, and Habermas, and on the topics of metaphor, science, and interpretive texts; with bibliography of works by Gadamer and of works on Gadamer and hermeneutics.

740. Warnke, Georgia. *Gadamer: Hermeneutics, Tradition, and Reason.* Cambridge: Polity, 1987.

741. Weinsheimer, Joel. *Gadamer's Hermeneutics: A Reading of Truth and Method.* New Haven: Yale UP, 1985. Excellent introduction to Gadamer's magnum opus.

742. Wright, Kathleen, ed. *Festivals of Interpretation: Essays on Hans-Georg Gadamer's Work.* Albany: State U of New York P, 1990. Includes essays on Gadamer's theory and modern poetry.

PAUL RICOEUR (1913–   )

Paul Ricoeur began as a translator and commentator on Edmund Husserl. He then tried to extend phenomenological description to the relation not of consciousness to the world of our experience but of human will to that world. This investigation led him to study fallibility and evil. In the process, his method of approach changed. From direct descriptions of the will, he turned to explore the varieties of evil recorded in Western poetry, mythology, and philosophy. He came to recognize that tradition provided a greater range of phenomena than pure reflection could have imagined. He therefore began to stress the importance of culturally created and transmitted symbols in our mental life. He pursued the study of symbols in a major interpretation of Sigmund Freud, confronting Freud's suspicion that unconscious and instinctual forces lay behind cultural symbols and also exploring the similar suspicion directed by Nietzsche and Marx toward cultural phenomena. Ricoeur argued that these symbols are not simply masks for sexual drives, economic interests, or an arbitrary will to power. They contain significance whose recovery and appreciation is vital to our life. Ricoeur went on to write an important book on metaphor, which finds in metaphor not simply a figure of speech but the very process by which meaning is created and brought into language. In his three-volume work *Time and Narrative*, he maintains that narrative is the way human beings grasp the meaning of their existence in time. The philosophical depth of Ricoeur's thought gives an unsurpassed richness and power to the works in which he touches on themes of fundamental importance to critical theory. In addition, he has written extensively on the interpretation of biblical texts and has commented on a variety of political and social issues.

743.   *The Conflict of Interpretations: Essays on Hermeneutics.* Ed. Don Ihde. Evanston: Northwestern UP, 1974. Hermeneutics and structuralism, psychoanalysis, religion, and other topics.

744.   *Essays on Biblical Interpretation.* Ed. and introd. Lewis S. Mudge. Philadelphia: Fortress, 1980.

745.   *Freud and Philosophy: An Essay on Interpretation.* Trans. Denis Savage. New Haven: Yale UP, 1970.

746.   *Hermeneutics and the Human Sciences: Essays on Language, Action, and Interpretation.* Ed. and trans. John B. Thompson. Cambridge: Cambridge UP, 1981. Includes essays on interpretation and generalizes the concept of text from the humanities to the social sciences.

747.   *History and Truth.* Trans. Charles A. Kelbley. Evanston: Northwestern UP, 1965. Essays on various topics.

748.   *Interpretation Theory: Discourse and the Surplus of Meaning.* Dallas: Texas Christian UP, 1976.

749. *Lectures on Ideology and Utopia.* Ed. George H. Taylor. New York: Columbia UP, 1986. Traces two key Marxist political themes.

750. *Main Trends in Philosophy.* New York: Holmes, 1979.

751. *Paul Ricoeur on Biblical Hermeneutics.* Ed. John Dominic Crossan. Rpt. of a spec. issue of *Semeia.* Missoula: Scholars, 1975. An excellent illustration of his interpretive theory and practice.

752. *The Philosophy of Paul Ricoeur.* Ed. Charles E. Reagan and David Stewart. Boston: Beacon, 1978. Essays and excerpts from Ricoeur presenting the full range of his work.

753. *Political and Social Essays.* Ed. David Stewart and Joseph Bien. Columbus: Ohio State UP, 1974.

754. *A Ricoeur Reader: Reflection and Imagination.* Ed. Mario J. Valdés. Toronto: U of Toronto P, 1991.

755. *The Rule of Metaphor: Multi-disciplinary Studies of the Creation of Meaning in Language.* Trans. Robert Czerny with Kathleen McLaughlin and John Costello. Toronto: U of Toronto P, 1977.

756. *The Symbolism of Evil.* Trans. Emerson Buchanan. New York: Harper, 1967. Studies the representation of evil in the Bible, mythology and philosophical works.

757. *Time and Narrative.* Trans. Kathleen (McLaughlin) Blamey and David Pellauer. 3 vols. Chicago: U of Chicago P, 1984–88. Monumental study of narrative in historical and literary writing and its philosophical bases and importance.

758. Kearney, Richard. *Dialogues with Contemporary Continental Thinkers: The Phenomenological Heritage: Paul Ricoeur, et al.* Manchester, Eng.: Manchester UP, 1984. Dialogues with Ricoeur, Levinas, Marcuse, Stanislas Breton, and Derrida.

Books on Ricoeur

759. Clark, S. H. *Paul Ricoeur.* London: Routledge, 1991.

760. Gerhart, Mary. *The Question of Belief in Literary Criticism: An Introduction to the Hermeneutical Theory of Paul Ricoeur.* Stuttgart: Heinz, 1979. Surveys the question of belief in New Criticism, Frye, Hirsch, Gadamer, and extensively in Ricoeur.

761. Kemp, T. Peter, and David Rasmussen, eds. *The Narrative Path: The Later Works of Paul Ricoeur.* Cambridge: MIT P, 1989. Four essays on narrative and metaphor, a response by Ricoeur, and a bibliography of his work in English.

762. Klemm, David. *The Hermeneutical Theory of Paul Ricoeur: A Constructive Analysis.* Lewisburg: Bucknell, UP, 1983.

763. Thompson, John B. *Critical Hermeneutics: A Study in the Thought of Paul Ricoeur and Jürgen Habermas.* Cambridge: Cambridge UP, 1981.

764.   Wood, David, ed. *On Paul Ricoeur: Narrative and Interpretation.* New York: Routledge, 1992.

Hermeneutics: Individual Critical Theorists

MAURICE BLANCHOT (1907–   )

Maurice Blanchot is so enigmatic and unusual a figure that his inclusion in this section is certainly open to challenge. But his philosophical debt to Martin Heidegger is especially clear in books like *Literary Space.* Himself a novelist of a subtle and modernist style, Blanchot's extensive critical writings are concerned with issues of importance to him as an artist. He argues that fictive narration is freed from immediate reference to the ordinary world and, equally, that it is freed from the author's biographical personality: one begins writing fiction, he says, not with the word "I . . ." but with the impersonal "He . . ." Given this liberation from reality and from the author's self, what can give to fiction that sense of necessity and inevitability that are indispensable to convincingly great art? Blanchot seeks the "necessity of writing" in the very nature of writing as an act and in the profoundly existential experience of the writer, who faces the task of creating in language works that seem to come from nowhere yet, once created, also seem as solid as reality.

There is evidence that Blanchot flirted with right-wing political movements during the 1930s. That experience and his absolute dedication to criticism and writing have led him to follow an extremely reclusive life. The importance of his work has long been recognized in France, where he was a decisive influence on Jacques Derrida and deconstruction. He is only beginning to be fully appreciated in the United States as well.

765.   *The Gaze of Orpheus and Other Literary Essays.* Trans. Lydia Davis. Ed. P. Adams Sitney. Barrytown: Station Hill, 1981.

766.   *The Sirens' Song: Selected Essays of Maurice Blanchot.* Trans. Sacha Rabinovitch. Ed. Gabriel Josipovici. Bloomington: Indiana UP, 1982.

767.   *The Space of Literature: A Translation of* L'Espace Littéraire. Trans. Ann Smock. Lincoln: U of Nebraska P, 1982.

768.   *The Writing of the Disaster.* Trans. Ann Smock. Lincoln: U of Nebraska P, 1986. On the Holocaust.

Foucault/Blanchot. See entry 1289.

Book on Blanchot

Shaviro, Steven. *Passion and Excess: Blanchot, Bataille, and Literary Theory.* See entry 603.

GEOFFREY HARTMAN (1929–)

Geoffrey Hartman was a student of the philologist Erich Auerbach in the 1950s, but from his earliest books he has shown an intelligence deeply versed in the philosophic currents of phenomenology and hermeneutics. His study *Wordsworth's Poetry* revolutionized the interpretation of that poet, but its critical method was kept in the background. In the years since, he has been more explicit about his ideas of interpretation, chiefly through engagements with the dominant schools of structuralism and poststructuralism. Though he is often grouped with Jacques Derrida and Paul de Man as part of the Yale school, the label is inappropriate to Hartman, whose special gift is a subtly responsive reading of poetry, which concentrates on categories of the representation of space, time, acts of the will and what he calls "word consciousness"—the writer's sensitivity to the sounds and syntax as well as the meanings of language. This range of themes bears obvious connections to the phenomenological tradition, though Hartman has enriched that tradition with ideas from psychoanalysis as well. Hartman is a thinker of enormous range and acumen and a particularly rewarding commentator on poetry. Recently he has also contributed to new appreciation of ancient, particularly Jewish, traditions of interpretation.

769. *Criticism in the Wilderness: The Study of Literature Today.* New Haven: Yale UP, 1980. Survey of contemporary criticism, particularly in the context of American culture.

770. *Easy Pieces.* New York: Columbia UP, 1985.

771. *The Fate of Reading and Other Essays.* Chicago: U of Chicago P, 1975.

772. *Minor Prophecies: The Literary Essay in the Culture Wars.* Cambridge: Harvard UP, 1991. Discusses the history of criticism since 1700 and, in particular, Leavis and de Man.

773. *Saving the Text: Literature/Derrida/Philosophy.* Baltimore: Johns Hopkins UP, 1982. A sympathetic study of Derrida followed by reflections on language and literature.

774. *The Unmediated Vision.* 1954. Corrected ed. New York: Harcourt, 1966. Studies poems by Wordsworth, Hopkins, Rilke, and Valéry.

775. *The Unremarkable Wordsworth.* Minneapolis: U of Minnesota P, 1987. Collects essays on Wordsworth, illustrating a variety of theoretical issues and approaches.

776. *Wordsworth's Poetry: 1787–1814.* Rev. ed. New Haven: Yale UP, 1967.

Hartman, Geoffrey H., and Sanford Budick, eds. *Midrash and Literature.* See entry 245.

Book on Hartman

777. Atkins, G. Douglas. *Geoffrey Hartman: Criticism as Answerable Style.* London: Routledge, 1991.

E. D. HIRSCH, JR. (1928–   )

E. D. Hirsch advocates an older tradition in hermeneutics, reaching back to Friedrich Schleiermacher and the German Romantic theorists. He distinguishes sharply between a text's "meaning" and its "significance." He argues that meaning can be determined within the limits set by our ordinary uncertainty about all human affairs. The correct procedure is to give close attention to the kind or genre of the text and to attempt to discover as far as possible its author's intention. By contrast, the text's significance is its relation to its own historical milieu or its value or importance to us. Significance is indeterminately various, though it must be based on and responsive to a text's meaning. Hirsch thus seeks principles for validating interpretation, principles whose reliability will be unshaken by any practical difficulties we may encounter in understanding. Hirsch's summaries of and borrowings from other critics and philosophers are not always dependable guides to the original thinker, but his defense of a traditional conviction—or hope—that the meaning of even the most complex work of literature is a determinate and determinable thing has appealed to many literary professionals who are seeking legitimation for their claim to expertise and are distrustful of the unconventional and often unsettling speculations of much current critical theory. More recently, Hirsch has achieved wide reputation arguing that understanding presupposes possession of a substantial body of information, which he labels "cultural literacy" and which he maintains can be specified and taught. This claim has been accused of narrow elitism and theoretical naïveté, but it remains persuasive to many and influential in current cultural and educational policy-making.

778.   *The Aims of Interpretation.* Chicago: U of Chicago P, 1978. Essays, including reconsiderations of his earlier theories.

779.   *Cultural Literacy: What Every American Needs to Know.* Boston: Houghton, 1987. Argues that understanding requires possession of specific background information.

780.   *The Philosophy of Composition.* Chicago: U of Chicago P, 1981. Considers the teaching of writing and draws conclusions that have been controversial.

Phenomenological Critical Theory

For a brief discussion, see the headnote to this chapter.

Books and Collections

781.   Alexander, Ian W. *French Literature and the Philosophy of Consciousness: Phenomenological Essays.* Ed. A. J. L. Busst. Cardiff: U of Wales P, 1984.

Anozie, Sunday O. *Phenomenology in Modern African Studies.* See entry 1466.

782.   Lawall, Sarah. *Critics of Consciousness: The Existential Structures of Literature.* Cambridge: Harvard UP, 1968. General introduction to critics who describe how an author's consciousness structures the world presented in his or her work.

783.   LeSage, Laurent, ed. *The French New Critics: An Introduction and Sampler.* University Park: Pennsylvania State UP, 1963. Essays on the Geneva school of phenomenological critics (see note on Georges Poulet below), with bibliographies and brief selections from their works.

784.   Magliola, Robert. *Phenomenology and Literature: An Introduction.* West Lafayette: Purdue UP, 1977.

785.   Martínez-Bonati, Felix. *Fictive Discourse and the Structures of Literature: A Phenomenological Approach.* Trans. Philip W. Silver. Ithaca: Cornell UP, 1981.

786.   Simon, John K., ed. *Modern French Criticism.* Chicago: U of Chicago P, 1972. Includes essays on the philosopher Merleau-Ponty, the Geneva school, Blanchot, and others.

787.   Tymieniecka, Anna-Teresa, ed. *The Existential Coordinates of the Human Condition: Poetic-Epic-Tragic: The Literary Genre.* Dordrecht: Reidel, 1984. Large collection of essays.

788.   ———, ed. *The Philosophical Reflection of Man in Literature.* Dordrecht: Reidel, 1987.

Individual Authors

GASTON BACHELARD (1884–1962)

Gaston Bachelard began as a historian and philosopher of science, but he was eventually attracted to poetry's contrasting way of dealing with physical matter through imaginative engagements. He sought in Freudian psychoanalysis, but found more fully in Jungian psychoanalysis, a recognition of the mind's power, in "waking reverie," to elicit our secret relations with the material world we inhabit. Following the ancient categories of alchemy and premodern science, Bachelard studied the poetic response to the four elements—fire, air, water, and earth. He added further studies of space and of feelings of rest and active willing. What marks these studies as phenomenological is Bachelard's uncanny capacity to follow closely the movements of the poet's mind—not quite conscious and not quite unconscious, revealed in isolated words and images—as it engages with the appearances of the material world. Bachelard's method is descriptive: he conducts his meditations and invites the reader to enter into his readings and moods and share his perceptions. So subtle and insightful is Bachelard that even thinkers as skeptically inclined as Jacques Derrida have found his appeal irresistible.

Reading him seems to renew one's responsiveness not only to poetry but to the material world itself.

789. *Gaston Bachelard, Subversive Humanist: Texts and Readings.* Ed. Mary McAllester Jones. Madison: U of Wisconsin P, 1991. Selections from Bachelard, with essays by the editor on the development of Bachelard's ideas and on their relation to contemporary theorists such as Foucault and Derrida.

790. *The New Scientific Spirit.* Trans. Arthur Goldhammer. Boston: Beacon, 1985.

791. *On Poetic Imagination and Reverie.* Trans. and introd. Colette Gaudin. Indianapolis: Bobbs, 1971. Selections from his works.

792. *The Philosophy of No: A Philosophy of the New Scientific Mind.* Trans. G. C. Waterston. New York: Orion, 1968.

793. *The Poetics of Reverie: Childhood, Language, and the Cosmos.* Trans. Daniel Russell. New York: Orion, 1969. Origins of poetic imagery in reverie.

794. *The Poetics of Space.* Trans. Maria Jolas. New York: Orion, 1964.

795. *The Psychoanalysis of Fire.* Trans. Alan C. M. Ross. Boston: Beacon, 1964.

796. *The Right to Dream.* Trans. J. A. Underwood. New York: Grossman, 1971. A collection of essays on art, literature, and other topics.

797. *Water and Dreams: An Essay on the Imagination of Matter.* Trans. Edith R. Farrell. Dallas: Pegasus, 1983.

Books on Bachelard

Lecourt, Dominique. *Marxism and Epistemology: Bachelard, Canguilhem, and Foucault.* See entry 1312.

798. McAllester Jones, Mary. *The Philosophy and Poetics of Gaston Bachelard.* Chicago: Center for Advanced Research in Phenomenology; Washington: UP of America, 1989.

799. Smith, Roch Charles. *Gaston Bachelard.* Boston: Twayne, 1982.

ROMAN INGARDEN (1893–1970)

A student of Edmund Husserl, Roman Ingarden added to his philosophical and mathematical studies an active career as a drama critic. In *The Literary Work of Art* he undertakes a description of the literary object and finds four strata in its structure: the levels of sounds; meaning; represented objects; and "schematized aspects." This highly technical study was followed by an equally rigorous book on the actual process of cognizing a literary work. Ingarden's work was used by René Wellek to support his conception of the literary work, presented in the widely influential book he wrote with Austin Warren, *The Theory of Literature* (though Ingarden later insisted he had been misrepresented). Ingarden's ideas were also adapted by Wolfgang Iser in his reader-response theory (see chapter 7, "Reader-Response Theory").

800. *The Cognition of the Literary Work of Art.* 1937. Trans. Ruth Ann Crowley and Kenneth Olson. Evanston: Northwestern UP, 1973. Technical but stimulating phenomenological analysis.

801. *The Literary Work of Art: An Investigation on the Borderlines of Ontology, Logic, and the Theory of Literature.* 1931. Trans. George G. Grabowicz. Evanston: Northwestern UP, 1973. Phenomenological analysis of the literary work.

802. *Selected Papers in Aesthetics.* Ed. Peter McCormick. Munich: Philosophia; Washington: Catholic U of America P, 1983. With full bibliography of works by and about Ingarden.

Books on Ingarden

803. Dziemidok, Bohdan, and Peter McCormick, eds. *On the Aesthetics of Roman Ingarden: Interpretations and Assessments.* Lancaster, Eng.: Kluwer, 1989.

804. Falk, Eugene. *The Poetics of Roman Ingarden.* Chapel Hill: U of North Carolina P, 1981.

Wellek, René. *Four Critics: Croce, Valéry, Lukács, and Ingarden.* See entry 358.

GEORGES POULET (1902–   )

Georges Poulet, the most important of the Geneva school of critics, adapted phenomenology to the study of literature. Focusing on the fundamental categories of our experience of the world, Poulet studied the way individual writers' minds gave a unique and specific shape to their representation of space and time. Poulet and the other Geneva school critics of consciousness (see Lawall, entry 782 above) studied a writer's entire body of work, published and unpublished, and sometimes examined biographical facts as well. They then synthesized this material to reveal characteristic patterns that permeated the author's consciousness. In *Metamorphoses of the Circle*, Poulet extended his method and approached the image of the circle rather from the perspective of cultural history, but he did not pursue this innovation. The vogue of Poulet's approach has declined in the United States, though he remains influential in the French-speaking world. In two books, *Les chemins actuels de la critique* (1968) and *La conscience critique* (1971), he applied his phenomenological method to a reading of literary critics. Unfortunately, these works remain untranslated.

805. *Exploding Poetry: Baudelaire-Rimbaud.* Trans. Françoise Meltzer. Chicago: U of Chicago P, 1984.

806.   *The Interior Distance.* Trans. Elliott Coleman. Baltimore: Johns Hopkins UP, 1959.

807.   *The Metamorphoses of the Circle.* Trans. Carley Dawson and Elliott Coleman in collaboration with the author. Baltimore: Johns Hopkins UP, 1967.

808.   *Proustian Space.* Trans. Elliott Coleman. Baltimore: Johns Hopkins UP, 1977.

809.   *Studies in Human Time.* Trans. Elliott Coleman. Baltimore: Johns Hopkins UP, 1956.

J. HILLIS MILLER (1928–   )

For a general headnote and recent works by J. Hillis Miller adopting deconstructive criticism, see his entry in chapter 5, "Poststructuralism and Deconstruction."

810.   *Charles Dickens: The World of His Novels.* Cambridge:Harvard UP, 1958. Phenomenological reading of Dickens.

811.   *The Disappearance of God: Five Nineteenth-Century Writers.* Cambridge: Harvard UP, 1976. Phenomenological readings of De Quincey, Browning, Emily Brontë, Arnold, and Hopkins.

812.   *Poets of Reality: Six Twentieth-Century Writers.* New York: Atheneum, 1969. Readings of Conrad, Yeats, Eliot, Dylan Thomas, Stevens, and William Carlos Williams.

7. Reader-Response Theory

Reader-response criticism is not an autonomous approach but an orientation or emphasis within other critical schools. Presented below are its chief varieties: formalist, or New Critical; hermeneutic and phenomenological; and psychological or psychoanalytic. A few cultural critics have also emphasized the reader, particularly in the light of the social processes that influence and develop reading practices. While studies of reading are multitudinous in educational psychology, literary theorists have largely ignored them, but a few works are listed below under the heading "Psychoanalytic and Empirical Studies of Reading."

Introductory Books and Collections

813.   Freund, Elizabeth. *Return of the Reader: Reader-Response Criticism*. London: Methuen, 1987.

814.   Holub, Robert C. *Reception Theory: A Critical Introduction*. London: Methuen, 1984. Introduction to theories that look at how literary works were received by readers.

815.   Suleiman, Susan R., and Inge Crosman, eds. *The Reader in the Text: Essays on Audience and Interpretation*. Princeton: Princeton UP, 1980. Stimulating collection of essays by leading critics, with bibliography.

816.   Tompkins, Jane P., ed. *Reader-Response Criticism: From Formalism to*

Structuralism. Baltimore: Johns Hopkins UP, 1980. A collection of key essays with an excellent introduction and analysis by the editor and an annotated bibliography.

General

Bouson, J. Brooks. *The Empathetic Reader: A Study of the Narcissistic Character of the Drama of the Self.* See entry 878.

817.   Clark, Gregory. *Dialogue, Dialectic, and Conversation: A Social Perspective on the Function of Writing.* Carbondale: Southern Illinois UP, 1990.

818.   Collins, Christopher. *The Poetics of the Mind's Eye: Literature and the Psychology of Imagination.* Philadelphia: U of Pennsylvania P, 1991. Describes six "cognitive modes" in reading: perception, retrospection, assertion, introspection, expectation, and judgment.

819.   ———. *Reading the Written Image: Verbal Play, Interpretation, and the Roots of Iconophobia.* University Park: Pennsylvania State UP, 1992. Discusses how readers construct an imagined, internal world.

820.   Forsyth, Neil, ed. *Reading Contexts.* Tübingen: Narr, 1988.

821.   Foster, Dennis A. *Confession and Complicity in Narrative.* Cambridge: Cambridge UP, 1987. Argues that the reader has not a passive but a complex and active relation with the author.

822.   Freedberg, David. *The Power of Images: Studies in the History and Theory of Response.* Chicago: U of Chicago P, 1989.

823.   Garvin, Harry, and Steven Mailloux, eds. *Theories of Reading, Looking, and Listening.* Lewisburg: Bucknell UP, 1981. Eleven essays by leading critics on reader-response theory.

824.   Gloversmith, Frank, ed. *The Theory of Reading.* New York: Barnes, 1984. Essays on modernist texts and the kind of reading they invite.

Hawthorn, Jeremy. *Identity and Relationship: A Contribution to the Marxist Theory of Literary Criticism.* See entry 1148.

825.   Mailloux, Steven. *Interpretive Conventions: The Reader in the Study of American Fiction.* Ithaca: Cornell UP, 1982.

826.   ———. *Rhetorical Power.* Ithaca: Cornell UP, 1989. Argues for a hermeneutic theory based on rhetoric, that is, reader-response seen in its institutional and cultural context.

827.   McGregor, Graham, and R. S. White. *Reception and Response: Hearer Creativity and the Analysis of Spoken and Written Texts.* London: Routledge, 1990.

828.   Rosenblatt, Louise M. *Literature as Exploration.* 1938. 4th ed. New York: MLA, 1983. Discusses importance of students' responses to literature.

829.   ———. *The Reader, the Text, the Poem: The Transactional Theory of the*

Literary Work. Carbondale: Southern Illinois UP, 1978. Pioneering critical reflections on the psychology of reading.

830. Rosenblatt (book on). Farrell, Edmund J., and James R. Squire, eds. *Transactions with Literature: A Fifty-Year Perspective.* Urbana: NCTE, 1990. Contributors examine Rosenblatt's contribution and compare her approach to reader-response theories.

831. Slatoff, Walter. *With Respect to Readers: Dimensions of Literary Response.* Ithaca: Cornell UP, 1970. Pioneering study of reader's role in producing literary meaning.

832. Spolsky, Ellen, ed. *The Uses of Adversity: Failure and Accommodation in Reader Response.* Lewisburg: Bucknell UP, 1990.

833. Steig, Michael. *Stories of Reading: Subjectivity and Literary Understanding.* Baltimore: Johns Hopkins UP, 1988. Accepts emphasis on the reader, but argues that the reader's knowledge of history, the author's intent, and literary influences enter into interpretation.

834. Trotter, D. *The Making of the Reader.* London: Macmillan, 1984.

Formalist Approach

I. A. Richards's theory of poetry (see chapter 3, "New Criticism") already emphasized the response of an abstractly posited reader to the complex language of a poem. His highly speculative version of an empirical psychology was not pursued by the New Critics, who returned instead to the rhetorical tradition's more idealized way of thinking about the interrelations among speaker, speech, and audience. What keeps this reader-response orientation within formalism is the kind of reader posited, essentially one attentive and responsive to the language of the poem or literary work. We are speaking not of an actual reader, or even of an individual posited with the help of psychological, psychoanalytic, or sociological categories, but only of a reader skilled in the rules of language generally and the rules of literary language in particular. The responses of such a reader are postulated according to rules that are public and generally recognized, though ordinarily implicit. Even where a theorist like Stanley Fish (see below) may insist that "interpretive communities" set these rules for responding and interpreting, the notion of community remains entirely abstract, circularly defined by the rules the community is claimed to establish. While a reader-response emphasis within formalism always threatens to break into psychology or specific social categories, it can also lend renewed energy to what remain discernibly formalist analyses.

Individual Author

STANLEY FISH (1938–   )

Stanley Fish's views have evolved through a series of stages within a single orientation. He began with what he called "affective stylistics," which made two claims: it analyzed not the text but the reader's experience of the text as the reader moved through it in linear fashion, from word to word. That experience, it turned out, was always one of the frustration of expectations that the text itself had aroused, so that the text was "self-consuming"— or rather the reader's experience was of a constantly revised meaning. Fish applied this approach mainly to English Renaissance texts, particularly John Milton and George Herbert. It seems clear, however, that this approach is simply formalism in a slightly different vocabulary, even repeating Richards's and the Russian formalists' idea that literature forces us to revise clichéd expectations. Fish went on to argue that in fact reading is not merely something the reader is in charge of; rather, reading follows rules established by an "interpretive community." There can be no autonomous validation of either the rules or the readings they sponsor. And this is generally true of human experience: it is always seen to have a particular form or meaning, which is generated by the interpretive rules or principles held by the group that interprets experience a certain way. We have no direct contact with texts or any other experience, since these are constituted by the very rules and procedures by which we interpret them. Nevertheless, Fish asserts that his view is not relativistic or solipsistic, for each individual is restrained by the interpretive community, and the community is constituted as a "profession," which both enables and controls the processes of interpretation. Fish claims to be just describing a fact of life, not prescribing or recommending a procedure that anyone could follow or turn to advantage. His concept of community is obviously abstract and based on a logical definition rather than on historical, psychological, or sociological data. Fish has increasingly been interested in showing how interpretive principles are articulated and applied within given professional communities and has recently written extensively about legal interpretation.

835.   *Doing What Comes Naturally: Change, Rhetoric, and the Practice of Theory in Literature and Legal Studies.* Durham: Duke UP, 1989. Collects essays of the 1980s on a wide range of topics.

836.   *Is There a Text in This Class? The Authority of Interpretive Communities.* Cambridge: Harvard UP, 1980. Collects essays over a fifteen-year period, showing Fish's evolution from formalist reader-response to interpretive-communities theory.

837.   *The Living Temple: George Herbert and Catechizing.* Berkeley: U of California P, 1978. Analyzes the seventeenth-century poet in the light of Fish's theories.

838.   *Self-Consuming Artifacts: The Experience of Seventeenth-Century Literature.* Berkeley: U of California P, 1973. Analyzes literary works as subvert-
ing readers' expectations.

839.   *Surprised by Sin: The Reader in* Paradise Lost. London: Macmillan, 1967.
Milton's epic lures the reader into sinful expectations, then subverts them
to impel the growth of religious and moral insight.

Hermeneutic and
Phenomenological Approach

Individual Authors

WOLFGANG ISER (1926–)

Wolfgang Iser developed a reader-response theory out of the phenomenology of Roman Ingarden (see chapter 6, "Hermeneutics and Phenomenology"). Ingarden claimed that a literary work was a multilayered structure
containing "spots of indeterminacy" that readers could fill in freely, so long
as they did not violate or distort the basic structure. Iser argues that a literary
text exists as only a "virtual" object until a reader "concretizes" it in the act
of reading. The reading process is described as an interaction between a
text, which anticipates and invites response, and an "implied reader," whose
response is thus controlled by the text. What distinguishes this variety of
reader-response theory from formalism is the specific philosophical model
used to characterize the reading process.

840.   *The Act of Reading: A Theory of Aesthetic Response.* Baltimore: Johns
Hopkins UP, 1979.

841.   *The Implied Reader: Patterns of Communication in Prose Fiction from
Bunyan to Beckett.* Baltimore: Johns Hopkins UP, 1974. Analyzes changes
over time in how literary texts invite readers to respond.

842.   *Prospecting: From Reader Response to Literary Anthropology.* Baltimore:
Johns Hopkins UP, 1989. Develops a theory of the literary text as "play"
and as enactment of human possibilities.

843.   *Walter Pater: The Aesthetic Moment.* Trans. David Henry Wilson. Cambridge: Cambridge UP, 1987. Study of the nineteenth-century English
critic.

HANS-ROBERT JAUSS (1921–)

Hans-Robert Jauss drew from Hans-Georg Gadamer (see chapter 6,
"Hermeneutics and Phenomenology") and from Felix Vodička (one of the
Prague structuralists—see chapter 2, "Russian Formalism and Prague Struc-

turalism") the idea that a literary work has real existence only in the various interpretations given it as it is passed down in historical tradition. He attempted to develop a concrete "aesthetic of reception," describing on the basis of historical evidence how actual readers responded to works over time. With Gadamer, he sees this as a process of growth and even correction in our experience. Our first approach to a work is always made against the background of expectations absorbed from our social milieu, but the individual work corrects these expectations in a process that brings the work's unique structure to the foreground. While no interpretation is absolute or definitive, each reveals something about the work and its meaning and something about the social circumstances that both obscure and enable us to understand it. Jauss's theory thus responded to the gap between formalism and Marxism and aimed to combine sophisticated analysis of texts with the actual history of texts' receptions, so as to avoid an aestheticist concentration on the text for its own sake and at the same time a naively positivistic or dogmatic political approach to history.

844.   *Aesthetic Experience and Literary Hermeneutics.* Trans. Michael Shaw. Minneapolis: U of Minnesota P, 1982. General statement and application of his approach, tracing how readers at various times responded to literary works.

845.   *Question and Answer: Forms of Dialogic Understanding.* Trans. Michael Hays. Minneapolis: U of Minnesota P, 1990.

846.   *Toward an Aesthetic of Reception.* Trans. Timothy Bahti. Minneapolis: U of Minnesota P, 1982.

Psychological and Psychoanalytic Approach
Individual Authors
DAVID BLEICH (1940–   )

In formalist and phenomenological reader-response criticism, both the reader and the reading process are abstractions, specified according to a theoretical model. For David Bleich, the reader is a real human being, and the process of reading and interpreting takes place in transactions between readers. He concentrates above all on the readers he actually knows—his students—and the classroom is the decisive starting and ending point for all his theoretical reflections. He does not commit himself to a single model of psychology or a single description of the interactive process in the classroom but draws freely on a variety of thinkers. In Bleich's view, the aim of reading and of the social process of interpreting is not so much knowledge of literary works as self-knowledge and the development of a humane and responsible community.

847. *The Double Perspective: Language, Literacy, and Social Relations.* New York: Oxford UP, 1988. Argues that language is not individual but transactional; draws on Bakhtin, feminists, and others to develop a collaborative style of teaching and learning based on Bleich's psychological reader-response theory.

848. *Literature and Self-Awareness: Critical Questions and Emotional Responses.* New York: Harper, 1977.

849. *Readings and Feelings: An Introduction to Subjective Criticism.* Urbana: NCTE, 1975.

850. *Subjective Criticism.* Baltimore: Johns Hopkins UP, 1978.

NORMAN H. HOLLAND (1927–)

Norman Holland's psychoanalytic criticism follows the classic emphasis on the self, character, or personal identity. He himself distinguishes three phases of psychoanalytic theory. In the first phase, Freud found a latent content hidden beneath the manifest surface of dreams, jokes, and slips of the tongue. At this stage, psychoanalytic criticism consisted of a rather simple decoding of works for the emotional conflicts or wishes they concealed. In the second phase, Freud was more concerned with the mind's dynamic functioning in relation to external reality and to internal psychic structures and events. Holland applies this phase of Freud's theory in *The Dynamics of Literary Form*, arguing that as adults we retain the powerful but repressed impulses of childhood and that these impulses are active in and activated by literature. But poems transform these wishes and fears into meaning and coherence and thus protect or defend us against the fantasies poems also invite. This "regression in the service of the ego"—a phrase Holland takes from the psychoanalyst Ernst Kris—results in the pleasure we feel in mastery and control. The "meaning" of a literary work lies in this dynamic process it instigates and guides, not in any detachable theme or general statement. The theory is evaluative as well, for a "bad" poem is simply one that offers a less complex defense and is therefore unable to arouse and govern our deepest and strongest fantasies. Holland's third phase emphasizes the "psychology of identity" of Heinz Lichtenstein, Erik Erikson, and others. Each reader has a character, set early in life and dominant throughout his or her life and career. The reading process is "transactive," a complex interaction between the individual's dominant "identity theme" and the themes and structures embodied in the work. The reader's own identity may make it possible to respond to some aspects of a poem but not others. No generalized "right reading" is possible, and Holland's *Five Readers Reading* traces the individualized responses of five (admittedly highly skilled and conscious) students of literature. Holland is representative of a relatively orthodox continuation of psychoanalytic theory, which emphasizes the individual personality and differs sharply from Jacques Lacan's structuralist reconstruction of psychoanalysis (see chapter 8, "Psychological and Psychoanalytic Critical Theory").

851.   *The Brain of Robert Frost: A Cognitive Approach to Literature*. New York: Routledge, 1988. Goes beyond Freud to contemporary cognitive psychology and its relevance to literary pedagogy, theory, and criticism.

852.   *The Dynamics of Literary Response*. New York: Oxford UP, 1968. Psychoanalytic approach to reading literature.

853.   *Five Readers Reading*. New Haven: Yale UP, 1975. Psychoanalytic reports on five experienced readers' responses to poems.

         Holland's Guide to Psychoanalytic Psychology and Literature-and-Psychology. See entry 865.

854.   *The I*. New Haven: Yale UP, 1985.

855.   *Laughing: A Psychology of Humor*. Ithaca: Cornell UP, 1982.

856.   *Poems in Persons: An Introduction to the Psychoanalysis of Literature*. New York: Norton, 1973.

857.   *Psychoanalysis and Shakespeare*. New York: McGraw, 1966.

Psychoanalytic and Empirical Studies of Reading

858.   Bettelheim, Bruno. *On Learning to Read: The Child's Fascination with Meaning*. New York: Knopf, 1982. Psychoanalytic approach to learning to read and to errors in reading.

859.   Dillon, George. *Language Processing and the Reading of Literature: Towards a Model of Comprehension*. Bloomington: Indiana UP, 1978. Technical but stimulating analysis of readers' perceptual strategies, with numerous literary illustrations.

860.   Gibson, Eleanor J., and Harry Levin. *The Psychology of Reading*. Cambridge: MIT P, 1975. An empirical study.

861.   Nell, Victor. *Lost in a Book: The Psychology of Reading for Pleasure*. New Haven: Yale UP, 1988. Analyzes the responses of about one hundred readers to whom the author provided passages.

8. Psychological and Psychoanalytic Critical Theory

Like every aspect of modern culture, literary criticism has been power-fully influenced by the psychoanalytic theories of Sigmund Freud (1856–1939). Only a few of his writings directly address literary writers or literary works, but those few already exhibit in germ the later range of development of psychoanalytic criticism: biographical studies of creativity and of authors' works in relation to their lives; analyses of literary characters, who are treated as though they were real persons; etymological and mythological research into the origins of literary structures and symbols, resulting in the discovery, so the theory claims, that these symbols have the power to move us because they resonate with traces of prehistoric psychic experience.

Recent criticism has added to this agenda psychoanalytic study of the reader and the reading process. But, more important, interest has shifted away from Freud's ideas about human character. Under the influence of Jacques Lacan, who posited that the unconscious was "structured like a language," critics have turned to Freud's *The Interpretation of Dreams*, *The Psychopathology of Everyday Life*, and *Jokes and Their Relation to the Unconscious* to find both a theory and techniques to guide the interpretation of literary devices and language. The application of psychoanalysis not to persons—whether authors, characters, or readers—but to language and to texts themselves has allowed Freudian criticism to link up with formalist, structuralist, and other critical approaches that use models and terms from linguistic theory to scrutinize the language and meanings of literary works. Some critics have used Freud's broader cultural speculations or applied some of his ideas in cultural theory and a few have made them a dominant theme, but more often these ideas have been absorbed into the general background of poststructuralist thinking.

Meanwhile, Freud himself and his texts have come under scrutiny by critics using his own and other methods. A number of books have traced Freud's intellectual milieu and background. His case histories have proved interesting to narrative theorists as a source of ideas and as themselves objects for analysis. Some of these analyses have been distinctly polemical, often inspired by feminist suspicion of Freud's patriarchal and conventional attitudes toward women and by a conviction that a psychological orientation neglects or even resists political and cultural approaches. The work of Jacques Lacan has received similar criticisms. Psychological criticism itself has become diversified as theorists turn to other versions of psychoanalysis, such as those of Sandor Ferenczi, Melanie Klein, or D. W. Winnicott, including versions Freud himself attacked. Relatively few critics adopt the approach of Carl Jung (see below), despite the extensive writing by him and his followers on mythology, literature, and other cultural works and symbolic processes. A few theorists take a psychological approach distinct from any variety of psychoanalysis.

Individual works by Freud are not included here, since the bibliographies and books listed will lead the reader to them. The section "Books and Collections" also includes works whose orientation is nonpsychoanalytic or psychoanalytic but broader than Freud's specific theory. Chapter 7, "Reader-Response Theory," includes subheadings relevant to this topic: see the listings for Norman Holland and David Bleich, as well as the subsequent section, "Psychoanalytic and Empirical Studies of Reading." A substantial body of feminist criticism and theory has made use of psychological and psychoanalytic approaches. A few broad or prominent studies are cross-listed here, but see also chapter 15, "Feminist and Gender Criticism."

Bibliographies

862.   Kiell, Norman, ed. *Psychoanalysis, Psychology, and Literature: A Bibliography.* 2nd ed. 2 vols. Metuchen: Scarecrow, 1982. Extremely comprehensive; no annotations.

863.   Natoli, Joseph P., and Frederik L. Rusch, comps. *Psychocriticism: An Annotated Bibliography.* Westport; Greenwood, 1984.

Introductory Surveys

864.   Hartman, Geoffrey, ed. *Psychoanalysis and the Question of the Text.* Se-

lected Papers from the English Institute, 1976–77, ns 2 New York: Columbia UP, 1979. Essays by leading critics showing contemporary approaches.

865.   Holland, Norman H. *Holland's Guide to Psychoanalytic Psychology and Literature-and-Psychology*. New York: Oxford UP, 1990. Succinct survey of all types of current psychoanalysis and their applications to literary criticism; with extensive bibliographies.

866.   Kaplan, Morton, and Robert Kloss. *The Unspoken Motive: A Guide to Psychoanalytic Literary Criticism*. New York: Free, 1973.

867.   Kurzweil, Edith, and William Phillips, eds. *Literature and Psychoanalysis*. New York: Columbia UP, 1983. Traces psychoanalytic criticism from Freud to the present.

868.   Laplanche, Jean, and J-B. Pontalis. *The Language of Psychoanalysis*. Trans. Donald Micholson-Smith. New York: Norton, 1974. Alphabetically arranged glossary explains key psychoanalytic terms.

869.   Mollinger, Robert N. *Psychoanalysis and Literature: An Introduction*. Chicago: Nelson, 1981.

870.   Natoli, Joseph P., ed. *Psychological Perspectives on Literature: Freudian Dissidents and Non-Freudian, A Casebook*. Hamden: Archon, 1984.

871.   Skura, Meredith. *The Literary Use of the Psychoanalytic Process*. New Haven: Yale UP, 1981.

872.   Wright, Elizabeth. *Psychoanalytic Criticism: Theory in Practice*. London: Methuen, 1985. Broad survey of psychoanalytic critical theory to the present.

Books and Collections

873.   Berg, Temma F., Anna Shannon Elfenbein, Jeanne Larsen, and Elisa Kay Sparks, eds. *Engendering the Word: Feminist Essays in Psychosexual Politics*. Urbana: U of Illinois P, 1989. Twelve essays on various literary works.

874.   Berman, Jeffrey. *The Talking Cure: Literary Representations of Psychoanalysis*. New York: New York UP, 1985.

875.   Bersani, Leo. *Baudelaire and Freud*. Berkeley: U of California P, 1978.

876.   ———. *The Freudian Body: Psychoanalysis and Art*. New York: Columbia UP, 1986.

877.   Binswanger, Ludwig. *Being in the World: Selected Papers of Ludwig Binswanger*. Trans. Jacob Needleman. New York: Torchbook-Harper, 1967. Phenomenological psychology; includes an analysis of Ibsen's dramas.

878.   Bouson, J. Brooks. *The Empathetic Reader: A Study of the Narcissistic Character of the Drama of the Self*. Amherst: U of Massachusetts P, 1989.

879.   Brennan, Teresa, ed. *Between Feminism and Psychoanalysis*. London:

Routledge, 1989. Fifteen essays critically examine French feminism; contributors include Gallop, Irigaray, Jardine, Moi, Spivak.

880.   Bresky, Dushan, and Miroslav Malik. *Literary Practice.* Vol. 1: *Esthetic Qualities and Values in Literature: A Humanistic and Biometric Appraisal.* New York: Lang, 1984. Vol. 2: Bresky, Dushan, with Brian Gill and Miroslav Malik. *Esthetics of Style.* New York: Lang, 1989. Reviews traditional humanist approaches and then introduces biometric and biocybernetic measures and models.

881.   Brooks, Peter. *Reading for the Plot.* New York: Knopf, 1984. Psychoanalytic theory that plot is generated by readers' desires.

882.   Camden, Vera J. *Compromise Formations: Current Directions in Psychoanalytic Criticism.* Kent: Kent State UP, 1989.

883.   Crews, Frederick. *Out of My System: Psychoanalysis, Ideology, and Critical Method.* New York: Oxford UP, 1975. Essays on psychoanalytic and social approaches to literature.

884.   ———, ed. *Psychoanalysis and the Literary Process.* Berkeley: U of California P, 1970. Contains Crews's "Anesthetic Criticism" and psychoanalytic essays on Dickens, Pater, and others.

885.   Easthope, Antony. *Poetry and Phantasy.* Cambridge: Cambridge UP, 1989. Examines English poetry in the light of psychoanalysis and Marxist ideological analysis.

886.   Edel, Leon. *The Stuff of Sleep and Dreams: Experiments in Literary Psychology.* New York: Harper, 1982.

887.   Edelson, Marshall. *Hypothesis and Evidence in Psychoanalysis.* Chicago: U of Chicago P, 1984. By emphasizing language and narrative, Edelson brings literature and psychoanalysis into conjunction.

888.   ———. *Language and Interpretation in Psychoanalysis.* Chicago: U of Chicago P, 1984. Draws a parallel between poetry as the critic hears it and the language of analysis as the psychoanalyst hears it.

889.   Eissler, Kurt R. *Discourse on Hamlet: A Psychoanalytic Inquiry.* New York: International P, 1971. By the dean of contemporary psychoanalysts.

890.   Feldstein, Richard, and Henry Sussman, eds. *Psychoanalysis and . . ..* New York: Routledge, 1989. Thirteen essays on psychoanalysis and feminism, Marxism, deconstruction.

891.   Feldstein, Richard, and Judith Roof, eds. *Feminism and Psychoanalysis.* Ithaca: Cornell UP, 1989. Sixteen essays by leading theorists.

892.   Felman, Shoshana. *The Literary Speech Act: Don Juan with J. L. Austin, or Seduction in Two Languages.* Trans. Catherine Porter. Ithaca: Cornell UP, 1983. A mythical encounter between Molière's Don Juan and British philosopher J. L. Austin; explores speech and the erotic.

893.   ———. *Writing and Madness: Literature/Philosophy/Psychoanalysis.* Trans.

Martha Noel Evans and the author, with Brian Massumi. Ithaca: Cornell UP, 1985.

894.   Fizer, John. *Psychologism and Psychoaesthetics: A Historical and Critical View of Their Relations.* Amsterdam: Benjamins, 1981.

895.   Flax, Jane. *Thinking Fragments: Psychoanalysis, Feminism, and Postmodernism in the Contemporary West.* Berkeley: U of California P, 1990.

896.   Frieden, Ken. *Freud's Dream of Interpretation.* Albany: State U of New York P, 1989. Compares psychoanalytic dream interpretation with Jewish biblical dream interpretation.

Garner, Shirley Nelson, Claire Kahane, and Madelon Sprengnether, eds. *The (M)Other Tongue: Essays in Feminist Psychoanalytic Interpretation.* See entry 1595.

897.   Girard, René. *Deceit, Desire, and the Novel: Self and Other in Literary Structure.* Trans. Yvonne Freccero. Baltimore: Johns Hopkins UP, 1966. Sees reading as parallel to the interplay of desire in triangular love relationships.

898.   Gordon, David J. *Literary Art and the Unconscious.* Baton Rouge: Louisiana State UP, 1976.

899.   Gunn, Daniel. *Psychoanalysis and Fiction: An Exploration of Literary and Psychoanalytic Borders.* Cambridge: Cambridge UP, 1988. Argues that psychoanalysis and literature have common concerns, objectives, and procedures.

900.   Harris, Jay, and Jean Harris. *The Roots of Artifice: On the Origin and Development of Literary Creativity.* New York: Human Sciences, 1981.

901.   Hertz, Neil. *The End of the Line: Essays on Psychoanalysis and the Sublime.* New York: Columbia UP, 1985. Essays on literature and psychoanalysis; from Longinus to Freud.

902.   Hirsch, Marianne. *The Mother/Daughter Plot: Narrative, Psychoanalysis, Feminism.* Bloomington: Indiana UP, 1989.

903.   Horden, Peregrine, ed. *Freud and the Humanities.* London: Duckworth, 1985. Essays on topics from ancient to modern literature.

904.   Irwin, John T. *Doubling and Incest—Repetition and Revenge: A Speculative Reading of Faulkner.* Baltimore: Johns Hopkins UP, 1975. Uses poststructuralist psychoanalytic ideas.

905.   Keitel, Evelyne. *Reading Psychosis: Readers, Texts and Psychoanalysis.* Oxford: Blackwell, 1989. A theory and analysis of psychotic literature.

906.   Kofman, Sarah. *The Childhood of Art: An Interpretation of Freud's Aesthetics.* Trans. Winifred Woodhull. New York: Columbia UP, 1988.

———. *The Enigma of Woman: Woman in Freud's Writings.* See entry 1621.

907.   ———. *Freud and Fiction.* Trans. Sarah Wykes. Boston: Northeastern UP, 1991. Argues that Freud edited and distorted literary texts to support his

theories; reconsiders the Greek and nineteenth-century works Freud discussed.

908.   Layton, Lynne, and Barbara Ann Schapiro, eds. *Narcissism and the Text: Studies in Literature and the Psychology of the Self.* New York: New York UP, 1986. Applies a contemporary school of psychoanalysis, "object-relations" theory, to literary works of the nineteenth and twentieth centuries.

909.   Lindauer, Martin S. *The Psychological Study of Literature: Limitations, Possibilities, and Accomplishments.* Chicago: Nelson, 1974. On the empirical psychological study of the literary work, the author, and the reader.

910.   Lukacher, Ned. *Primal Scenes: Literature, Philosophy, and Psychoanalysis.* Ithaca: Cornell UP, 1986.

911.   Maitre, Doreen. *Literature and Possible Worlds.* London: Middlesex Polytechnic P, 1983.

912.   Mauron, Charles. *Aesthetics and Psychology.* Trans. Roger Fry and Katherine John. 1935. Port Washington: Kennikat, 1970. An important French critic who brought together psychoanalysis and the formalist analysis of literature.

913.   Mauron (book on). Hutcheon, Linda. *Formalism and the Freudian Aesthetic: The Example of Charles Mauron.* Cambridge: Cambridge UP, 1984.

914.   May, Keith M. *Out of the Maelstrom: Psychology and the Novel in the Twentieth Century.* New York: St. Martin's, 1977. Surveys psychological approaches to the novel, from Freud to the existentialists.

915.   Meltzer, Françoise, ed. *The Trial(s) of Psychoanalysis.* Chicago: U of Chicago P, 1988. Fifteen essays, many on Freud and issues in literary theory.

916.   Møller, Lis. *The Freudian Reading: Analytical and Fictional Constructions.* Philadelphia: U of Pennsylvania P, 1992. Examines four texts by Freud and criticizes his approach to literary and other kinds of interpretation.

917.   Morrison, Claudia C. *Freud and the Critic: The Early Use of Depth Psychology in Literary Criticism.* Chapel Hill: U of North Carolina P, 1968. Concentrates on the period through the 1920s.

918.   Nägele, Rainer. *Reading after Freud: Essays on Goethe, Hölderlin, Habermas, Nietzsche, Brecht, Celan, and Freud.* New York: Columbia UP, 1987.

919.   Orlando, Francesco. *Toward a Freudian Theory of Literature: With an Analysis of Racine's* Phèdre. Trans. Charmaine Lee. Baltimore: Johns Hopkins UP, 1979. Theory developed through analysis of Freud on jokes, applied to Racine.

920.   Paris, Bernard J. *Third Force Psychology and the Study of Literature.* Rutherford: Fairleigh Dickinson, 1986. Fourteen essays describing and applying the psychological ideas of Horney and Maslow to nineteenth- and twentieth-century British and American novels and poetry.

921.   Rimmon-Kenan, Shlomith, ed. *Discourse in Psychoanalysis and Literature*. London: Methuen, 1987. Focuses not on "personality" but on rhetorical structures and strategies and discourse in texts.

922.   Roland, Alan, ed. *Psychoanalysis, Creativity, and Literature: A French-American Inquiry*. New York: Columbia UP, 1978. Sixteen essays by leading critics on creativity, literature, and recent developments in French and American psychoanalysis.

923.   Schafer, Roy. *Language and Insight: The Sigmund Freud Lectures at University College London*. New Haven: Yale UP, 1978.

924.   ————. *Narrative Actions in Psychoanalysis: Narratives of Space and Narratives of Time*. Worcester: Clark UP, 1981.

925.   ————. *A New Language for Psychoanalysis*. New Haven: Yale UP, 1976. By emphasizing language and narrative, Schafer brings literature and psychoanalysis into close relation.

926.   Smith, Joseph H., ed. *Psychiatry and the Humanities*. Vol. 1. New Haven: Yale UP, 1976. Includes essays by Ricoeur, Heller, and others; other volumes of this annual have separate titles.

927.   ————, ed. *Psychoanalysis and Language*. Psychiatry and the Humanities 3. New Haven: Yale UP, 1978. Includes essays by Ricoeur and Holland.

928.   Smith, Joseph H., and Gloria H. Parloff, eds. *The Literary Freud: Mechanisms of Defense and the Poetic Will*. Psychiatry and the Humanities 4. New Haven: Yale UP, 1980. Twelve essays by leading critics.

Smith, Joseph H., and William Kerrigan, eds. *Taking Chances: Derrida, Psychoanalysis, and Literature*. See entry 641.

929.   Spector, Jack J. *The Aesthetics of Freud: A Study in Psychoanalysis and Art*. New York: Praeger, 1972.

930.   Spence, Donald P. *Narrative Truth and Historical Truth: Meaning and Interpretation in Psychoanalysis*. New York: Norton, 1983. Argues that psychoanalysis deals in literary, narrative truth, not the truth of actual fact in the patient's life.

931.   Sprengnether, Madelon. *The Spectral Mother: Freud, Feminism, and Psychoanalysis*. Ithaca: Cornell UP, 1990. Critiques the marginal role Freud assigns the mother.

932.   Strelka, Joseph P., ed. *Literary Criticism and Psychology*. Yearbook of Comparative Criticism 7. University Park: Pennsylvania State UP, 1976. Theoretical and applied essays, with reviews of work in France, Germany, and England; with a bibliography.

933.   Tennenhouse, Leonard, ed. *The Practice of Psychoanalytic Criticism*. Detroit: Wayne State UP, 1976. Essays on Thomas More, Shakespeare, and modern works.

934.   Timpanaro, Sebastiano. *The Freudian Slip: Psychoanalysis and Textual Criticism*. London: New Left, 1976. Critical of Freud.

Vološinov, V. N. *Freudianism: A Marxist Critique.* See entry 342.

Waugh, Patricia. *Feminine Fictions: Revisiting the Postmodern.* See entry 1686.

935.   Weber, Samuel. *The Legend of Freud.* Minneapolis: U of Minnesota P, 1982. A reading of Freud by a literary theorist influenced by Derrida and poststructuralist thought.

936.   Weiss, Allen S. *The Aesthetics of Excess.* Albany: State U of New York P, 1989. Blends deconstruction and psychoanalysis to study the relation of rhetorical figures to libidinal activity.

937.   Wyatt, Jean. *Reconstructing Desire: The Role of the Unconscious in Women's Reading and Writing.* Chapel Hill: U of North Carolina P, 1990. Uses Freud, Lacan, Kristeva, and others; explores function of the unconscious in reading and creative processes, considering, for example, the appeal of romantic love fantasy for female readers.

Individual Authors

CARL GUSTAV JUNG (1875–1961)

At first a colleague of Freud, Carl Jung finally concluded that Freud's focus on childhood experience and sexuality gave a narrowly reductive view of the human mind. Jung read widely in literature and philosophy and also studied art, alchemy, and mythology. Starting from a romantic conception of the imagination, he posited a "collective unconscious," a repository of "archetypes," or basic patterns, that found expression in dreams, personality, and cultural artifacts of all kinds.

His followers Karl Kerenyi, Erich Neumann, Joseph Campbell, and others investigated the patterns of mythology, seeking the fundamental structures of the human mind and its development both in the individual and in cultural history. Maud Bodkin sought archetypal patterns in poetry. Jung was an important influence on Northrop Frye (see chapter 13, "Myth, Anthropology, and Critical Theory"), but Frye saw in Jung simply a modern extension of the Romantic theories with which he was already familiar.

Despite a tendency to gain committed disciples, Jung's thought has not been widely influential. He may have suffered some taint from his too ready cooperation with the Nazis and from revelations of irresponsible erotic relations with more than one patient, notably Sabina Spielrein. Contemporary critics have also tended to sympathize with Freud's sarcastic image of himself as a mere psychologist in contrast with those—referring implicitly but unmistakably to Jung—who set themselves up as prophets.

Only a few relevant anthologies that provide introductions to Jung's work are listed here; individual works are not included.

938.   *The Basic Writings of C. G. Jung.* Ed. Violet S. de Laszlo. New York: Modern Library, 1959.

939. *The Essential Jung.* Ed. Anthony Storr. Princeton: Princeton UP, 1983.

940. *Man and His Symbols.* New York: Dell, 1968.

941. *The Portable Jung.* Ed. Joseph Campbell. Trans. R. F. C. Hull. New York: Viking, 1971.

942. *The Spirit in Man, Art, and Literature.* Vol. 15 of *The Collected Works.* Trans. R. F. C. Hull. 2nd ed. Princeton: Princeton UP, 1966.

Jung Bibliography

943. Van Meurs, Jos. *Jungian Literary Criticism, 1920–1980: An Annotated Bibliography of Works in English (with a Selection of Titles after 1980).* Metuchen: Scarecrow, 1988.

Books on Jung and on the Application of His Theories

944. Barnaby, Karin, and Pellegrino D'Acierno, eds. *C. G. Jung and the Humanities: Toward a Hermeneutics of Culture.* Princeton: Princeton UP, 1990. Contributors discuss such issues as creativity, gender, religion, popular culture, and hermeneutics.

945. Bodkin, Maud. *Archetypal Patterns in Poetry: Psychological Studies of Imagination.* London: Oxford UP, 1934. One of the earliest applications of Jung to literature.

946. ———. *Studies of Type-Images in Poetry, Religion, and Philosophy.* New York: Oxford UP, 1951.

947. Jones, Joyce Meeks. *Jungian Psychology in Literary Analysis: A Demonstration Using T. S. Eliot's Poetry.* Washington: UP of America, 1979.

948. Knapp, Bettina L. *A Jungian Approach to Literature.* Carbondale: Southern Illinois UP, 1984.

949. ———. *Word/Image/Psyche.* University: U of Alabama P, 1985.

950. Spivey, Ted R. *The Journey beyond Tragedy: A Study of Myth and Modern Fiction.* Gainesville: UP of Florida, 1980. A Jungian approach.

JACQUES LACAN (1901–81)

Returning to a close reading of Freud's texts, Jacques Lacan reconstructed psychoanalysis by drawing on ideas from structural linguistics and the philosophy of Martin Heidegger. His basic formula, that "the unconscious is structured like a language," led him to emphasize the works in which Freud deals with the unconscious and the symbols that mediate its disguised appearance in symptoms, dreams, jokes, slips of the tongue, and similar phenomena. Lacan traced the formation of our sense of self-identity to the "mirror stage," a point where the child fashions a self-image on the basis of statues, the child's image in the mirror, and other representations of an integral, coherent self. The very fact that the coherent self can be created only by the use of an external mediating image undoes its alleged coherence. Subsequently, the child is brought into the cultural realm of language at the "symbolic stage," corresponding to the Oedipal stage of Freud. By mastering the key linguistic device of negation, the child is enabled to think in terms of what is *not* and becomes liberated as a human being from the immediacy of nature. But equally, the child is subjected to cultural taboos and restrictions, including the grammatical restrictions inherent to language, which Lacan label generally "the law of the Father." The object of psychoanalytic investigation, for Lacan, is the adventures and misadventures of this illusorily unified self, negotiating its way through the simultaneous empowerment and constrictions imposed by language and culture on its instinctual drives. Lacan's use of structural linguistics linked him with the larger structuralist movement. Some theorists tried to apply to critical theory and to the analysis of literary works Lacan's ideas about the nature and role of language and about the fissured self. Similarly, they tried to borrow and adapt to the reading of other kinds of texts Lacan's penetrating but somewhat idiosyncratic way of reading Freud's works.

951. *Ecrits: A Selection.* Trans. Alan Sheridan. New York: Norton, 1977. Nine essays (about half the original French volume) selected by the author.

952. *The Ego in Freud's Theory and in the Technique of Psychoanalysis, 1954–1955.* Trans. Sylvana Tomaselli with notes by John Forrester. Cambridge: Cambridge UP, 1988. Vol. 2 of *Seminars.*

953. *The Four Fundamental Concepts of Psychoanalysis.* Trans. Alan Sheridan. Ed. Jacques Alain-Miller. New York: Norton, 1978. On the unconscious, repetition, transfer, and drive.

954. *Freud's Papers on Technique, 1953–1954.* Trans. with notes by John Forrester. Cambridge: Cambridge UP, 1988. Vol. 1 of *Seminars.* Essays compiled from seminars Lacan conducted; published after his death.

955. *Speech and Language in Psychoanalysis: The Language of the Self.* Trans. with notes and commentary by Anthony Wilden. Baltimore: Johns Hopkins UP, 1981. Lacan on language, with extensive and helpful material by Wilden.

Lacan Bibliography

956. Clark, Michael. *Jacques Lacan: An Annotated Bibliography.* New York: Garland, 1988.

957. Nordquist, Joan, comp. *Jacques Lacan: A Bibliography.* Santa Cruz: Reference and Research Services, 1987.

Books on Lacan

958. Barr, Marleen S., and Richard Feldstein. *Discontented Discourses: Feminism/Textual Intervention/Psychoanalysis.* Twelve essays on Lacanian psychoanalysis and French feminist theory.

Reading of Lacan. Trans. David Pettigrew and François Raffoul. Albany: State U of New York P, 1992.

Ragland-Sullivan, Ellie. *Jacques Lacan and the Philosophy of Psychoanalysis*. Urbana: U of Illinois P, 1986.

Ragland-Sullivan, Ellie, and Mark Bracher. *Lacan and the Subject of Language*. New York: Routledge, 1990.

Roudinesco, Elisabeth. *Jacques Lacan and Co.: A History of Psychoanalysis in France, 1925–1985*. Trans. Jeffrey Mehlman. Chicago: U Chicago P, 1990.

Schneiderman, Stuart. *Jacques Lacan: The Death of an Intellectual Hero*. Cambridge: Harvard UP, 1983.

Smith, Joseph H., and William Kerrigan, eds. *Interpreting Lacan*. Psychiatry and the Humanities 6. New Haven: Yale UP, 1983.

Stanton, Martin. *Outside the Dream: Lacan and the French Styles of Psychoanalysis*. London: Routledge, 1983.

Turkle, Sherry. *Psychoanalytic Politics: Jacques Lacan and Freud's French Revolution*. 2nd ed. New York: Guilford, 1992. Lively account of polemics centered on Lacan and his school.

Weber, Samuel. *Return to Freud: Jacques Lacan's Dislocation of Psychoanalysis*. Trans. Michael Levine. Cambridge: Cambridge UP, 1991.

Books Applying Lacan's Theories

Davis, Robert Con, ed. *Lacan and Narrative: The Psychoanalytic Difference in Narrative Theory*. Baltimore: Johns Hopkins UP, 1983. Essays applying Lacanian psychoanalysis to narratives; includes bibliography of works by Lacan and about Lacan and narrative.

Green, André. *The Tragic Effect*. Trans. Alan Sheridan. Cambridge: Cambridge UP, 1979.

Laplanche, Jean. *Life and Death in Psychoanalysis*. Trans. Jeffrey Mehlman. Baltimore: Johns Hopkins UP, 1976. Discusses Freud's ideas from a Lacanian perspective.

Mellard, James M. *Using Lacan, Reading Fiction*. Urbana: U of Illinois P, 1992. Applies Lacan to works by Hawthorne, James, Woolf.

Pagano, Jo Anne. *Exiles and Communities: Teaching in the Patriarchal Wilderness*. See entry 1645.

JULIA KRISTEVA (1941–)

The early phase of Julia Kristeva's work was structuralist, and books that orientation are listed in chapter 4, "Structuralism and Semiotics." er work was also responsive to a variety of figures, including Mikhail in (see chapter 2, "Russian Formalism and Prague Structuralism") and

959. Benvenuto, Bice. *The Work of Jacques Lacan: An In*
      Free, 1986.

960. Borch-Jacobsen, Mikkel. *Lacan: The Absolute Mas*
      Brick. Stanford: Stanford UP, 1991.

961. Bowie, Malcolm. *Freud, Proust, and Lacan: Theory as*
      Cambridge UP, 1987.

962. ———. *Lacan*. Cambridge: Harvard UP, 1991.

963. Clément, Catherine. *The Lives and Legends of Jacqu*
      thur Goldhammer. New York: Columbia UP, 1983.

964. ———. *The Weary Sons of Freud*. London: Verso,
      disciples of Lacan and argues for a feminist and cultu

965. Davis, Robert Con, ed. *The Fictional Father: Laca*
      Text. Amherst: U of Massachusetts P, 1981.

966. Felman, Shoshana. *Jacques Lacan and the Adventu*
      analysis in Contemporary Culture. Cambridge: Har

967. Gallop, Jane. *Reading Lacan*. Ithaca: Cornell UP, 1

968. Grosz, Elizabeth. *Jacques Lacan: A Feminist Introdu*
      ledge, 1990.

969. Hogan, Patrick Colm, and Lalita Pandit. *Criticism a*
      Dialogue on Language, Structure, and the Unconscio
      gia P, 1990. Sixteen essays by Frye, Holland, and o
      relevance to clinical psychology, art, and literature.

970. Lee, Jonathan Scott. *Jacques Lacan*. Boston: Hall,

971. Lemaire, Anika. *Jacques Lacan*. Trans. David Macc
      can. London: Routledge, 1977.

972. MacCabe, Colin, ed. *The Talking Cure: Essays in P*
      guage. New York: St. Martin's, 1981. Nine essays
      the self, language, and representation.

973. MacCannell, Juliet Flower. *Figuring Lacan: Crit*
      Unconscious. London: Croom Helm, 1986.

974. Macey, David. *Lacan in Contexts*. London: Verso,

975. Mitchell, Juliet, and Jacqueline Rose, eds. *Femi*
      Lacan and the Ecole Freudiènne. London: Macmi

976. Muller, John P., and William J. Richardson. *L*
      Reader's Guide to Ecrits. New York: Internationa

977. ———. *The Purloined Poe: Lacan, Derrida, and*
      Baltimore: Johns Hopkins UP, 1988. Includes Po
      Letter," Lacan's reading of it, Derrida's critique
      essays by Barbara Johnson, Jane Gallop, Holland,
      on the controversy.

978. Nancy, Jean-Luc, and Philippe Lacoue-Labarthe.

Jacques Derrida (see chapter 5,"Poststructuralism and Deconstruction"). More recently, her work has been immersed in varieties of psychoanalytic theory, including that of Lacan but also of Melanie Klein and British analysts. Kristeva outlines a preoedipal stage of development where the child is attached to the mother, has not formed an integrated subject that can stand over against rigid objects, and expresses feelings in fluid, free linguistic forms. Following Lacan, she argues that the child in the succeeding oedipal stage absorbs the more rigid "symbolic" forms of language and culture and repudiates and represses the earlier stage. But that stage and its derivatives emerge again in certain literary phenomena, such as the experience of "abjection" or the wordplay of Joyce. Recently, she has extended her approach to religious experience as well. Kristeva has explicitly distanced her thinking from Marxism and feminism, though her analysis of a "maternal" stage has been of particular interest to feminists.

991.   *Black Sun: Depression and Melancholia.* Trans. Leon S. Roudiez. New York: Columbia UP, 1989. Examines works of art and literature.

    Desire in Language: A Semiotic Approach to Literature and Art. See entry 541.

992.   *In the Beginning Was Love: Psychoanalysis and Faith.* Trans. Arthur Goldhammer. New York: Columbia UP, 1987.

993.   *The Kristeva Reader.* Ed. and introd. Toril Moi. Oxford: Blackwell, 1986.

994.   *Language the Unknown.* New York: Columbia UP, 1989.

995.   *The Powers of Horror: An Essay on Abjection.* Trans. Leon S. Roudiez. New York: Columbia UP, 1982.

    Revolution in Poetic Language. See entry 543.

996.   *Strangers to Ourselves.* Trans. Leon Roudiez. New York: Columbia UP, 1991. Psychological and literary dimensions of the "stranger," from Greek literature to the present.

997.   *Tales of Love.* Trans. Leon S. Roudiez. New York: Columbia UP, 1987.

Books on Kristeva

998.   Fletcher, John, and Andrew Benjamin, ed. *Abjection, Melancholia and Love: The Work of Julia Kristeva.* London: Routledge, 1990. Essays on varied aspects of her work.

999.   Lechte, John. *Julia Kristeva.* London: Routledge, 1990.

HAROLD BLOOM (1930–)

Harold Bloom's career began with a spirited defense of the Romantics against the harsh estimates of them by the New Critics, F. R. Leavis, and others. His immediate debt was to M. H. Abrams and Northrop Frye, but his early study *Shelley's Mythmaking* drew on Martin Buber as well. Bloom's comprehensive study *The Visionary Company* already began to read Romantic poems as interrelated texts and especially as oblique polemics against each other. This synoptic approach gradually led him to formulate a new theory of the "greater Romantic lyric"—essentially, the English lyric after Milton. Supporting his claim by reference to Walter Jackson Bate's *The Burden of the Past and the English Poet*, Bloom argued that poets must struggle against the existing body of poetry to make room for their own writing and personal style. *The Anxiety of Influence* went beyond this general observation to list six steps or stages in the struggle with the poetic precursor. These are both stages in a single poet's career and—as *A Map of Misreading* argues—a sequence of figures or defensive relations to a specific earlier poem that provides the structure for a specific later lyric poem. The scheme is explicitly evaluative: only poets who reach the final stage and only poems that pass through the whole sequence can achieve greatness. Bloom calls these poets or poems "strong." In *Kabbalah and Criticism*, he discovers the same fundamental sequence in the Jewish mystical writings studied by Gershom Scholem.

Bloom has theorized that critical reading is also defensive and involves the same process of deliberately misreading earlier works so as to open space for the critic's own commentary. While Bloom has elaborated his theory as a method for analyzing or reading individual poems, his instinctive loyalties are to the psychological structure of a poet's relation to great predecessors. Bloom's scheme retains the flavor of the Romantic quest, in which a hero, often not apparent as such, passes through a series of tests to achieve some spiritual or erotic goal along with fame or recognition. But Bloom interprets that quest in essentially psychological terms whose close relations to Freud reveal how much Freud himself was working out a psychology in the Romantic tradition.

Bloom has also written important books on W. B. Yeats, William Blake, and Wallace Stevens and has recently pursued the history of Gnostic and kabbalistic thought and biblical interpretation.

1000.   *Agon: Towards a Theory of Revisionism.* New York: Oxford UP, 1982.

1001.   *The Anxiety of Influence: A Theory of Poetry.* New York: Oxford UP, 1973.

1002.   *Kabbalah and Criticism.* New York: Continuum, 1975. Draws on Scholem's studies of Jewish mystical writings to extend Bloom's theories of poetic creation.

1003.   *A Map of Misreading.* New York: Oxford UP, 1975. Elaborates Bloom's theory of poetic creation to include imagistic, rhetorical, and psychological dimensions.

1004.   *Ruin the Sacred Truths: Poetry and Belief from the Bible to the Present.* Cambridge: Harvard UP, 1989.

1005.   *The Strong Light of the Canonical: Kafka, Freud, and Scholem as Revisionists of Jewish Culture and Thought.* New York: City Coll. of New York, 1987.

Books on Bloom

1006.   De Bolla, Peter. *Harold Bloom: Towards Historical Rhetorics.* London: Routledge, 1988.

1007.   Fite, David. *Harold Bloom: The Rhetoric of Romantic Vision.* Amherst: U of Massachusetts P, 1985. Good survey of Bloom's entire work.

1008.   Mileur, Jean-Pierre. *Literary Revisionism and the Burden of Modernity.* Berkeley: U of California P, 1985.

9. Cultural Criticism

The attempt to connect literature and criticism with larger cultural issues is one of the most vigorous movements in contemporary theory. It takes a much wider variety of forms than the conventional literary history or the rigidly orthodox Marxism that dominated earlier efforts. Indeed, the remainder of this bibliography may be regarded as concerned with cultural criticism and theory.

The present chapter treats books and theorists who are concerned with general cultural issues and whose approach is eclectic or at least does not easily fit into other more specific categories; included in this chapter are broad studies influenced by different strands in poststructuralist theory. Chapter 10 focuses on Marx and Marxist theories, including recent varieties that have reinterpreted Marx and sometimes diverged from orthodox Marxism. Chapter 11 deals with poststructuralist approaches to cultural criticism from theorists like Foucault and the new historicists. The specific areas of interest covered in the rest of the volume are literacy and orality (chapter 12), myth and anthropology (chapter 13), ethnic and postcolonial studies (chapter 14), and feminist and gender criticism (chapter 15). The last two chapters reflect a variety of theoretical approaches, but in both fields a deep concern with confronting cultural issues and with effecting changes in society provides a dominant and defining context for theorizing.

Introductory Studies and Anthologies

1009. Belsey, Catherine. *Critical Practice*. London: Methuen, 1980. On structuralist and poststructuralist views of language, ideology, and the media and mass culture.

1010. Burns, Elizabeth, and Tom Burns, eds. *Sociology of Literature and Drama: Selected Readings*. Harmondsworth, Eng.: Penguin, 1973. Excellent selections from a wide range of leading figures.

1011. Grossman, Lawrence, Cary Nelson, and Paula A. Treichler, eds. *Cultural Studies*. New York: Routledge, 1992. Wide-ranging collection exhibiting current state of the field.

1012. Lentricchia, Frank. *After the New Criticism*. Chicago: U of Chicago P, 1980. On developments in literary theory since the 1960s, emphasizing the social and political context.

1013. ———. *Criticism and Social Change*. Chicago: U of Chicago P, 1984.

1014. Saluszinsky, Imre, ed. *Criticism in Society: Interviews with Jacques Derrida, Northrop Frye, Harold Bloom, Geoffrey Hartman, Frank Kermode, Edward Said, Barbara Johnson, Frank Lentricchia, and J. Hillis Miller*. London: Routledge, 1987.

1015. Sammons, Jeffrey L. *Literary Sociology and Practical Criticism: An Inquiry*. Bloomington: Indiana UP, 1978. Good general study, with substantial bibliography divided into topical sections.

Books and Collections

1016. Arac, Jonathan, ed. *Postmodernism and Politics: New Directions*. Minneapolis: U of Minnesota P, 1986.

1017. Barker, Francis, et al., eds. *Literature, Politics, and Theory: Papers from the Essex Conference, 1976–84*. London: Methuen, 1986. Essays by Williams, Jameson, Said, and others, selected from important conferences at the University of Essex; with a complete list of papers presented.

1018. ———, eds. *Literature, Sociology, and the Sociology of Literature: Proceedings of the Conference Held at the University of Essex, July 1976*. Colchester, Eng.: U of Essex, 1977.

1019. ———, eds. *The Politics of Theory: Proceedings of the Essex Conference on the Sociology of Literature, July 1982*. Colchester, Eng.: U of Essex, 1983.

1020. Batsleer, Janet, Tony Davies, Rebecca O'Rourke, and Chris Weedon. *Rewriting English: Cultural Politics of Gender and Class*. London: Methuen, 1985. Argues that literary study needs to be resituated within cultural politics and feminist criticism.

1021.   Baudrillard, Jean. *For a Critique of the Political Economy of the Sign.* Trans. Charles Levin. St. Louis: Telos, 1981. By an influential theorist of the political and economic dimensions of culture.

1022.   ———. *The Mirror of Production.* Trans. Mark Poster. St. Louis: Telos, 1975.

1023.   ———. *Selected Writings.* Ed. Mark Poster. Oxford: Polity, 1988.

1024.   Baudrillard (book on). Gane, Mike. *Baudrillard: Critical and Fatal Theory.* New York: Routledge, 1991.

1025.   Baudrillard (book on). Gane, Mike. *Baudrillard's Bestiary: Baudrillard and Culture.* New York: Routledge, 1992. Examines Baudrillard's essays on literary works; discusses his theory of modernity, fiction, and consumer culture.

1026.   Baudrillard (book on). Kellner, Douglas. *Jean Baudrillard: From Marxism to Postmodernism and Beyond.* Stanford: Stanford UP, 1989.

1027.   Bennett, Sheila. *Imagination and Awareness: Literature as Society's Analyst.* New York: Vantage, 1988.

1028.   Bennett, Tony, ed. *Culture, Ideology and Social Process: A Reader.* London: Batsford, 1981.

1029.   Bourdieu, Pierre. *Distinction: A Social Critique of the Judgment of Taste.* Trans. Richard Nice. Cambridge: Harvard UP, 1984.

1030.   ———. *Language and Symbolic Power.* Ed. John B. Thompson. Cambridge: Harvard UP, 1991.

1031.   ———. *Outline of a Theory of Practice.* Trans. Richard Nice. Cambridge: Cambridge UP, 1977.

1032.   Bourdieu, Pierre, and Jean-Claude Passeron. *Reproduction: In Education, Society and Culture.* London: Sage, 1970.

1033.   Bourdieu (book on). Robbins, Derek. *The Work of Pierre Bourdieu.* Boulder: Westview, 1991.

1034.   Brantlinger, Patrick. *Bread and Circuses: Theories of Mass Culture as Social Decay.* Ithaca: Cornell UP, 1984.

1035.   Brenkman, John. *Culture and Domination.* Ithaca: Cornell UP, 1988.

1036.   Brogger, Fredrik Chr. *Culture, Language, Text: Culture Studies within the Study of English as a Foreign Language.* New York: Oxford UP, 1992. Focuses on the interplay between language and ideology to develop a theory and methodology of culture studies from the perspective of the study of English as a foreign language.

         Butler, Christopher. *Interpretation, Deconstruction, and Ideology: An Introduction to Some Current Issues in Literary Theory.* See entry 76.

1037.   Cottom, Daniel. *Text and Culture: The Politics of Interpretation.* Minneapolis: U of Minnesota P, 1989. Argues for necessity of multiple readings;

restriction to a single interpretation is a political move. Analyzes Dickens's *Great Expectations*.

1038. Craige, Betty Jean, ed. *Literature, Language, and Politics*. Athens: U of Georgia P, 1988. Essays by Gates, Graff, feminist theorists, and others.

1039. Cros, Edmond. *Theory and Practice of Sociocriticism*. Trans. Jerome Schwartz. Minneapolis: U of Minnesota P, 1988. Draws on Foucault, Bakhtin, and Goldmann to uncover semiotic and ideological elements in texts; examples from Spanish and Latin American literature.

1040. Davis, Lennard J., and M. Bella Mirabella, eds. *Left Politics and the Literary Profession*. New York: Columbia UP, 1990. Discusses the integration of New Left politics into the literary profession in the 1970s and the resulting changes in literary study.

1041. De Bolla, Peter. *The Discourse of the Sublime: History, Aesthetics and the Subject*. Oxford: Blackwell, 1989. Relations between capitalism and the "subject" in aesthetics.

1042. Desan, Philippe, Priscilla Parkhurst Ferguson, and Wendy Griswold, eds. *Literature and Social Practice*. Chicago: U of Chicago P, 1989. Seventeen essays by Eagleton, Bourdieu, and others on theory and on literary works from the eighteenth century to the present.

1043. Dews, Peter. *Logics of Disintegration: Post-structuralist Thought and the Claims of Critical Theory*. London: Verso, 1988. Critique of poststructuralism, drawing on Adorno and Habermas's theory of "communicative action."

1044. Docherty, Thomas. *After Theory: Postmodernism/Postmarxism*. London: Routledge, 1990. Opposes institutionalization of theory and seeks radical but post-marxist criticism in the wake of poststructuralism.

1045. Easthope, Antony. *Literary into Cultural Studies*. New York: Routledge, 1992. Aims to develop a method for analyzing both canonical and popular works; discusses Conrad's *Heart of Darkness* and Burroughs's *Tarzan of the Apes*.

1046. Fekete, John. *The Critical Twilight: Explorations in the Ideology of Anglo-American Literary Theory from Eliot to McLuhan*. London: Routledge, 1977. Analyzes Eliot, Ransom (New Criticism), Frye, and McLuhan as forms of "bourgeois" critical theory.

1047. ———. *Life after Postmodernism: Essays on Value and Culture*. New York: St. Martin's, 1987.

1048. Fleming, Richard, and Michael Payne, eds. *Criticism, History, and Intertextuality*. Lewisburg: Bucknell, UP, 1988.

1049. Gaitet, Pascale. *Political Stylistics: Popular Language as Literary Artifact*. New York: Routledge, 1992. Situates texts' formal properties within social power relations; uses Bourdieu, Goody, Watt, and Bakhtin.

1050. Garvin, Harry R., and James M. Heath, eds. *Literature and Ideology*. Lewisburg: Bucknell UP, 1982. Essays on ideology in relation to writers, critics, and women.

1051.   Gloversmith, Frank, ed. *The Theory of Reading*. Brighton, Eng.: Harvester, 1985. Essays rejecting the "autonomy" of the literary text postulated by New Criticism and using Bakhtin and others to develop a cultural approach.

1052.   Goux, Jean-Joseph. *Symbolic Economies: After Marx and Freud*. Trans. Jennifer Curtiss Gage. Ithaca: Cornell UP, 1990. On notions of value and exchange, image and representation; integrates poststructuralist approaches.

1053.   Graff, Gerald. *Literature against Itself: Literary Ideas in Modern Society*. Chicago: U of Chicago P, 1979. A controversial polemic on political grounds against the pretenses of modernist literature and critical theory.

1054.   Hodge, Robert. *Literature as Discourse: Textual Strategies in English and History*. Baltimore: Johns Hopkins UP, 1990. On social semiotics, history, and culture.

1055.   Hohendahl, Peter U. *The Institution of Criticism*. Ithaca: Cornell UP, 1982. Social context of German criticism from the eighteenth century to the present.

1056.   Hughes, Kenneth James. *Signs of Literature: Languages, Ideology, and the Literary Text*. Vancouver: Talon, 1986.

1057.   Inglis, Fred. *Ideology and Imagination*. Cambridge: Cambridge UP, 1975.

1058.   Jackson, J. R. De J. *Historical Criticism and the Meaning of Texts*. London: Routledge, 1989. Argues that historical criticism is the prerequisite for all other approaches.

1059.   Kennedy, Alan. *Reading Resistance Value: Deconstructive Practice and the Politics of Literary Critical Encounters*. London: Macmillan, 1990. Focusing on concept of resistance, argues that deconstruction can be engaged with history and politics; draws on de Man.

1060.   Laurenson, Diana, and Alan Swingewood. *The Sociology of Literature: Applied Studies*. New York: Schocken, 1972.

1061.   Lyotard, Jean-François. *The Differend: Phrases in Dispute*. Trans. Georges Van Der Abbeele. Minneapolis: U of Minnesota P, 1988. By an influential philosopher who brings a poststructuralist perspective to questions of law, justice, and social processes.

1062.   ———. *Peregrinations: Law, Form, Event*. New York: Columbia UP, 1988.

1063.   ———. *The Post-modern Condition: A Report on Knowledge*. Trans. Geoff Bennington and Brian Massumi. Minneapolis: U of Minnesota P, 1984. A searching analysis of the nature of knowledge in the modern era.

1064.   Lyotard (book on). Bennington, Geoffrey. *Lyotard: Writing the Event*. New York: Columbia UP, 1988.

1065.   Lyotard (book on). Readings, Bill. *Introducing Lyotard*. London: Routledge, 1991.

         Marcus, George E., and Michael M. J. Fischer. *Anthropology as Cultural Critique: An Experimental Moment in the Human Sciences*. See entry 1449.

1066. McGann, Jerome J. *The Beauty of Inflections: Literary Investigations in Historical Method and Theory.* Oxford: Clarendon–Oxford UP, 1985.

1067. ———, ed. *Historical Studies and Literary Criticism.* Madison: U of Wisconsin P, 1985. Essays by critics on works from the eighteenth century to the present.

1068. ———. *The Romantic Ideology: A Critical Investigation.* Chicago: U of Chicago P, 1983. Criticizes Romantic poets and their critics, using Marxist concept of ideology.

1069. ———. *Social Values and Poetic Acts: A Historical Judgment of Literary Work.* Cambridge: Harvard UP, 1988. Tries to reconcile formalism, deconstruction, and Marxism to rehabilitate historical criticism; draws on Adorno and criticizes de Man, Frye, and Fish.

1070. ———. *Towards a Literature of Knowledge.* Oxford: Clarendon–Oxford UP, 1989. Argues that criticism has postulated a literature of power, but defends the possibility of a literature that gives knowledge.

1071. Merod, Jim. *The Political Responsibility of the Critic.* Ithaca: Cornell UP, 1987.

1072. Miller, Jane. *Seductions: Studies and Readings in Culture.* Cambridge: Harvard UP, 1991. Discusses ways women experience literature and cultural traditions that both exclude and include them.

1073. Mitchell, W. J. T., ed. *The Politics of Interpretation.* Chicago: U of Chicago P, 1983. Essays from the journal *Critical Inquiry.*

1074. Mohanty, S. P. *Literary Theory and the Claims of History.* Oxford: Blackwell, 1990. Combines Marxism, feminism, and poststructuralism; discusses de Man, Jameson, and Althusser and examines politics of cross-cultural inquiry.

1075. Morson, Gary Saul. *Literature and History: Theoretical Problems and Russian Case Studies.* Stanford: Stanford UP, 1986. Non-Marxist approach.

1076. Nemoianu, Virgil. *A Theory of the Secondary: Literature, Progress, and Reaction.* Baltimore: Johns Hopkins UP, 1989. Draws on Girard and Serres; argues that literature is part of the "secondary," or margin of a society, and ordinarily opposes the progressive movement of its era.

1077. Parrinder, Patrick. *The Failure of Theory: Essays on Criticism and Contemporary Fiction.* Brighton, Eng.: Harvester, 1987. Criticizes recent Marxists while supporting his own interpretation of Raymond Williams's approach; with essays on contemporary British fiction.

1078. Pefanis, Julian. *Heterology and the Postmodern: Bataille, Baudrillard, and Lyotard.* Durham: Duke UP, 1991.

1079. Poyatos, Fernando, ed. *Literary Anthropology: A New Interdisciplinary Approach to People, Signs, and Literature.* Amsterdam: Benjamins, 1988.

1080. Punter, David. *The Hidden Script: Writing and the Unconscious.* London: Routledge, 1985. Draws mainly on Barthes, Foucault, and poststructuralist psychoanalysis to argue that contemporary theory and fiction unconsciously respond to destructive social processes while attempting to imagine a future.

1081.   Ridless, Robin. *Ideology and Art: Theories of Mass Culture from Walter Benjamin to Umberto Eco.* New York: Lang, 1984.

1082.   Said, Edward, ed. *Literature and Society.* Selected Papers from the English Institute, 1978, ns 3. Baltimore: Johns Hopkins UP, 1980.

1083.   Schulze, Leonard, and Walter Wetzels, eds. *Literature and History.* Lanham: UP of America, 1983. Nine essays, theoretical and applied.

1084.   Shell, Marc. *The Economy of Literature.* Baltimore: Johns Hopkins UP, 1978. Interprets texts from Greeks to Rousseau and Ruskin, bringing together literature, philosophy, and economics.

1085.   Simpson, David, ed. *Subject to History: Ideology, Class, Gender.* Ithaca: Cornell UP, 1991. Essays take various "materialist" approaches to mainly nineteenth-century works.

1086.   Solomon, J. Fisher. *Discourse and Reference in the Nuclear Age.* Norman: U of Oklahoma P, 1988. Discusses theoretical issues in the debate over critical responses to nuclear arms, particularly the problem of referentiality and the relation of criticism to politics and society.

1087.   Stallybrass, Peter, and Allon White. *Politics and Poetics of Transgression.* London: Methuen, 1986. Draws on Bakhtin and French critical theorists to analyze the idea of hierarchies in Western society.

1088.   Strelka, Joseph, ed. *Literary Criticism and Sociology.* Yearbook of Comparative Criticism 5. University Park: Pennsylvania State UP, 1973. Thirteen informative essays.

1089.   Terdiman, Richard. *Discourse/Counter-Discourse: The Theory and Practice of Symbolic Resistance in Nineteenth-Century France.* Ithaca: Cornell UP, 1985. Combines Marxism and semiotics to analyze the cultural function of texts.

1090.   Thurley, Geoffrey. *The Romantic Predicament.* London: Macmillan, 1983. Draws on recent neo-Marxism while critical of dialectical materialism.

1091.   Von Hallberg, Robert, ed. *Politics and Poetic Value.* Chicago: U of Chicago P, 1987. Essays by poets and theorists.

1092.   Weimann, Robert. *Structure and Society in Literary History: Studies in the History and Theory of Historical Criticism.* Enl. ed. Baltimore: Johns Hopkins UP, 1984. Includes new final chapter on poststructuralist criticism.

1093.   White, George Abbott, and Charles Newman, eds. *Literature in Revolution.* New York: Holt, 1972. Essays on the responsibilities of literature, popular culture, and critical consciousness.

1094.   Zavarzadeh, Mas'ud, and Donald Morton. *Theory, (Post) Modernity, Opposition: An "Other" Introduction to Literary and Cultural Theory.* Washington: Maisonneuve, 1991. Critiques the arguments that a range of critics and theorists have expounded against theory.

Individual Authors

WAYNE BOOTH (1921–   )

Wayne Booth is the most enduring representative of the *Chicago*, or *neo-Aristotelian*, approach to literature. This group presented its ideas in the important anthology *Critics and Criticism* (1952). The contributors, including the editor, R. S. Crane, proposed to follow Aristotle's example by seeing various literary works as wholes intended to produce a certain effect and by developing an analytic vocabulary for describing and evaluating how well the work used the available artistic resources to achieve that effect. In *The Rhetoric of Fiction*, Booth followed out this study of artistic resources by analyzing the ways the narrator of a story can guide readers directly or indirectly toward a certain understanding and emotional response. His purpose was to defend a wider variety of narrative stances than current criticism, based on Henry James's practice, allowed for. But he went beyond the Chicago school's more formal analyses to make in addition a historical and a moral point. Over time, an explicit and reliable narrator has evolved into a "persona," a narrator who is simply another character no more authoritative than any other. The result is that the reader becomes increasingly unsure how to understand and evaluate the action and the characters in the story. And this historical development, Booth suggested, is morally questionable. Or at least, he argued, there is no reason to prefer the modern uncertainty of moral response to the traditional definiteness.

Throughout his work, Booth shows exactly this capacity to be intelligently responsive to the full range of literary possibilities—for narration, for irony, for critical approaches, and so on—and yet refuses to acquiesce uncritically in the assumption that the modern is superior or that an unwillingness or inability to hold to clear moral values is the same as moral sophistication. Combining subtle formal analysis with a concern for larger issues of value, both personal and social, Booth is also dedicated to traditional values of clear writing and reasoning in critical theory. His gentle insistence that critics should produce intelligible and defensible reasons for their views has given him an important role as a rational conscience for contemporary theory.

1095.   *The Company We Keep: An Ethics of Fiction.* Berkeley: U of California P, 1988. Continues the argument of the *Rhetoric of Fiction*, but in the context of recent interest in moral philosophy, literary theory, and literature.

1096.   *Critical Understanding: The Powers and Limits of Pluralism.* Chicago: U of Chicago, 1979.

1097.   *Modern Dogma and the Rhetoric of Assent.* Notre Dame: U of Notre Dame P, 1974.

1098.   *Now Don't Try to Reason with Me: Essays and Ironies for a Credulous Age.* Chicago: U of Chicago P, 1970.

1099.   *The Rhetoric of Fiction.* 1961. Rev. ed. Chicago: U of Chicago P, 1983.

1100.   *A Rhetoric of Irony.* Chicago: U of Chicago, 1974.

1101.   *The Vocation of a Teacher: Rhetorical Occasions, 1967–1988.* Chicago: U of Chicago P, 1988.

KENNETH BURKE (1897–   )

Omnivorously eclectic, Kenneth Burke has found in the analysis of human symbolic activities a key to the largest cultural issues. As symbol-making animals, human beings depend on their symbols to enable them to encompass the situations, natural and social, into which they are thrust. As inventors of the negative, human beings are free to imagine what is not and to obey or violate the restrictions of communal life. Separated from the merely natural by cultural, symbolic systems, human beings are "goaded by the spirit of hierarchy" and "moved by a sense of order," and they steadily pursue a perfection formulated in "god terms," the ideas that bear ultimate value, hope, and consolation.

Burke's social analysis makes a strong connection between social hierarchy and mystery or guilt. Establishing order inevitably entails the sense of sin or failure inherent in the social hierarchy's "losers" or outcasts. Order consequently demands a sacrificial principle, involving victimization and catharsis. Human beings "fall" whenever they follow "the impulse towards abstraction which reason and language make possible, and conceive of ideals ('god-terms') which are incapable of being perfectly realized." The secular analogue for the sacrificial redemption envisioned in the story of Christ is symbolic action. Literature, the most prominent and sophisticated form of symbolic action, provides "equipment for living" by allowing us to adopt hypothetically various strategies for encompassing situations.

A Grammar of Motives offers key terms to analyze literature's purgative and curative social function: "act," "scene," "agent," "agency," "purpose," and the various "ratios" between these elements. *Counter-statement* describes the formal arrangements by which works arouse and satisfy an audience's expectations. Extensive, complex, and wide-ranging, Burke's writing has had considerable influence, particularly among theorists of communication and students of social processes.

1102.   *Attitudes toward History.* 1937. 3rd ed. Berkeley: U of California P, 1984.

1103.   *Counter-statement.* 1931. 2nd rev. ed. 1953. Berkeley: U of California P, 1968.

1104.   *Dramatism and Development.* Barre: Clark UP, 1972.

1105.   *A Grammar of Motives.* 1945. Berkeley: U of California P, 1969.

1106.   *Language as Symbolic Action: Essays on Life, Literature, and Method.* Berkeley: U of California P, 1966.

1107.   *On Symbols and Society.* Ed. Joseph R. Gusfield. Chicago: U of Chicago P, 1989.

1108.   *Permanence and Change: An Anatomy of Purpose.* 1936. 3rd ed. Berkeley: U of California P, 1984.

1109.   *Perspectives by Incongruity.* Ed. Stanley Edgar Hyman with Barbara Karmiller. Bloomington: Indiana UP, 1964. Selections from his criticism and creative writing.

1110.   *The Philosophy of Literary Form: Studies in Symbolic Action.* 1941. 3rd ed. Berkeley: U of California P, 1974.

1111.   *A Rhetoric of Motives.* 1950. Berkeley: U of California P, 1969.

1112.   *The Rhetoric of Religion: Studies in Logology.* Berkeley: U of California P, 1970.

1113.   *Terms for Order.* Ed. Stanley Edgar Hyman with Barbara Karmiller. Bloomington: Indiana UP, 1964.

1114.   *Towards a Better Life: Being a Series of Epistles, or Declamations.* 1932. Berkeley: U of California P, 1966.

Books on Burke

1115.   Frank, Armin Paul. *Kenneth Burke.* New York: Twayne, 1969.

1116.   Heath, Robert L. *Realism and Relativism: A Perspective on Kenneth Burke.* Macon: Mercer UP, 1986.

1117.   Henderson, Greig E. *Kenneth Burke: Literature and Language as Symbolic Action.* Athens: U of Georgia P, 1988.

1118.   Knox, George. *Critical Moments: Kenneth Burke's Categories and Critiques.* Seattle: U of Washington P, 1957.

1119.   Rueckert, William H., ed. *Critical Responses to Kenneth Burke, 1924–1961.* Minneapolis: U of Minnesota P, 1969.

1120.   ———. *Kenneth Burke and the Drama of Human Relations.* 2nd ed. Berkeley: U of California P, 1982.

1121.   Simons, Herbert W., and Trevor Melia, eds. *The Legacy of Kenneth Burke.* Madison: U of Wisconsin P, 1988. Fifteen essays from various disciplines.

1122.   Southwell, Samuel B. *Kenneth Burke and Martin Heidegger: With a Note against Deconstruction.* Gainesville: UP of Florida, 1987.

1123.   White, Hayden, and Margaret Brose, eds. *Representing Kenneth Burke.* Selected Papers from the English Institute, ns 6. Baltimore: Johns Hopkins UP, 1983.

10. Marxist Critical Theory

Though Karl Marx (1818–83) and his collaborator Friedrich Engels (1820–95) were highly cultured, their labors in political economy left them little leisure to write about art and literature. But their scattered comments have been gathered in anthologies listed here, and such is the nature of the orthodoxy to which their systems gave rise that the merest scraps by either of them or by their successors Lenin, Stalin, and Mao Tse-tung have been dutifully and reverentially pored over by those committed to elaborating a Marxist criticism.

Far more important are their general economic and political ideas, particularly the beliefs that a base of economic production sets the determining conditions for all phases of social activity, including the cultural superstructure, and that each dominant class holds an ideology, a warped vision of the world that grows out of and masks unacknowledged economic interests. It is endemic to Marx and Marxists to measure literature for its ability to aid in the emergence of a classless society, yet Marx acknowledges and admits his puzzlement over the seeming autonomy and continuing power of aesthetic objects and values despite the most radical historical and social changes.

The headnotes under individual authors and schools in this chapter give a brief overview of some varieties of Marxist critical theory. While orthodox traditional Marxists like Georg Lukács or Christopher Caudwell continue to attract interest, contemporary theory has been more responsive to the ideas of the Frankfurt school (especially Walter Benjamin), to the structuralist Marxism of Louis Althusser, and recently to the "hegemonic" theory of culture of Antonio Gramsci. Fredric Jameson attempts a powerful and comprehensive approach under the general rubric of Marxism.

Bibliographies

1124.   Baxandall, Lee. *Marxism and Aesthetics: A Selective Annotated Bibliography. Books and Articles in the English Language.* New York: Humanities, 1968.

1125.   Bullock, Chris, and David Peck, comps. *Guide to Marxist Literary Criticism.* Bloomington: Indiana UP, 1980. Annotated bibliography of primary texts and sources.

Introductory Anthologies and Surveys

1126.   Baxandall, Lee, ed. *Radical Perspectives in the Arts.* Harmondsworth, Eng.: Penguin, 1972. Nineteen essays on the arts under capitalism and socialism and on the "future of culture."

1127.   Craig, David, ed. *Marxists on Literature: An Anthology.* Harmondsworth, Eng.: Penguin, 1975. Twenty-six selections from leading Marxist critics, Engels to the present.

1128.   Demetz, Peter. *Marx, Engels, and the Poets: Origins of Marxist Literary Theory.* Trans. Jeffrey L. Sammons. Rev. ed. Chicago: U of Chicago P, 1967. Extensive discussion of Marx and Engels and later theorists, including Lukács, Plekhanov, Adorno, Goldmann, and others.

Eagleton, Terry. *Marxism and Literary Criticism.* See entry 1242.

Jameson, Fredric. *Marxism and Form: Twentieth-Century Dialectical Theories of Literature.* See entry 1265.

1129.   Lang, Berel, and Forrest Williams, eds. *Marxism and Art: Writings in Aesthetics and Criticism.* New York: McKay, 1972. Thirty-five well-chosen selections from Marx to the present.

1130.   Marx, Karl. *On Literature and Art.* Moscow: Progress, 1978.

1131.   Marx, Karl, and Friedrich Engels. *Marx and Engels on Literature and Art: A Selection of Writings.* Ed. Lee Baxandall and Stefan Morawski. St. Louis: Telos, 1973. Passages by Marx and Engels, a long introduction.

1132.   Nelson, Cary, and Lawrence Grossberg, eds. *Marxism and the Interpretation of Culture.* Urbana: U of Illinois P, 1988. Massive and comprehensive collection of essays on current issues.

1133.   Solomon, Maynard, ed. *Marxism and Art: Essays Classic and Contemporary.* New York: Knopf, 1973.

1134.   Swingewood, Alan. *Sociological Poetics and Aesthetic Theory.* Basingstoke,

Eng.: Macmillan, 1986. Broad discussion of Marxist theory of literature.

Williams, Raymond. *Marxism and Literature.* See entry 1274.

Books and Collections

1135.   Anderson, Perry. *Arguments within English Marxism.* London: New Left, 1980. Replies to an attack on poststructuralist Marxism by the famous Marxist historian E. P. Thompson in his *Poverty of Theory.*

1136.   ———. *In the Tracks of Historical Materialism.* Chicago: U of Chicago P, 1984. Traces recent developments in European Marxist theory.

Bakhtin, Mikhail M., and Medvedev, P. N. *The Formal Method in Literary Scholarship: A Critical Introduction to Sociological Poetics.* See entry 341.

Bennett, Tony. *Formalism and Marxism.* See entry 306.

1137.   ———. *Outside Literature.* New York: Routledge, 1990. Discusses Lukács, Jameson, Eagleton, Lentricchia, and other Marxists; critiques poststructuralism and shows relation of literature to social institutions.

1138.   Bloch, Ernst. *The Utopian Function of Art and Literature: Selected Essays.* Trans. Jack Zipes and Frank Mecklenburg. Cambridge: MIT P, 1988. Essays on art and literature by one of the outstanding Marxist philosophers of the century.

1139.   Caudwell, Christopher. [Christopher St. John Sprigg] (book on). Margolies, David N. *The Function of Literature: A Study of Christopher Caudwell's Aesthetics.* New York: International, 1969. On the theories of a leading Marxist critic of the 1930s.

1140.   Caudwell (book on). Pawling, Christopher. *Christopher Caudwell: Towards a Dialectical Theory of Literature.* New York: St. Martin's, 1989.

1141.   Caudwell (book on). Sullivan, Robert. *Christopher Caudwell.* London: Croom Helm, 1987.

1142.   Caute, David. *The Illusion: An Essay on Politics, Theatre and the Novel.* London: Deutsch, 1971. Marxist approach to theater and the novel.

1143.   Coward, Rosalind, and John Ellis. *Language and Materialism: Developments in Semiology and the Theory of the Subject.* London: Routledge, 1977. A synthesis of Marxism with recent psychoanalytic theory, especially that of Lacan, and with deconstruction.

1144.   Ermolaev, Herman. *Soviet Literary Theories, 1917–1934: The Genesis of Socialist Realism.* Berkeley: U of California P, 1963.

1145.   Fekete, John, ed. *The Structural Allegory: Reconstructive Encounters with the New French Thought.* Minneapolis: U of Minnesota P, 1984. Essays by and on French Marxists and poststructuralists, attempting to absorb the work of Derrida, Foucault, and Barthes into a broadened Marxist cultural criticism.

1146.   Frow, John. *Marxism and Literary History*. New Haven: Yale UP, 1986. Examines work of Macherey, Eagleton, Jameson.

1147.   Goldstein, Philip. *The Politics of Literary Theory: An Introduction to Marxist Criticism*. Gainesville: UP of Florida, 1990.

1148.   Hawthorn, Jeremy. *Identity and Relationship: A Contribution to the Marxist Theory of Literary Criticism*. London: Lawrence, 1973. A Marxist approach to reader-response criticism.

1149.   Johnson, Pauline. *Marxist Aesthetics: The Foundations within Everyday Life for an Emancipated Consciousness*. London: Routledge, 1984. On Lukács, Benjamin, Brecht, Adorno, Marcuse, Althusser, Macherey, and Eagleton.

1150.   Lewis, Thomas E. *Fiction and Reference*. London: Methuen, 1986. Synthesizes semiotic and Marxist approaches to argue that literature does refer.

1151.   Lunn, Eugene. *Marxism and Modernism: An Historical Study of Lukács, Brecht, Benjamin, and Adorno*. Berkeley: U of California P, 1982.

1152.   Poster, Mark. *Existential Marxism in Postwar France: From Sartre to Althusser*. Princeton: Princeton UP, 1975. Important historical background for the renaissance of Marxist literary theories.

1153.   Ryan, Michael. *Marxism and Deconstruction: A Critical Articulation*. Baltimore: Johns Hopkins UP, 1982.

1154.   ———. *Politics and Culture: Working Hypotheses for a Post-revolutionary Society*. Baltimore: Johns Hopkins UP, 1989. Combines Marxist approach with ideas from deconstruction.

1155.   Selden, Raman. *Criticism and Objectivity*. London: Allen, 1984.

1156.   Sharratt, Bernard. *Reading Relations: Structures of Literary Productions: A Dialectical Text/Book*. Brighton, Eng.: Harvester, 1982. A book whose witty postmodernist form defies description, but which draws on Marxism to discuss the social relations of literary production.

1157.   Slaughter, Cliff. *Marxism, Ideology and Literature*. London: Macmillan, 1980.

1158.   Sprinker, Michael. *Imaginary Relations: Aesthetics and Ideology in the Theory of Historical Materialism*. London: Verso, 1987. Analyzes Marx's *Grundrisse* on the concept of the subject and discusses works of literature and theory up to Jameson and Sartre.

Vološinov, V. N. *Freudianism: A Marxist Critique*. See entry 342.

———. *Marxism and the Philosophy of Language*. See entry 343.

1159.   Wells, Susan. *The Dialectics of Representation*. Baltimore: Johns Hopkins UP, 1986. Playing off de Man against Jameson, defends a Marxist theory of representation while acknowledging that the reader's interpretation is historical and indeterminate.

Willis, Susan. *Specifying: Black Women Writing the American Experience*. See entry 1525.

Individual Author

GEORG LUKACS (1885–1971)

The philosophical career of Georg Lukács (the spelling "György Lu-kács" is now standard for libraries) recapitulates one strand in the German tradition. His early *Soul and Form* adopted a Kantian approach to the relations between aesthetic forms, on the one hand, and the soul's faculties and power to intuit ultimate realities, on the other; he applied this approach to the genre of the essay. *Theory of the Novel* followed Hegel by emphasizing the importance for narrative form of the central hero's biography, the career of the character's spiritual development in interaction with and opposition to the natural and social environment. With *History and Class Consciousness*, Lukács took his permanent stand with Marx, and all his further work flows from that commitment.

Like all Marxists, he believes he has learned from Marx the essential pattern and forces of history. Literature, like every other aspect of human culture, is to be read in the light of that unshakable knowledge. Contrary to our ordinary ways of thinking and acting, Lukács asserts, the institutions and everyday objects in our world are less solid than we imagine, for they are in fact determined by the historical forces that have produced them. Literature must reflect those underlying forces, not the mere surface appearance of the world—a doctrine surprisingly close to what Aristotle means by "mimesis," or "imitation." Literature does so by presenting "typical" characters and situations. "Typical" refers not to what is merely statistically frequent but rather to that in which the inescapable conflicts between historical forces reach a decisive point of intensity and clarity. Lukács has no use for experimental literary works that simply record the flow of experience or evade formulating a conscious response to historical situations. For him, history is not a meaningless play of forces but a conflict whose direction is certain: toward the emergence of a classless society. Literature can be great only if it fosters this inexorable historical movement or at least does not set itself against it.

In Lukács's hands, Marxism becomes a means of both analyzing and evaluating works of literature. Fully committed to the realist literary tradition, he has no patience for modernist literature in any of its forms. But his theory stands as the richest Marxist approach to the literature most congenial to its own way of thinking. Of his many works, only those most relevant to critical and theoretical issues are listed here.

1160.   *Conversations with Lukács.* Ed. Theo. Pinkus. Cambridge: MIT P. 1975.

1161.   *Essays on Realism.* Trans. David Fernbach. Ed. Rodney Livingstone. Cambridge: MIT P, 1981.

1162. *Goethe and His Age.* Trans. Robert Anchor. 1947. New York: Grossett, 1969.

1163. *The Historical Novel.* Trans. Hannah Mitchell and Stanley Mitchell. Boston: Beacon, 1963.

1164. *History and Class Consciousness.* 1923. Trans. Rodney Livingstone. Cambridge: MIT P. 1971.

1165. *The Meaning of Contemporary Realism.* Trans. John Mander and Necke Mander. London: Marlin, 1963. Published in the United States under the title *Realism in Our Time: Literature and the Class Struggle.* New York: Harper, 1964. Attacks modernism, with a famous comparison between Kafka and Mann.

1166. *Reviews and Articles from* Die Rote Fahne. Trans. Peter Palmer. London: Merlin, 1983. Pieces from 1922.

1167. *Solzhenitsyn.* Trans. William D. Graf. Cambridge: MIT P, 1971.

1168. *Soul and Form.* 1910. Trans. Anna Bostock. Cambridge: MIT P, 1974.

1169. *Studies in European Realism: A Sociological Survey of the Writings of Balzac, Stendhal, Zola, Tolstoy, Gorki, and Others.* Trans. Edith Bone. New York: Grosset, 1964.

1170. *The Theory of the Novel.* 1916. Trans. Anna Bostock. Cambridge: MIT P, 1971.

1171. *Writer and Critic.* Ed. and trans. Arthur D. Kahn. London: Merlin, 1970. Important essays from the 1930s.

Lukács Bibliography

1172. Lapointe, François. *Georg Lukács and His Critics: An International Bibliography with Annotations (1910–1982).* Westport: Greenwood, 1983.

Books on Lukács

1173. Bahr, Erhard, and Ruth Goldschmidt Kunzer. *George Lukács.* New York: Ungar, 1972.

1174. Bernstein, J. M. *The Philosophy of the Novel: Lukács, Marxism, and the Dialectics of Form.* Minneapolis: U of Minnesota P, 1984. Ties Lukács's early study of the novel to his later Marxism.

1175. Corredor, Eva L. *György Lukács and the Literary Pretext.* New York: Lang, 1988. Examines his theory broadly and his views on French literature; supplies biographical information and a bibliography.

1176. Holzman, Michael. *Lukács's Road to God: The Early Criticism against Its Pre-Marxist Background.* Washington: Center for Advanced Research in Phenomenology; Lanham: UP of America, 1985. Argues that Lukács's early works escaped neo-Kantian dilemmas by a leap into messianic religion; discusses other theorists, including New Critics.

1177.   Joos, Ernest, ed. *George Lukács and His World: A Reassessment.* New York: Lang, 1988.

1178.   Kiralyfalvi, Bela. *The Aesthetics of Gyorgy Lukacs.* Princeton: Princeton UP, 1975.

1179.   Marcus, Judith. *Georg Lukács and Thomas Mann: A Study in the Sociology of Literature.* Amherst: U of Massachusetts P, 1987.

1180.   Pike, David. *Lukács and Brecht.* Chapel Hill: U of North Carolina P, 1985.

1181.   Rockmore, Tom, ed. *Lukács Today: Essays in Marxist Philosophy.* Dordrecht: Reidel, 1988.

Wellek, René. *Four Critics: Croce, Valéry, Lukács, and Ingarden.* See entry 358.

The Frankfurt School

In the period after World War I, a group of thinkers formed the Institute for Social Research in Frankfurt, Germany, to elaborate and apply a Marxist analysis of society and politics. Its chief theorists were Theodor Adorno and Max Horkheimer, but Herbert Marcuse, Leo Lowenthal, and—more loosely—Walter Benjamin were also associated with its thinking. The *Frankfurt school* did not aim at conventional sociology or even at orthodox Marxism but sought a transformation of the social and political order through "practice" informed by a "critical theory" that would reveal and repudiate the oppressive workings of the status quo. The institute and its theorists moved to the United States after the rise of the Nazis and returned to Germany only after World War II.

From the beginning, these theorists were interested in cultural phenomena, particularly music and literature. They examined the ways the psychological makeup of the individual and the influence of escapist commercial mass culture (the culture industry) conspired to produce both acquiescence in oppressive and destructive political and economic conditions and indifference or even resistance to efforts at making liberating changes or revolution. Radically experimental modern art resisted being converted into a cultural commodity, they believed, and consequently it provided a key point of opposition to the status quo. The Frankfurt school thus blended Marxist social and political analysis, Freudian psychology, a sympathetic attention to radical modernist art, and analysis and critique of contemporary communications, especially in the distorted form of commercial mass culture. This combination of interests has made it particularly influential in contemporary theory.

The school's heritage has been continued by the philosopher and sociologist Jürgen Habermas. But in elaborating his own theory of communicative action, Habermas has moved in directions that put the explicit Marxism of the Frankfurt school further and further in the background. Most recently, his book *The Philosophical Discourse of Modernity* presented a broad attack on poststructuralism and postmodernism, and his sharp critique has provoked a continuing debate.

Books and Collections

1182.   Benjamin, Andrew, ed. *The Problems of Modernity: Adorno and Benjamin.* London: Routledge, 1989.

1183.   Berman, Russell A. *Modern Culture and Critical Theory: Art, Politics, and the Legacy of the Frankfurt School.* Madison: U of Wisconsin P, 1989.

1184.   Buck-Morss, Susan. *The Origin of Negative Dialectics: Theodor W. Adorno, Walter Benjamin, and the Frankfurt Institute.* New York: Free, 1977.

1185.   Hohendahl, Peter Uwe. *Reappraisals: Shifting Alignments in Postwar Critical Theory.* Ithaca: Cornell UP, 1991. Discusses Lukács, Adorno, Habermas, the Frankfurt school.

1186.   Jay, Martin. *The Dialectic Imagination: A History of the Frankfurt School and the Institute of Social Research, 1923–1950.* Boston: Little, 1973. Excellent introductory survey of the Frankfurt school's cultural theorists, including Adorno, Horkheimer, Marcuse, Benjamin, and Lowenthal.

1187.   Kellner, Douglas. *Critical Theory, Marxism, and Modernity.* Baltimore: Johns Hopkins UP, 1989.

1188.   Taylor, Ronald, ed. *Aesthetics and Politics.* Introd. Fredric Jameson. London: New Left, 1977. Presents debates among Bloch, Lukács, Brecht, Benjamin, and Adorno from the 1930s.

Individual Authors

THEODOR W. ADORNO (1903–69)

The core of Theodor Adorno's thought is a resistance to any simplifying syntheses or systematization. His philosophy extolled the "negative" or "critical" moment that undermines totality. A staunch advocate of radically experimental modern art, he praised fragmented or ruptured structures that destroy the soothing unity and aesthetic enjoyment which cover over or compensate for a historical reality of conflict, oppression, and barbarism. The difficulty of the form and content of modernist art, he asserted, resists "commodification," that is, the reduction to a commercial mass entertainment that, like Roman circuses, diverts most people from seriously facing their social reality. Adorno scornfully rejected art that seeks to serve social causes directly, and he likewise rejected the orthodox Marxist idea that art simply reflects the world and the class interests of its creators and consumers. Through dissonance and critical resistance, radical modernist art alone keeps alive the utopian hope for a more just world. A composer who wrote extensively about modern music, Adorno championed Arnold Schönberg, whose twelve-tone, or serial, compositions challenge the conventional audience's wish for pacifying aesthetic pleasure. He denounced Igor Stravinsky, whose music at first seemed experimental but turned out to be quickly digested and made profitable by the "culture industry." Adorno thus saw political dimensions in modernist art's self-reflexive preoccupation with form and its resistance to traditional ideals of organic unity and pleasure. Of Adorno's varied writings, only those most directly relevant to literary theory are listed here.

1189.   *Aesthetic Theory*. Trans. C. Lenhardt. Ed. Gretel Adorno and Rolf Tiedemann. London: Routledge, 1984.

1190.   *The Culture Industry: Selected Essays on Mass Culture*. Ed. J. M. Bernstein. New York: Routledge, 1991.

1191.   *Kierkegaard: Construction of the Esthetic*. Trans. and ed. Robert Hullot-Kentor. 1933. Minneapolis: U of Minnesota P, 1989.

1192.   *Minima Moralia: Reflections from Damaged Life*. Trans. E. F. N. Jephcott. London: New Left, 1974.

1193.   *Negative Dialectics*. Trans. E. B. Ashton. New York: Continuum, 1973. His major philosophical work.

1194.   *Notes to Literature*. Vol. 1. Ed. Rolf Tiedemann. Trans. Shierry Weber Nicholsen. New York: Columbia UP, 1991. Vol. 2. Trans. Shierry Weber Nicholsen. New York: Columbia UP, 1992.

1195.   *Prisms*. Trans. Samuel Weber and Shierry Weber. London: Spearman, 1967. Aphorisms and essays.

1196.   Adorno, Theodor W., and Max Horkheimer. *Dialectic of the Enlightenment*. Trans. John Cumming. 1944. New York: Herder, 1972. A critique of modern "rationalism" and of the "culture industry."

Adorno Bibliography

1197.   Nordquist, Joan, comp. *Theodor Adorno*. Santa Cruz: Reference and Research Services, 1988.

Books on Adorno

1198.   Jameson, Fredric. *Late Marxism: Adorno; or, The Persistence of the Dialectic*. London: Verso, 1990.

1199.   Jay, Martin. *Adorno*. Cambridge: Harvard UP, 1984.

1200.   Zuidervaart, Lambert. *Adorno's Aesthetic Theory: The Redemption of Illusion*. Cambridge: MIT P, 1991.

WALTER BENJAMIN (1892–1940)

Walter Benjamin's work was related to that of the Frankfurt school, but its sources were so unorthodox and varied that its allegiances and implications were a subject of controversy in his lifetime and remain so today. He absorbed Marxist ideas but not the practice of communism, although he sympathized with communist antifascism. His main interest was in modern industrial and urban life, which led to a transformation of literary motifs and forms developed in an earlier, largely agriculture society. The same interest attracted him to new artistic forms, such as film, where the older idea of an original and copy was rendered obsolete by mechanical processes of reproduction in which all copies were equivalent. Modern conditions have thus changed both art and our relation to it by changing the processes of artistic production and consumption. Benjamin's way of eliciting historical conditions through reading particular literary works was not an orthodox matching of content with Marxist categories of historical analysis. Instead, he traced oblique relations of form and content to highly specific historical realities with a subtlety that some have argued was indebted more to Jewish kabbalistic practices than to Marxism (and Benjamin was a close friend of Gershom Scholem, the major historian of Kabbalah). His friend Theodor Adorno criticized him for the unorthodoxy of his analyses, yet to modern theorists they have seemed an important extension of Marxist thought, precisely because of their originality.

1201.   *Charles Baudelaire: A Lyric Poet in the Era of High Capitalism.* Trans. Harry Zohn and Quintin Hoare. London: New Left, 1973. A unique approach to setting Baudelaire in his historical context.

1202.   *Illuminations.* Trans. Harry Zohn. Ed. and introd. Hannah Arendt. New York: Harcourt, 1968. Important essays on translation, narration, film, Baudelaire.

1203.   *One-Way Street and Other Writings.* Trans. Edmund Jephcott. London: New Left, 1979.

1204.   *The Origin of German Tragic Drama.* Trans. John Osborne. London: New Left, 1977.

1205.   *Reflections: Essays, Aphorisms, Autobiographical Writings.* Trans. Edmund Jephcott. New York: Harvest-Harcourt, 1979.

1206.   *Understanding Brecht.* Trans. Anna Bostock. London: New Left, 1973.

Books on Benjamin

1207.   Buck-Morss, Susan. *The Dialectics of Seeing: Walter Benjamin and the Arcades Project.* Cambridge: MIT P, 1989.

1208.   Bullock, Marcus Paul. *Romanticism and Marxism: The Philosophical Devel-*

opment of Literary Theory and Literary History in Walter Benjamin and Friedrich Schlegel. New York: Lang, 1987.

1209.   Eagleton, Terry. Walter Benjamin; or, Towards a Revolutionary Criticism. London: New Left, 1981.

1210.   Frisby, David. Fragments of Modernity: Theories of Modernity in the Work of Simmel, Kracauer, and Benjamin. Cambridge, Eng.: Polity, 1985.

         Handelman, Susan A. Fragments of Redemption: Jewish Thought and Literary Theory in Benjamin, Scholem, and Levinas. See entry 243.

1211.   Jennings, Michael W. Dialectical Images: Walter Benjamin's Theory of Literary Criticism. Ithaca: Cornell UP, 1987.

1212.   Nägele, Rainer, ed. Benjamin's Ground: New Readings of Walter Benjamin. Detroit: Wayne State UP, 1989.

1213.   ———. Theater, Theory, Speculation: Walter Benjamin and the Scenes of Modernity. Baltimore: Johns Hopkins UP, 1991. Concentrates on Benjamin's account of the baroque period and the modern theater.

1214.   Roberts, Julian. Walter Benjamin. London: Macmillan, 1982.

1215.   Smith, Gary, ed. Benjamin: Philosophy, Aesthetics, History. Chicago: U of Chicago P, 1989.

1216.   ———, ed. On Walter Benjamin: Critical Essays and Recollections. Cambridge: MIT P, 1988.

1217.   Witte, Bernd. Walter Benjamin: An Intellectual Biography. Detroit: Wayne State UP, 1991.

1218.   Wolin, Richard. Walter Benjamin: An Aesthetic of Redemption. New York: Columbia UP, 1982.

HERBERT MARCUSE (1898–1979)

Herbert Marcuse achieved his greatest renown in the 1960s and 1970s, when his writings were the means for infusing Frankfurt school ideas into the student protest movement. In the 1930s, he had written critical essays arguing that the doctrines of Martin Heidegger and other German philosophers were reactionary and potentially or actually fascist. Along with Theodor Adorno, Marcuse connected Freud with social theory and maintained that contemporary society is more repressive than is justifiable, so that the expression of repressed desires can have a politically liberating significance. In One-Dimensional Man he tried to show that techniques of mass communication and manipulation, such as advertising, distorted people's desires, producing the false wants and "needs" that drive a commercial, consumer economy. He welcomed the student protest movement and its resistance to consumer values, to social and psychological repression, and to militarism. He even argued that hope for revolutionary change had to be found in a countercultural intelligentsia rather than in the working class, since workers had been pacified by material success and mass entertainment. Certain kinds of art could both resist the oppressive status quo and serve as the utopian bearer of hope for a better future. Such claims were sharply criticized by more orthodox Marxists.

1219.   *The Aesthetic Dimension: Towards a Critique of Marxist Aesthetics.* Trans. Herbert Marcuse. Boston: Beacon, 1978.

1220.   *Counterrevolution and Revolt.* Boston: Beacon, 1972. Includes the chapter "Art and Revolution."

1221.   *Eros and Civilization: A Philosophical Inquiry into Freud.* Boston: Beacon, 1974. Connects Freud with social theory and presents idea of "repressive desublimation."

1222.   *Essay on Liberation.* Boston: Beacon, 1969. Emphasizes art's role in liberation.

1223.   *Five Lectures: Psychoanalysis, Politics, and Utopia.* Trans. Jeremy J. Shapiro and Shierry M. Weber. Boston: Beacon, 1970.

1224.   *One-Dimensional Man.* Boston: Beacon, 1966. Best brief introduction to Marcuse's thought.

Marxism: Poststructuralist and Contemporary

Individual Authors

LOUIS ALTHUSSER (1918–)

Louis Althusser reinterpreted Marxism in terms that frequently drew on structuralism and post-Lacanian psychoanalysis. Adopting a concept from Michel Foucault (see the listings in chapter 11, "Poststructuralist Cultural Criticism"), he argued that there was an "epistemological break" in Marx from the "humanist" *1844 Manuscripts*, where Marx vividly expressed his hopes for a liberated utopian society. In contrast, *Capital* developed a rigorous and "scientific" analysis of social processes that differed from the distorted and incoherent "ideological" notions lived out in daily experience. Althusser saw rigorous "theory" not as a closed or totalized set of dogmatic propositions but as a "practice" that could locate possibilities of real change in history. He insisted on maintaining the distinction between a "base" of economic relations of production and a "superstructure" of cultural practices, but he described the relations between the two with extraordinary complexity. Such practices had a restricted autonomy, even though they were determined "in the last analysis" by economics.

The implications of Althusser's extremely difficult thought for literary

analysis were most cogently developed by Pierre Macherey. A work of literature, Macherey argued, is both the outcome of a productive process and for
its readers itself part of an ongoing social process of production. Authors
begin with ideas, images, and materials drawn from their historical contexts
and in particular from their class "ideologies," or lived experiences of a
historical world. But the process of shaping these ideological materials within
a literary form produces ruptures or breaks in them, which it is the critic's
business to locate and disclose. In doing so, the critic both shows how the
work's production manifests the limitations or incoherences of its ideology
and extends this liberating disruption into the reading process. In later work,
Althusser emphasized the role of "ideological state apparatuses" such as
education in a particular class's control over and conservative reproduction
of existing social structures. Althusser's ideas about Marx were criticized as
unorthodox by other communist theorists and he later acknowledged the
validity of many of these objections.

1225.   *Essays in Self-Criticism.* Trans. Graham Lock. London: New Left, 1976.
        Replies to critics of his version of Marxist theory.

1226.   *Essays on Ideology.* London: Verso, 1984.

1227.   *For Marx.* Trans. Ben Brewster. New York: Pantheon, 1969. Includes essays
        on theater and on Marxist philosophy.

1228.   *Lenin and Philosophy and Other Essays.* Trans. Ben Brewster. London:
        New Left, 1971. Contains the important essay "State Ideological Appara-
        tuses."

1229.   *Philosophy and the Spontaneous Philosophy of the Scientists.* London:
        Verso, 1989.

1230.   *Politics and History: Montesquieu, Rousseau, Hegel, Marx.* Trans. Ben
        Brewster. London: New Left, 1978.

1231.   Althusser, Louis, and Etienne Balibar. *Reading Capital.* Trans. Ben Brew-
        ster. London: New Left, 1970. His central work, important not only for its
        analysis of Marx's ideas but also because its particular way of reading Marx
        can be applied to other texts as well.

Althusser Bibliography

1232.   Nordquist, Joan, comp. *Louis Althusser: A Bibliography.* Santa Cruz: Refer-
        ence and Research Services, 1986.

Books on Althusser and Books Applying His Theory

1233.   Clarke, Simon, et al. *One-Dimensional Marxism: Althusser and the Politics
        of Culture.* London: Allison, 1980.

        Dowling, William C. *Jameson, Althusser, Marx: An Introduction to "The
        Political Unconscious."* See entry 1268.

1234.   Macherey, Pierre. *A Theory of Literary Production.* Trans. Geoffrey Wall.

London: Routledge, 1978. Application of Althusser's Marxism to literary analysis, with discussions of Verne, Defoe, Borges, and Balzac.

1235.   O'Neill, John. *For Marx against Althusser and Other Essays.* Washington: Center for Advanced Research in Phenomenology and UP of America, 1983.

1236.   Smith, Steven B. *Reading Althusser: An Essay on Structural Marxism.* Ithaca: Cornell UP, 1984.

TERRY EAGLETON (1943–)

A prolific and influential English Marxist, Terry Eagleton began his work under the influence of Raymond Williams (see below) and in opposition to the humanist criticism of F. R. Leavis. For him, literature and literary forms are historical and social products, neither transcending time to state eternal truths and values nor expressing the artist's individuality but playing a specific role in social production and reproduction. He absorbed Althusser's and Macherey's (see above) concepts of ideology and production and elaborated them in subtle and original ways. Eagleton went on to review the varieties of contemporary theory and to locate in each what he regarded as usable elements for fashioning a revised and broadened but still committed Marxism. Advocates of other theories have accused Eagleton of treating their approaches as merely subordinate to his and of criticizing their theories as determined by social and political conditions without recognizing that his own are similarly determined. Under current political conditions, Eagleton has defended traditional criticism and even the idea of an autonomous aesthetic sphere as attempts to create within the public realm a base for resisting various forms of oppression. In our era, he argues, feminist criticism comes closest to re-creating this sphere within which the critic can move beyond analysis of the text to social and political practice.

1237.   *Against the Grain: Essays, 1975–1985.* London: Verso, 1986.

1238.   *Criticism and Ideology: A Study in Marxist Literary Theory.* London: New Left, 1978.

1239.   *The Function of Criticism: From the Spectator to Post-structuralism.* London: Verso, 1984.

1240.   *Ideology: An Introduction.* New York: Verso, 1991.

1241.   *The Ideology of the Aesthetic.* Oxford: Blackwell, 1990. History and critique of the concept of the aesthetic since the eighteenth century.

Literary Theory: An Introduction. See entry 40.

1242.   *Marxism and Literary Criticism.* Berkeley: U of California P, 1976.

The Rape of Clarissa: Writing, Sexuality, and Class Struggles in Richardson. See entry 1581.

1243.   *The Significance of Theory.* Oxford: Blackwell, 1990. Broad overview of his work, with a new essay on Adorno.

Walter Benjamin; or, Towards a Revolutionary Criticism. See entry 1209.

Eagleton, Terry, Fredric Jameson, and Edward Said. *Nationalism, Colonialism, and Literature.* See entry 1487.

LUCIEN GOLDMANN (1913–70)

Lucien Goldmann's earlier work analyzed the complex interplay between society, religion, and literature in the era of Pascal and Racine. Many hoped he would be able to develop convincingly but more subtly than orthodox Marxists had done the theory that literature "reflected" its society. His belief that literature reflects not just society or even economic production but the structure of production seemed promising. But his final formulation asserted a close parallelism—"homology" was his term—between the structures of society and those of contemporary literary works. This theory seemed to revert to simple ideas of structure and reflection and to abandon the potential of structuralist thought to develop a Marxism more adequate to the complexities of both social and literary structure and their interrelations.

1244.   *Cultural Creation in Modern Society.* Trans. Bart Grahl. St. Louis: Telos, 1976.

1245.   *Essays on Method in the Sociology of Literature.* Trans. and ed. William Q. Boelhower. St. Louis: Telos, 1980.

1246.   *The Hidden God.* Trans. Philip Thody. London: Routledge, 1964. Seventeenth-century French literature, especially Pascal and Racine, in its cultural and religious context.

1247.   *The Human Sciences and Philosophy.* Trans. Hayden V. White and Robert Anchor. London: Cape, 1969.

1248.   *Lukács and Heidegger: Towards a New Philosophy.* Trans. William Q. Boelhower. London: Routledge, 1977. Finds parallels between the Marxist and existentialist thinkers.

1249.   *The Philosophy of the Enlightenment: The Burgess and the Enlightenment.* Trans. Henry Maas. Cambridge: MIT P, 1973.

1250.   *Racine.* Trans. Alastair Hamilton. Introd. Raymond Williams. Cambridge, Eng.: Rivers, 1972.

1251.   *Toward a Sociology of the Novel.* Trans. Alan Sheridan. London: Tavistock, 1975. Marxist approach to the relations between novels and the social situation they reflect and that produces them.

ANTONIO GRAMSCI (1891–1937)

One of the founders of the Italian Communist party, Antonio Gramsci was arrested by Mussolini's government in 1926. Although his short journalistic writings appeared in print, his most important works, the notebooks that he wrote in prison, were not published until after World War II. His most significant doctrine for literary study is the concept of "hegemony," which is intended to explain "how a particular social and economic system maintains its hold and retains its support. Gramsci saw, in a way that few other Marxists have done, that the rule of one class over another does not depend on economic or physical power alone but rather on persuading the ruled to accept the system of beliefs of the ruling class and to share its social, cultural, and moral values" (James Joll). Gramsci wrote extensively about the relation of culture, both elite and popular, to the state and society. The subtlety with which he developed his ideas, his rejection of the simplistic treatment of literary works as mere reflections of economic conditions or vehicles for political views, and his way of engaging culture in the struggle for a broad transformation of society and of human beings have made his work particularly appealing to contemporary theorists of literature and politics.

1252.   *Antonio Gramsci: Selections from Political Writings (1910–1920).* Ed. and trans. Quintin Hoare. New York: International, 1977.

1253.   *Antonio Gramsci: Selections from Political Writings (1921–1926).* Ed. and trans. Quintin Hoare. New York: International, 1978.

1254.   *A Gramsci Reader: Selected Writings, 1916–1935.* Ed. David Forgacs. London: Lawrence, 1988.

1255.   *Gramsci's Prison Letters/Lettere dal Carcere: A Selection.* Trans. Hamish Hamilton. London: Zwan, 1988.

1256.   *History, Philosophy, and Culture in the Young Gramsci.* Ed. Pedro Cavalcanti and Paul Piccone. St. Louis: Telos, 1975. Selections from his early writings.

1257.   *Letters from Prison.* Trans. and introd. Lynne Lawner. New York: Harper, 1973. A selection.

1258.   *The Modern Prince and Other Writings.* Trans. L. Marks. New York: International, 1959.

1259.   *Prison Notebooks: Selections.* Ed. and trans. Quintin Hoare and Geoffrey Nowell-Smith. New York: International, 1971. Notes on philosophy, history, party formation, intellectuals, and other subjects.

1260.   *Selections from Cultural Writings.* Trans. William Boelhower. Ed. David Forgacs and Geoffrey Nowell-Smith. Cambridge: Harvard UP, 1985. Writings selected from Gramsci's journalism and prison notebooks.

Gramsci Bibliography

1261.   Nordquist, Joan. *Antonio Gramsci.* Santa Cruz: Reference and Research Services, 1987.

Books on Gramsci

1262.   Dombrowski, Robert S. *Antonio Gramsci.* Boston: Hall, 1989.

1263.   Joll, James. *Antonio Gramsci.* New York: Penguin-Viking, 1978.

FREDRIC JAMESON (1934–   )

In his early work, Fredric Jameson wrote about the French philosopher, novelist, and dramatist Jean-Paul Sartre and expounded the varieties of Marxist criticism and of formalism and structuralism. In *The Political Unconscious,* he began to articulate his own view, which is captured in the book's opening words: "Always historicize." Jameson made room for other critical approaches, but always as steps toward a grasp of the historical dimension of literature and its service in a struggle toward a liberated utopia. Jameson rejected any closed or totalized system and argued that the virtue of Marxism is not to formulate dogmatic answers but to return us constantly to the "untranscendable horizon" of our historical existence. Literature is an ideological process that reflects and also conceals or represses its historical circumstances. In addition to locating the fissures and contradictions in a literary work's ideology, the critic locates the "utopian" element of hope the work conveys. More recently, Jameson was sharply critical of postmodernism, seeing it as the cultural expression and instrument of "late capitalism," which regulates and dominates life in both industrialized and Third World countries. Yet he later reversed his judgment, at least in some major respects. Jameson gathers a wide range of intellectual movements into his work, from Freud to poststructuralism, but always preserves a recognizable Marxist center.

1264.   *The Ideologies of Theory: Essays 1971–1986.* 2 vols. Minneapolis: U of Minnesota P, 1988. Vol. 1: *Situations of Theory;* vol. 2: *Syntax of History.*

   Late Marxism: Adorno; or, The Persistence of the Dialectic. See entry 1198.

1265.   *Marxism and Form: Twentieth-Century Dialectical Theories of Literature.* Princeton: Princeton UP, 1974.

1266.   *The Political Unconscious: Narrative as a Socially Symbolic Art.* Ithaca: Cornell UP, 1981. The most comprehensive presentation of Jameson's own ideas.

1267.   *The Prison-House of Language: A Critical Account of Structuralism and Russian Formalism.* Princeton: Princeton UP, 1972.

   Eagleton, Terry, Fredric Jameson, and Edward Said. *Nationalism, Colonialism, and Literature.* See entry 1487.

Books on Jameson

1268.   Dowling, William C. *Jameson, Althusser, Marx: An Introduction to The Political Unconscious.* Ithaca: Cornell UP, 1984.

1269.   Kellner, Douglas, ed. *Postmodernism/Jameson/Critique*. Washington: Maison-neuve, 1989. Fourteen essays with a reply by Jameson, comprehensive bibliography of his work, and bibliography on Marxist theory and postmodernism.

RAYMOND WILLIAMS (1921–88)

The driving force behind Raymond Williams's criticism is the commitment to work (by arguing and seeking consensus if at all possible but acceding to violence if unavoidable) toward the transformation of capitalism into a just and classless economic system. This commitment makes literary criticism inseparable from cultural criticism and also assigns theory and its more abstract flights a properly subordinate role. Without abandoning what seems indispensable in traditional Marxist theory, Williams does not hesitate to create his own vocabulary and to state directly the convictions about the meaning and purpose of human history that inform his discussion and evaluation of fiction, drama, and popular culture. In practice, he downplays the notion that the cultural superstructure is determined by the base of economic production. He emphasizes instead the interaction between consciousness or lived experience and social relations. Williams reads literary works for the insight they give into a society's "structures of feeling," defined as views about the world held so deeply and unconsciously that they are never questioned (the term seems close to the Marxist concept of ideology). Literary techniques or forms are conventions for expressing meaning. Because they emerge through social exchange, the critic can describe their social significance as well as that of a work's content or subject matter. Following Antonio Gramsci (see above), Williams recognizes that a particular group or class may exercise dominance, or hegemony, over a culture and may prefer some contents and forms and exclude others. Changes in these dominant "structures of feeling" or preferences and exclusions can be brought about only by changes in economic and social conditions, and literature reflects in an illuminating way the tensions and the suffering such changes inevitably produce. For Williams, it is important to see that the suffering caused by a class-based society is unnecessary and thus to return readers to a recognition of their power to improve their historic situation. The study of literature invites us to understand the structures of feeling reflected in it but also to judge those structures in relation to humankind's striving for a just social order. Working within Marxist values and ways of thought, but not constricted by orthodoxy or lost in scholastic abstractions, Williams is for many the exemplary cultural critic of our era. To his critics, however supple his cultural criticism, his political opinions remain rigidly Marxist and too sympathetic to an outmoded rhetoric of revolution.

1270.   *The Country and the City*. Oxford: Oxford UP, 1973.

1271.   *Culture and Society, 1780–1950*. New York: Columbia UP, 1958.

1272.   *Keywords: A Vocabulary of Culture and Society.* New York: Oxford UP, 1976.

1273.   *The Long Revolution.* London: Chatto, 1961.

1274.   *Marxism and Literature.* Oxford: Oxford UP, 1977.

1275.   *Politics and Letters: Interviews with New Left Review.* London: New Left, 1979.

1276.   *The Politics of Modernism: Against the New Conformists.* Ed. Tony Pinkney. London: Verso, 1989. Distinguishes modernism from the avant-garde and discusses the "ideology of modernism" and its impact on cultural theory.

1277.   *Problems in Materialism and Culture: Selected Essays* London: New Left, 1980.

1278.   *Resources of Hope: Culture, Democracy, Socialism.* Ed. Robin Gable. London: Verso, 1989.

1279.   *The Sociology of Culture.* New York: Schocken, 1982.

1280.   *Television: Technology and Cultural Form.* New York: Schocken, 1975.

1281.   *Writing in Society.* London: Verso, 1983. Essays developing his theory of cultural materialism and examining contemporary critical schools and literary works.

Books on Williams

1282.   Eagleton, Terry, ed. *Raymond Williams: A Critical Reader.* Boston: Northeastern UP, 1989. Essays on the whole range of Williams's work.

1283.   Gorak, Jan. *The Alien Mind of Raymond Williams.* Columbia: U of Missouri P, 1988.

1284.   O'Connor, Alan. *Raymond Williams: Writing, Culture and Politics.* Oxford: Blackwell, 1989.

11. Poststructuralist Cultural Criticism

Among the emerging varieties of Marxism, critics have considerable room for maneuver, but the relations between Marxism and the line of structuralist and poststructuralist thought have remained problematic. Orthodox Marxists accuse structuralist and poststructuralists of neglecting historical, political, and social realities and losing themselves in a pointless self-reflection on language, its devices and its ruses. Structuralists and poststructuralists have replied that orthodox Marxism is philosophically naive and ignores the actual complexities of both literary works and social processes. They find objectionable the totalizing and totalitarian practices of Communist regimes and Communist parties. While absorbing what they find convincing in Marxism, some cultural critics are even more committed to structuralist and poststructuralist thinking. They see it as more likely to reveal not only political or economic but every kind of restrictive structure and thus to disclose—if possible—strategies for maneuvering within and around the inevitability of structure without simply replacing one constraint with another. The leading inspiration for this approach has been the work of Michel Foucault. Books of cultural criticism developed broadly on a poststructuralist base are included in the general listing in chapter 9, "Cultural Criticism."

Individual Authors

MICHEL FOUCAULT (1926–84)

In *The Order of Things*, Michel Foucault presented the history of European culture since the Renaissance as a series of discontinuous "epistemes," meaning integrated structures of premises, methods, and doctrines, one of which characterized and dominated each successive period. This ambitiously general and somewhat rigid scheme seemed to bring the structuralist style of thought to the largest questions of cultural history. The book was at the same time influential and frequently criticized as tendentious.

Foucault's later work moved in a quite different direction, for which *The Archaeology of Knowledge* provided a methodological reflection. The key idea is that of "discourses" or "discursive practices." These are languages developed to organize particular fields—psychiatry, penology, medicine, law, sexuality—that are not only conceptual entities but fields of social practice: the treatment of the insane in mental hospitals, the confinement of criminals in prisons, the care of the ill in clinics and hospitals, the adjudication of criminal responsibility in courts of law, the presentation of human sexuality in a variety of specialized and daily practices. Foucault's most influential books analyzed these discursive practices, their presuppositions, linguistic devices, and—as he saw it—inevitable incoherences and uses for purposes of power or domination.

For many contemporary theorists, Foucault has thus managed to combine the linguistic and analytic sophistication of structuralism and poststructuralism with empirical historical and cultural analysis and to do so in a way that maintains a nondoctrinaire commitment to liberating human possibilities. Foucault in fact spoke out strongly for the rights of women and homosexuals and in favor of prison reform, while criticizing repressive regimes, whether right or left, fascist or communist. Some theorists, including Jacques Derrida, have, however, criticized Foucault for evading the full rigor of deconstruction; others—such as Edward Said, Timothy J. Reiss, and Frank Lentricchia—have defended Foucault's openness to history or, like Wesley Morris and David Carroll, have attempted to find alternative ways to integrate historical and deconstructive work.

1285. *The Archaeology of Knowledge: Including the Discourse on Language.* Trans. A. M. Sheridan Smith. New York: Pantheon, 1972.

1286. *The Birth of the Clinic: An Archaeology of Medical Perception.* Trans. A. M. Sheridan Smith. New York: Pantheon, 1973.

1287. *Death and the Labyrinth: The World of Raymond Roussel.* Trans. Charles Rus. Garden City: Doubleday, 1986. Foucault's one literary critical work, on an intriguing and strange French novelist.

1288. *Discipline and Punish: The Birth of the Prison.* Trans. Alan Sheridan. New York: Pantheon, 1977.

1289. *Foucault/Blanchot.* Trans. Brian Massumi and Jeffrey Mehlman. New York: Zone, 1987. An essay by Foucault on Blanchot and one by Blanchot on Foucault.

1290. *The Foucault Reader.* Ed. Paul Rabinow. New York: Pantheon, 1984. Excellent selection from the full range of his writings, with previously unpublished materials.

1291. *The History of Sexuality.* Trans. Robert Hurley. 3 vols. New York: Pantheon, 1978–87. Vol. 1: *Introduction* (1978); vol. 2: *The Uses of Pleasure* (1985); vol. 3: *The Care of the Self* (1987).

1292. *Language, Counter-Memory, Practice: Selected Essays and Interviews.* Trans. Donald Bouchard and Sherry Simon. Ed. and introd. Donald F. Bouchard. Ithaca: Cornell UP, 1977.

1293. *Madness and Civilization: A History of Insanity in the Age of Reason.* Trans. Richard Howard. New York: Pantheon, 1965.

1294. *Mental Illness and Psychology.* Trans. Alan Sheridan. New York: Colophon-Harper, 1976.

1295. *The Order of Things: An Archaeology of the Human Sciences.* New York: Pantheon, 1971.

1296. *Politics, Philosophy, Culture: Interviews and Other Writings, 1977–1984.* Trans. Alan Sheridan et al. Ed. Lawrence D. Kritzman. New York: Routledge, 1988.

1297. *Power/Knowledge: Selected Interviews and Other Writings, 1972–1977.* Trans. Colin Gordon et al. Ed. Colin Gordon. New York: Pantheon, 1981.

1298. *Power, Truth, Strategy.* Ed. Meaghan Morris and Paul Patton. Sydney, Austral.: Feral, 1979.

1299. *Technologies of the Self: A Seminar with Michel Foucault.* Ed. Luther H. Martin, Huck Gutman, and Patrick H. Hutton. Amherst: U of Massachusetts P, 1988.

1300. *This Is Not a Pipe: With Illustrations and Letters by René Magritte.* Trans. James Harkness. Berkeley: U of California P, 1982. On the work of the famous surrealist artist.

Foucault Bibliographies

1301. Clark, Michael P. *Michel Foucault, An Annotated Bibliography: Tool Kit for a New Age.* New York: Garland, 1983.

1302. Nordquist, Joan. *Michel Foucault.* Santa Cruz: Reference and Research Services, 1985.

Books on Foucault

1303. Arac, Jonathan, ed. *After Foucault: Humanistic Knowledge, Postmodern Challenges.* New Brunswick: Rutgers UP, 1988.

1304. Bernauer, James, and David Rasmusson, eds. *The Final Foucault.* Cambridge: MIT P, 1988. Includes a report of Foucault's last lectures on the concept of truth telling as a moral virtue, a Lacanian interpretation of his *History of Sexuality*, and others essays.

1305.   Carroll, David. *Paraesthetics: Foucault, Lyotard, Derrida.* New York: Methuen, 1987.

1306.   Cousins, Mark, and Athar Hussain. *Michel Foucault.* London: Macmillan, 1984. Lucid introduction, especially good on Foucault's treatment of and relation to Descartes and seventeenth-century Cartesianism.

1307.   Deleuze, Gilles. *Foucault.* Trans. Seán Hand. Minneapolis: U of Minnesota P, 1988. By an eminent contemporary French philosopher.

1308.   Diamond, Irene, and Lee Quinby, eds. *Feminism and Foucault: Reflections on Resistance.* Boston: Northeastern UP, 1988. Thirteen essays.

1309.   Dreyfus, Hubert L., and Paul Rabinow. *Michel Foucault: Beyond Structuralism and Hermeneutics.* 2nd ed. Chicago: U of Chicago P, 1983.

1310.   Eribon, Didier. *Michel Foucault.* Trans. Betsy Wing. Cambridge: Harvard UP, 1991.

1311.   Hoy, David Couzens, ed. *Foucault: A Critical Reader.* Oxford: Blackwell, 1986.

1312.   Lecourt, Dominique. *Marxism and Epistemology: Bachelard, Canguilhem, and Foucault.* Trans. Ben Brewster. London: New Left, 1975.

1313.   Lentricchia, Frank. *Ariel and the Police: Michel Foucault, William James, Wallace Stevens.* Madison: U of Wisconsin P, 1988. On the relations between imagination, power, and the personal subject.

Megill, Allan. *Prophets of Extremity: Nietzsche, Heidegger, Foucault, Derrida.* See entry 725.

1314.   Merquior, J. G. *Foucault.* London: Fontana, 1986.

1315.   Poster, Mark. *Foucault, Marxism and History: Mode of Production versus Mode of Information.* Cambridge: Polity, 1984.

1316.   Racevskis, Karlis. *Michel Foucault and the Subversion of Intellect.* Ithaca: Cornell UP, 1983.

1317.   Rajchman, John. *Michel Foucault: The Freedom of Philosophy.* New York: Columbia UP, 1985. Focuses on Foucault's later work.

1318.   Sheridan, Alan. *Michel Foucault: The Will to Truth.* London: Tavistock, 1980. Good general introduction.

1319.   Shumway, David. *Michel Foucault.* Boston: Hall, 1989.

1320.   Smart, Barry. *Foucault, Marxism, and Critique.* London: Routledge, 1983.

1321.   ———. *Michel Foucault.* Chichester, Eng.: Horwood, 1985. Useful on politics in the later Foucault.

EDWARD SAID (1935–   )

Born in Jerusalem before the creation of Israel, Edward Said was educated at Princeton and Harvard. His first book on Joseph Conrad fell well within the formalist tradition, but he rapidly became interested in new European currents in criticism, and the essays in *Beginnings* were an important mediator of those ideas to American academics. His further intellectual development as well as his personal involvement in the movement for a Palestinian homeland drew him to cultural issues and to a strong appreciation of the work of Michel Foucault. He has written on a variety of contemporary Middle Eastern issues, such as press coverage and its biases and inadequacies, and more generally in *Orientalism* on the way travel and other literature expressed and shaped negative European attitudes toward and misperceptions of the Arab world. His work continues to reflect his broad involvement in current critical movements, but he has argued steadily for more attention to cultural and political dimensions.

1322.   *Beginnings: Intention and Method.* New York: Basic, 1975. Poststructuralist critical reflections.

1323.   *Orientalism.* New York: Pantheon, 1978. Draws on critical approaches and Foucault to analyze the image of the Near East in Romantic and modern literature.

1324.   *The World, the Text, and the Critic.* Cambridge: Harvard UP, 1983.

Eagleton, Terry, Fredric Jameson, and Edward Said. *Nationalism, Colonialism, and Literature.* See entry 1487.

The New Historicism

A coinage introduced somewhat casually by Stephen Greenblatt in *Renaissance Self-Fashioning*, the *new historicism* evoked an immediate and strong response and has rapidly achieved a prominent, if not dominant, position in literary study. The approach has not yet received full theoretical formulation and examination, but it might be characterized as the kind of literary history that would be written in full awareness of recent developments in the theory and writing of history more generally. These have stressed social history and regard culture, whether elite or popular, as itself a practice grounded in material social life and in the ways of thought that emerge within that context (what one school of French historians calls the "mentality" of a particular group at a given time and place). Consequently, the new historicism sees literary works as both shaped by and influencing gender, class, and economic and power relations. It absorbs contemporary developments in Marxist theory and historiography but incorporates even more the work of Foucault and historians like Hayden White, Dominick LaCapra, and Carlo Ginzburg. Greenblatt also draws on Clifford Geertz's approach to anthropological description, and many new historicists have found inspiration in the writings of Mikhail Bakhtin. While the movement has fully assimilated formalist, structuralist, and deconstructive ways of analyzing texts, it aims to go beyond them by bringing texts into relation with historical contexts that are themselves analyzed and interpreted using these same contemporary theoretical approaches. Since Greenblatt is a scholar of the Renaissance, much new-historicist work has been done in that area, but the method is being applied to a steadily widening range of literature. Greenblatt was instrumental in founding the journal *Representations*, which is something of an organ for the movement.

Individual Author

STEPHEN GREENBLATT (1943–)

1325. *Learning to Curse: Essays in Early Modern Culture.* New York: Routledge, 1991.

1326. *Renaissance Self-Fashioning: From More to Shakespeare.* Chicago: U of Chicago P, 1980.

1327. *Representing the English Renaissance.* Berkeley: U of California P, 1988.

1328. *Shakespearean Negotiations: The Circulation of Social Energy in Renaissance England.* Berkeley: U of California P, 1988.

1329. Greenblatt, Stephen, ed. *Allegory and Representation.* Selected Papers from the English Institute, 1979–80, ns 5. Baltimore: Johns Hopkins UP, 1981.

1330. ———, ed. *The Power of Forms in the English Renaissance.* Norman: Pilgrim, 1982.

Books and Collections

1331. Crewe, Jonathan. *Hidden Designs: The Critical Profession and Renaissance Literature.* London: Methuen, 1987. New historicist and poststructuralist, but defends general criticism against professional specialization.

1332. Dollimore, Jonathan. *Radical Tragedy: Religion, Ideology and Power in the Drama of Shakespeare and His Contemporaries.* Brighton, Eng.: Harvester, 1984. Discusses broad theoretical questions as well as specific works.

1333. Dubrow, Heather, and Richard Strier, eds. *The Historical Renaissance: New Essays on Tudor and Stuart Literature and Culture.* Chicago: U of Chicago P, 1988. On literature, culture, and politics.

1334. Felperin, Howard. *The Uses of the Canon: Elizabethan Literature and Contemporary Theory.* New York: Oxford UP, 1990. A critical examination of the new-historicist approach.

1335. Ferguson, Margaret W., Maureen Quilligan, and Nancy Vickers, eds. *Rewriting the Renaissance: The Discourses of Sexual Difference in Early Modern Europe.* Chicago: U of Chicago P, 1986.

1336. Harvey, Elizabeth D., and Katharine Eisaman Maus, eds. *Soliciting Interpretation: Literary Theory and Seventeenth-Century English Poetry.* Chicago: U of Chicago P, 1990.

1337. Horowitz, Maryanne Cline, Anne J. Cruz, and Wendy A. Furman, eds. *Renaissance Rereadings: Intertext and Context.* Urbana: U of Illinois P, 1988.

1338. LaCapra, Dominick. *History and Criticism.* Ithaca: Cornell UP, 1985. Essays on rhetoric in history writing, the study of mass and popular culture, the novel, psychoanalysis, and other topics.

1339. ———. *Rethinking Intellectual History: Texts, Contexts, Language.* Ithaca: Cornell UP, 1983. Essays on recent work in intellectual history and its theory.

1340. ———. *Soundings in Critical Theory.* Ithaca: Cornell UP, 1989. Wide-ranging explorations on relations between history and critical theory, including Marxism, psychoanalysis, deconstruction, and new historicism.

1341. Michaels, Walter Benn. *The Gold Standard and the Logic of Naturalism: American Literature at the Turn of the Century.* Berkeley: U of California P, 1987.

1342. Nussbaum, Felicity, and Laura Brown, eds. *The New Eighteenth Century: Theory, Politics, English Literature.* London: Methuen, 1987.

1343. Parker, Patricia, and David Quint, eds. *Literary Theory/Renaissance Texts.* Baltimore: Johns Hopkins UP, 1986. Fifteen essays using Marxist, feminist, psychoanalytic, and new-historicist approaches.

1344. Patterson, Annabel. *Censorship and Interpretation: The Conditions of Writing and Reading in Early Modern England.* Madison: U of Wisconsin P, 1984.

1345. Pearce, Roy Harvey. *Gesta Humanorum: Studies in the Historicist Mode.* Columbia: U of Missouri P, 1987. Essays from the past twenty years by an early advocate of a historicist approach against formalism; discusses his relation to and difference from the new historicism.

1346. Siskin, Clifford H. *The Historicity of Romantic Discourse.* New York: Oxford UP, 1988. Along with Jerome J. McGann, a leading proponent of a new-historicist approach to Romantic literature.

1347. Tennenhouse, Leonard. *Power on Display: The Politics of Shakespeare's Genres.* London: Methuen, 1986.

1348. Thomas, Brook. *The New Historicism and Other Old-Fashioned Topics.* Princeton: Princeton UP, 1991. Locates new historicism within a tradition of pragmatic historiography but criticizes its reliance on a mimetic model for historical analysis.

1349. Veeser, H. Aram, ed. *The New Historicism.* London: Routledge, 1989. Twenty essays by Greenblatt, Fish, White, Spivak, and others.

1350. White, Hayden. *The Content of the Form: Narrative Discourse and Historical Representation.* Baltimore: Johns Hopkins UP, 1987.

1351.   ———. *Metahistory: The Historical Imagination in Nineteenth-Century Europe.* Baltimore: Johns Hopkins UP, 1974. Argues that four "master tropes" impose coherence on historical writing.

1352.   ———. *Tropics of Discourse: Essays in Cultural Criticism.* Baltimore: Johns Hopkins UP, 1985. On Vico, Croce, Derrida, Foucault and history, the novel, interpretation, and historicism.

12. Literacy, Orality, and Printing

The concept of *orality* emerged from the debate among classicists over whether the *Iliad* and *Odyssey* were composed by a single author or were collective and anonymous folk compositions. In the 1920s Milman Parry discovered in the Balkans a group of living poets who recited their long epics entirely from memory. They accomplished this feat not by simply memorizing poems but by memorizing formulaic scenes and verbal phrases and spontaneously composing poems out of these and similar components. Analysis of repetitive formulas in Homer supported the hypothesis that he worked the same way. After Parry's death, his student Albert Lord more fully presented his ideas. It remained for Eric Havelock to draw the broadest consequences for Greek culture. In early times, he argued, the only means of preserving the culture's stock of knowledge was to memorize it and transmit it through oral presentations to the next generation. To accomplish the feats of memory that oral culture required, individuals had to become completely absorbed in the collective material of the culture. In Plato, Havelock went on, there occurs a transition to a literate culture. Instead of carrying culture internally in memory, a society could now preserve cultural knowledge in the fixed, external form of a written record. Using written records to transmit culture thus makes possible the separation of the individual person from the collective culture, that is, of the knower from the known. Consequently, along with writing and reading there emerges the critical distance required for rational reflection and for the creation of a self-conscious identity. Similar ideas were developed by Harold Innis and Marshall McLuhan. These thinkers stressed the influence the media had on the cultural contents the media themselves presented and transmitted and especially the importance of shifts in medium from orality to a manuscript-based culture, then to a culture based on books and printing, and more recently to electronic forms—film, radio, television, and computers. Recent work has explored in detail these changes in the media of culture and their consequences.

The best general survey of the field is Walter Ong's *Orality and Literacy* (see below).

General Studies

1353.   Brandt, Deborah. *Literacy as Involvement: The Acts of Writers, Readers, and Texts.* Carbondale: Southern Illinois UP, 1989.

1354.   Burns, Alfred. *The Power of the Written Word: The Role of Literacy in the History of Western Civilization.* New York: Lang, 1989.

1355.   Chartier, Roger, ed. *The Culture of Print: Power and the Uses of Print in Early Modern Europe.* Trans. Lydia G. Cochrane. Princeton: Princeton UP, 1989.

1356.   Eisenstein, Elizabeth. *The Printing Press as an Agent of Change.* 2 vols. Cambridge: Cambridge UP, 1979. The leading study of the subject.

1357.   Finnegan, Ruth. *Literacy and Orality: Studies in the Technology of Communication.* Oxford: Blackwell, 1988. Collects papers written between 1969 and 1984; bibliography.

1358.   Foley, John Miles, ed. *Oral Tradition in Literature: Interpretation in Context.* Columbia: U of Missouri P, 1986.

1359.   ———. *The Theory of Oral Composition: History and Methodology.* Bloomington: Indiana UP, 1988.

1360.   Goody, Jack R. *The Domestication of the Savage Mind.* Cambridge: Cambridge UP, 1977. Studies writing's effects on thought and institutions.

1361.   ———. *The Interface between the Written and the Oral.* Cambridge: Cambridge UP, 1987.

1362.   ———, ed. *Literacy in Traditional Societies.* Cambridge: Cambridge UP, 1968. Includes an important broad survey, "The Consequences of Literacy," by Goody and Ian Watt.

1363.   ———. *The Logic of Writing and the Organization of Society.* Cambridge: Cambridge UP, 1986.

1364.   Havelock, Eric A. *The Literate Revolution in Greece and Its Cultural Consequences.* Princeton: Princeton UP, 1982. Collection of important essays since his path-breaking *Preface to Plato.*

1365.   ———. *The Muse Learns to Write: Reflections on Orality and Literacy from Antiquity to the Present.* New Haven: Yale UP, 1986.

1366.   ———. *Origins of Western Literacy*. Toronto: Ontario Inst. for Studies in Education, 1976.

1367.   ———. *Preface to Plato*. Cambridge: Belknap–Harvard UP, 1963. Epoch-making study of the influence of literacy on culture.

1368.   Heim, Michael. *Electric Language: A Philosophical Study of Word Processing*. New Haven: Yale UP, 1987. How computers affect written language.

1369.   Kernan, Alvin. *Printing Technology, Letters, and Samuel Johnson*. Princeton: Princeton UP, 1987. Synthesizes work on orality, literacy, and print and uses it to interpret Johnson and the shift to modern conditions of literary production and consumption.

1370.   Kittler, Friedrich A. *Discourse Networks, 1800/1900*. Trans. Michael Metteer with Chris Cullens. Stanford: Stanford UP, 1990. On the position of the self in relation to the materials and means of communication.

1371.   Landow, George P. *Hypertext: The Convergence of Contemporary Critical Theory and Technology*. Baltimore: John Hopkins UP, 1991.

1372.   Landow, George P., and Paul Delany, eds. *Hypermedia and Literary Studies*. Cambridge: MIT P, 1991. Hypermedia are a new computer-based way of presenting masses of data for easy manipulation.

1373.   Langer, Judith, ed. *Language, Literacy, and Culture: Issues of Society and Schooling*. Norwood: Ablex, 1987. Includes a section on literature and literacy.

1374.   Levenston, E. A. *The Stuff of Literature: Physical Aspects of Texts and Their Relation of Literary Meaning*. Albany: State U of New York P, 1992. Discusses relation of a work's literary meaning to physical aspects like spelling, punctuation, typography, and layout.

1375.   Lord, Albert B. *The Singer of Tales*. Cambridge: Harvard UP, 1960. Widely influential study of Homer as a preliterate oral poet.

1376.   McLuhan, Marshall. *Gutenberg Galaxy: The Making of Typographic Man*. Toronto: U of Toronto P, 1962.

1377.   ———. *Understanding Media: The Extensions of Man*. New York: McGraw, 1964.

1378.   McLuhan (book on). Marchand, Phillip. *Marshall McLuhan*. London: Ticknor, 1989.

         Ronell, Avital. *The Telephone Book: Technology–Schizophrenia–Electric Speech*. See entry 600.

1379.   Rosenberg, Bruce A. *Folklore and Literature: Rival Siblings*. Knoxville: U of Tennessee P, 1991. Discusses how theories and methods used to study oral folklore have influenced literary study.

1380.   Shevelow, Kathryn. *Women and Print Culture: Constructing Femininity in the Early Periodical*. London: Routledge, 1989.

1381.   Stock, Brian. *Listening for the Text: On the Uses of the Past*. Baltimore:

Johns Hopkins UP, 1990. Discusses orality and literacy, medieval theories of language, textual communities, and how we textualize the past.

1382.   Sussman, Henry S. *High Resolution: Critical Theory and the Problem of Literacy*. New York: Oxford UP, 1989. Issues of literacy in the wake of poststructuralist theory.

1383.   Swearingen, C. Jan. *Rhetoric and Irony: Western Literacy and Western Lies*. New York: Oxford UP, 1991. Examines shift from orality to literacy in antiquity and its implication for rhetoric, literacy, and the conception of literature down to the present.

1384.   Winterowd, W. Ross. *The Culture and Politics of Literacy*. New York: Oxford UP, 1989.

1385.   Zumthor, Paul. *Oral Poetry: An Introduction*. Trans. Kathy Murphy-Judy. Minneapolis: U of Minnesota P, 1990.

Individual Author

WALTER J. ONG (1912–   )

Walter Ong's earliest work was on the logic and rhetoric of Ramus, a Renaissance philosopher. To Ramus's influence Ong attributed the "decay of dialogue," a shift from oral and debating-style bases for thought to visual and diagrammatic bases, which are better suited to the print medium. Ong has gone on to develop a broad historical interpretation of this twin shift from the oral to the literate and from literate to print- and book-based culture and to describe the effect of these shifts in cultural media on literature and on cultural life generally.

1386.   *The Barbarian Within and Other Fugitive Essays and Studies*. New York: Macmillan, 1962.

1387.   *Interfaces of the Word: Studies in the Evolution of Consciousness and Culture*. Ithaca: Cornell UP, 1977.

1388.   *In the Human Grain*. New York: Macmillan, 1967.

1389.   *Orality and Literacy: The Technologizing of the World*. London: Methuen, 1982. Excellent introductory survey.

1390.   *The Presence of the Word: Some Prolegomena for Cultural and Religious History*. New Haven: Yale UP, 1967.

1391.   *Rhetoric, Romance, and Technology: Studies in the Interaction of Expression and Culture*. Ithaca: Cornell UP, 1971.

13. Myth, Anthropology, and Critical Theory

The bulk of studies of myth either collect and report myths from one culture or many cultures or trace a myth through its various presentations in literature. The most renowned modern compiler is Joseph Campbell, whose many books and series on public television have roused fresh interest in the continuing relevance of myths and mythic thinking to individual and social lives. Such compilations are not listed here, though bibliographies in the works listed provide a guide to them.

A number of thinkers have elaborated theories of myth and related it to literature and culture in a more general and philosophical way. German philosophers from the Romantic era to the present have been particularly interested in myth. Important figures include Friedrich Wilhelm Joseph von Schelling (1775–1854), Friedrich Nietzsche (1844–1900), and Ernst Cassirer (1874–1945). The anthology edited by Burton Feldman and Robert D. Richardson (listed below) surveys the historical tradition.

Carl Jung (see chapter 8, "Psychological and Psychoanalytic Critical Theory") used myths that recurred within and among cultures as evidence of the existence of archetypes—patterns of symbols found in the thinking of every individual. His theories, together with the work of the Cambridge school, were applied to literature by Northrop Frye (see below).

At mid-century, the radically different structuralist anthropology of Claude Lévi-Strauss (see listing below) introduced a new way of thinking. According to Lévi-Strauss, myth is a narrative that arranges sets of symbols in binary pairs, thus bringing them into analogous relations. The cultural function of myths, he argues, is to displace attention from irresolvable cultural or intellectual contradictions through a structure of parallel oppositions so as to give the myth's audience a feeling that the contradiction has been resolved. Lévi-Strauss applied his theories in a multivolume analysis of the myths of South American Indians. His ideas were an important part of the structuralist movement, but interest in them among literary theorists has declined recently.

Mircea Eliade (see listing below), a novelist and a scholar of the comparative history of religions, has surveyed myth and symbols in a wide range of cultures and argues that myth represents a repudiation of historical time and contingency. More recently, the German philosopher and historian of ideas Hans Blumenberg (see listing below) has proposed that myth deploys various patterns and strategies to help human beings cope with their fear of threats and dangers from environing reality.

Books and Collections

1392.   Blumenberg, Hans. *Work on Myth.* Trans. Robert Wallace. Cambridge: MIT P, 1985. The most important recent book. Argues that myth originates in efforts to cope with felt dangers in the environment; outlines myth's devices and, in contrast to earlier scholars' interest in its beginnings, emphasizes the transmission and adaptation of myth. Illustrates the theory by tracing the Prometheus myth from the Greeks to the present, with extensive discussion of Goethe.

1393.   Cook, Albert. *Myth and Language.* Bloomington: Indiana UP, 1980.

1394.   Cunningham, Adrian, ed. *The Theory of Myth: Six Studies.* London: Sheed, 1973. Essays on Mircea Eliade, Lévi-Strauss, Mary Douglas, classical mythology, and myth and story.

1395.   Doty, William G. *Mythography: The Study of Myths and Rituals.* University: U of Alabama P, 1986. Comprehensive survey with chapters on psychological, archetypal, and structuralist approaches, as well as on recent approaches that analyze ritual and culture. Extensive bibliography.

1396.   Dundes, Alan, ed. *Sacred Narratives: Readings in the Theory of Myth.* Berkeley: U of California P, 1984. Comprehensive compilation.

1397.   Eliade, Mircea. *Myth and Reality.* Trans. Willard R. Trask. New York: Harper, 1963. Brief introduction to his basic theory.

1398.   ———. *Myths, Rites, Symbols: A Mircea Eliade Reader.* Ed. Wendell C. Beane and William G. Doty. 2 vols. New York: Harper, 1976. Samples the entire range of Eliade's work.

1399.   ———. *Symbolism, the Sacred, and the Arts.* Ed. Diane Apostolos-Cappadona. New York: Crossroad, 1985. Selected essays.

1400.   Falck, Colin. *Myth, Truth and Literature: Towards a True Post-modernism.*

Cambridge: Cambridge UP, 1989. Argues that a mythic substratum, distinct from dogma, underlies all religion and has reappeared in modern culture.

1401.   Feldman, Burton, and Robert D. Richardson, eds. *The Rise of Modern Mythology, 1680–1860.* Bloomington: Indiana UP, 1972. Excellent survey of the historical background of myth theory.

1402.   Gould, Eric. *Mythical Intentions in Modern Literature.* Princeton: Princeton UP, 1981. Takes a structuralist and non-Jungian approach.

1403.   Leach, Edmund. *Genesis as Myth, and Other Essays.* London: Cape, 1969. Applies Lévi-Strauss's structural theory of myth.

1404.   Lévi-Strauss, Claude. *Myth and Meaning.* New York: Schocken, 1978. Radio talks briefly introducing his ideas.

1405.   ———. *The Savage Mind.* Chicago: U of Chicago P, 1966. Comprehensive introduction to his ideas.

1406.   ———. *Structural Anthropology.* Vol. 1 trans. Claire Jacobson and Brooke Grundfest Schoepf; vol. 2 trans. Monique Layton. New York: Basic, 1963–76. Comprehensive collection of essays on myth, ritual, kinship, and social organization. Volume 1 particularly influenced structuralist critical theory.

1407.   Manganaro, Marc. *Myth, Rhetoric, and the Voice of Authority: A Critique of Frazer, Eliot, Frye, and Campbell.* New Haven: Yale UP, 1992.

1408.   Maranda, Pierre, ed. *Mythology: Selected Readings.* Harmondsworth, Eng.: Penguin, 1972. Good collection of essays from Cassirer and Propp to Lévi-Strauss.

1409.   Murray, Henry, ed. *Myth and Mythmaking.* New York: Braziller, 1960.

1410.   Ohmann, Richard M., ed. *The Making of Myth.* New York: Putnam, 1962. Essays by Murray, Frye, Eliade, and others; with bibliography.

1411.   Righter, William. *Myth and Literature.* London: Routledge, 1975. Good brief introduction.

1412.   Ruthven, K. K. *Myth.* London: Methuen, 1976. Excellent brief survey of theories of myth in relation to literary study; full bibliography.

1413.   Sebeok, Thomas, ed. *Myth: A Symposium.* Bloomington: Indiana UP, 1958.

1414.   Slote, Bernice, ed. *Myth and Symbol: Critical Approaches and Applications.* Lincoln: U of Nebraska P, 1963. Four theoretical essays by Frye and others and eleven essays on applications.

1415.   Soyinka, Wole. *Myth, Literature and the African World.* Cambridge: Cambridge UP, 1976. Discusses the mythic element in African literature and its interaction with ideology and the social vision in contemporary African fiction.

1416.   Spivey, Ted R. *Beyond Modernism: Toward a New Myth Criticism.* Lanham: UP of America, 1988. Tries to relate myth criticism to poststructuralism.

1417.   Strelka, Joseph, ed. *Literary Criticism and Myth*. Yearbook of Comparative Criticism 9. University Park: Pennsylvania State UP, 1980.

1418.   Strenski, Ivan. *Four Theories of Myth in Twentieth-Century History: Cassirer, Eliade, Lévi-Strauss, and Malinowski*. Iowa City: U of Iowa P, 1987.

1419.   Vickery, John B., ed. *Myth and Literature: Contemporary Theory and Practice*. Lincoln: U of Nebraska P, 1966. Thirty-four contemporary essays arranged topically.

1420.   ———. *Myths and Texts: Strategies of Incorporation and Displacement*. Baton Rouge: Louisiana State UP, 1983.

Myth: Individual Author

NORTHROP FRYE (1912–91)

The sources of Northrop Frye's criticism, which began with a study of William Blake, are to be found in Romanticism. His interest is in the human imagination and its power to create patterns or shapes that guide our individual and social lives and our interaction with the world around us. These patterns are "myths" or "archetypes," and the totality of literature can be seen as embodying these archetypes, sometimes explicitly, sometimes in "displaced" or disguised form. Ultimately, there are four large patterns: romance, tragedy, comedy, and irony. The *Anatomy of Criticism* describes these in detail, since Frye insists that the critic's job is to provide a precise and comprehensive classification of the forms of literature. The critic thereby educates and liberates our imaginations and directs our thinking away from intolerance toward patterns or visions outside the restricted range of our own culture. It follows that the evaluation of literature is no part of the academic critic's work. As a cultural anthropologist describing the varieties of imaginative structure, the critic will be aware that society itself is organized around what Frye calls "myths of concern," but literary study aims finally at a broader, liberal (and therefore liberated) humane community.

Frye's theory drew heavily on the work of the *Cambridge school* of anthropology, a group of British classicists active around the time of World War I. They used anthropological reports to draw parallels and analogies with which to piece out the slender historical record of classical Greece. Their main idea was that Greek tragedy and comedy originated in agricultural and fertility myths and rites. James Frazer's *Golden Bough*, Jane Harrison's *Themis: A Study of the Social Origins of Greek Religion* (1912), and, more recently, Theodore Gaster's *Thespis: Ritual, Myth, and Drama in the Ancient Near East* (1950) are the best-known of their works, and their ideas widely influenced literary study. But their theories have been criticized tellingly and in detail by Gerald Else, Joseph Fontenrose, and Arthur W. Pickard-

Cambridge. The extent to which these criticisms undermine Frye's elaboration of Cambridge school ideas is debatable.

Frye's extensive writings draw a very wide range of authors and works into his powerfully encompassing schemes. He has relatively few close adherents in contemporary theory, but he remains a constant reference point for other theorists.

1421. *Anatomy of Criticism: Four Essays*. Princeton: Princeton UP, 1957. His magnum opus, a comprehensive system embracing the varieties of literature.

1422. *The Critical Path: An Essay on the Social Context of Literary Criticism*. Bloomington: Indiana UP, 1971.

1423. *The Double Vision: Language and Meaning in Religion*. Toronto: U of Toronto P, 1991.

1424. *The Educated Imagination*. Bloomington: Indiana UP, 1964.

1425. *Fables of Identity: Studies in Poetic Mythology*. New York: Harcourt, 1963.

1426. *The Great Code: The Bible and Literature*. New York: Harcourt, 1981.

1427. *Myth and Metaphor: Selected Essays, 1974–1988*. Ed. Robert D. Denham. Charlottesville: UP of Virginia, 1990.

1428. *Northrop Frye on Culture and Literature: A Collection of Review Essays*. Ed. Robert D. Denham. Chicago: U of Chicago P, 1978.

1429. *On Education*. Ann Arbor: U of Michigan P, 1988.

1430. *Reading the World: Selected Writings, 1935–1976*. Ed. Robert D. Denham. New York: Lang, 1990.

1431. *The Secular Scripture: A Study of the Structure of Romance*. Cambridge: Harvard UP, 1976.

1432. *Spiritus Mundi: Essays on Literature, Myth, and Society*. Bloomington: Indiana UP, 1976.

1433. *The Stubborn Structure: Essays on Criticism and Society*. Ithaca: Cornell UP, 1970.

1434. *The Well-Tempered Critic*. Bloomington: Indiana UP, 1963.

1435. *Words with Power: Being a Second Study of* The Bible and Literature. San Diego: Harcourt, 1990.

1436. *A World in a Grain of Sand: Twenty-Two Interviews with Northrop Frye*. Ed. Robert D. Denham. New York: Lang, 1991.

Frye Bibliography

1437. Denham, Robert D. *Northrop Frye: An Annotated Bibliography of Primary and Secondary Sources*. Toronto: U of Toronto P, 1987.

Books on Frye

1438.   Balfour, Ian. *Northrop Frye*. Boston: Twayne, 1988.

1439.   Cook, David. *Northrop Frye: A Vision of the New World*. New York: St. Martin's, 1985. Emphasizes the social and political implications of Frye's thought.

1440.   Cook, Eleanor, Chaviva Hosek, Jay Macpherson, Patricia Parker, and Julian Patrick, eds. *Centre and Labyrinth: Essays in Honour of Northrop Frye*. Toronto: U of Toronto P, 1983.

1441.   Denham, Robert D. *Northrop Frye and Critical Method*. University Park: Pennsylvania State UP, 1978.

1442.   ———, ed. *Visionary Poetics: Essays on Northrop Frye's Criticism*. New York: Lang, 1991.

1443.   Hamilton, A. C. *Northrop Frye: Anatomy of His Criticism*. Toronto: U of Toronto P, 1990.

1444.   Krieger, Murray, ed. *Northrop Frye in Modern Criticism*. Selected Papers from the English Institute, 1965. New York: Columbia UP, 1966.

Anthropology and Critical Theory

The unhappy fate of the Cambridge school does not, of course, suggest that anthropology may not have much to contribute to critical theory. The structural anthropology of Claude Lévi-Strauss (see the headnote to this chapter) exerted considerable influence, especially through his complex technique for analyzing myths, which he illustrated in a number of books. But he remained part of the general movement of structuralism and has received little attention from literary theorists recently. There has, however, been an important revival of theoretical interests within anthropology, and many of these developments are already influencing critical theory. The stress Clifford Geertz and Gregory Bateson put on the role of symbols in culture and on the complexities of interpretation have important connections with hermeneutics (see chapter 6, "Hermeneutics and Phenomenology"). Mary Douglas's studies of ideas such as purity and danger and Victor Turner's many books on "the ritual process" are similarly suggestive. But the links between critical theory and the most recent developments of anthropology are still in the process of formation.

Books and Collections

1445.   Ashley, Kathleen M., ed. *Victor Turner and the Construction of Cultural Criticism: Between Literature and Anthropology*. Bloomington: Indiana UP, 1990.

1446.   Brady, Ivan, ed. *Anthropological Poetics*. Savage: Rowman, 1990. Fourteen essays at the intersection of anthropology, literature, and theory.

1447.   Clifford, James. *The Predicament of Culture: Twentieth-Century Ethnography, Literature, and Art*. Cambridge: Harvard UP, 1988. Collected essays by a leader in the recent movement to examine ethnography from the perspective of current theory and bring out its cultural implications as a form of writing.

1448.   Clifford, James, and George E. Marcus, eds. *Writing Culture: The Poetics and Politics of Ethnography*. Berkeley: U of California P, 1986.

1449.   Marcus, George E., and Michael M. J. Fischer. *Anthropology as Cultural Critique: An Experimental Moment in the Human Sciences*. Chicago: U of Chicago P, 1986.

Individual Author

RENÉ GIRARD (1923–   )

René Girard's early book *Deceit, Desire, and the Novel* was a psychoanalytic investigation of the dynamic relations of love triangles in novels, where A's love for B is stimulated by C's love for B. This "triangular desire" could equally be projected onto the relations of author, reader, and a character, or indeed onto the entire novel. But Girard went on to develop a broader interest in the origins of literature and culture and turned eventually to anthropology. He elaborated a complex theory showing how all forms of representation emerged out of rituals that solidified the social group by expelling and sacrificing a scapegoat figure. He insisted that this is no mere speculation but an actual fact in the origin of culture, a fact that remains the decisive key to understanding both society and more delimited areas like literature. Somewhat taken aback by his "discovery" of the ritualized violence at the root of society, Girard more recently explored the contrasting idea of sacrificial redemption and reconciliation in the Christian story. Many of Girard's themes belong to the general movement of structuralist and post-structuralist thought, but his ideas diverge idiosyncratically from that movement. His theories bear a certain resemblance to those of Kenneth Burke (see listings in chapter 9, "Cultural Criticism") and Northrop Frye (see above), but he has so far gained few adherents.

1450.   *The Scapegoat*. Trans. Yvonne Freccero. Baltimore: Johns Hopkins UP, 1986.

1451.   *A Theater of Envy: William Shakespeare*. New York: Oxford UP, 1991.

1452.   *Things Hidden since the Foundation of the World*. Trans. Stephen Bann and Michael Metteer. London: Athlone, 1987. Research undertaken in collaboration with Jean-Michel Oughourlian and Guy Lefort.

1453.   *"To Double Business Bound": Essays on Literature, Mimesis, and Anthro-*

pology. Baltimore: Johns Hopkins UP, 1978. Traces origin of literature and culture to actual events in prehistory.

1454.   *Violence and the Sacred*. Trans. Patrick Gregory. Baltimore: Johns Hopkins UP, 1977. Anthropological theory of the origins of literature in ritual expulsions of a scapegoat.

Books on Girard or on Developing His Approach

1455.   Dumouchel Paul, ed. *Violence and Truth: On the Work of René Girard*. Stanford: Stanford UP, 1988.

1456.   Gans, Eric. *The End of Culture: Toward a Generative Anthropology*. Berkeley: U of California P, 1985. Traces all human representation—language, ritual, and art—to a prehistorical "scene" and its subsequent development.

1457.   ———. *The Origin of Language: A Formal Theory of Representation*. Berkeley: U of California P, 1981. Broad speculation drawing on anthropology and prehistory.

1458.   Hamerton-Kelly, Robert G., ed. *Violent Origins: Walter Burkert, René Girard, and Jonathan Z. Smith on Ritual Killing and Cultural Formation*. Stanford: Stanford UP, 1987.

1459.   Livingston, Paisley. *Models of Desire: René Girard and the Psychology of Mimesis*. Baltimore: Johns Hopkins UP, 1992.

1460.   McKenna, Andrew J. *Violence and Difference: Girard, Derrida, and Deconstruction*. Urbana: U of Illinois P, 1992. Attempts to redeem deconstruction from "sterility" by developing ideas of Girard.

1461.   *To Honor René Girard: On the Occasion of His Sixtieth Birthday*. Saratoga: Anma, 1986. Twenty essays, with primary and secondary bibliography.

14. Ethnic and Postcolonial Studies

Until recently, criticism of literature by black Americans concentrated on interpreting and evaluating African American writing for a wider audience, repudiating misperceptions and stereotypes emanating from the dominant white culture, and encouraging and sometimes trying to guide the development of African American literature. Old prejudices have by no means been eliminated, but the many outstanding achievements of both past and contemporary black writers are by now better acknowledged in the academy.

During the 1960s and later, important critical issues were sharply debated, including the social responsibilities of black writers, the relation of writing by blacks to that of whites, and the question of whether aesthetic standards and devices are universal or are or should be particular to cultural groups. Such debates and the wider burgeoning of literary theory led a new generation of scholars and critics to bring together contemporary theory and the study of African American writing. Among these scholars, Henry Louis Gates, Jr., and Houston Baker, Jr., (see below) are probably the most widely read and cited.

At the same time, in Africa, Asia, and throughout what has been called the Third World, writers and critics, many of whom have studied or spent time in the United States or Europe, have brought a high level of sophistication to the study of literature from formerly colonized regions. Their theoretical reflections often focus on questions of cultural analysis and social responsibility. Frequently they take a traditionally Marxist or a post-Marxist perspective, but Third World theorists have also drawn on structuralism, deconstruction, theories of myth and of orality, and studies of ethnography (see, for example, the work of James Clifford listed under "Anthropology and Critical Theory" in chapter 13). Gayatri Spivak, the translator of Jacques Derrida's *Of Grammatology* (see chapter 5, "Poststructuralism and Deconstruction"), is a leading example of this richly variegated approach.

In the United States, the literature of other ethnic groups, such as Hispanics or Asian Americans, is now gaining attention. In literary theoretical work, once again, post-Marxist cultural studies dominate. But important linkages connect the current study of American ethnic literatures with various regions of the Third World. There is considerable common ground also between ethnic studies and feminist and gender studies, and cross-listings here aim to underscore these connections.

1462.   Amanuddin, Syed. *Creativity and Reception: Toward a Theory of Third World Criticism*. New York: Lang, 1988.

1463.   Amuta, Chidi. *The Theory of African Literature: Implications for Practical Criticism*. London: Zed, 1989.

1464.   Anderson, Talmadge, ed. *Black Studies: Theory, Method, and Cultural Perspectives*. Pullman: Washington State UP, 1990. Collects articles from recent years; overview of the field.

1465.   Andrzejewski, B. W., Stanislaw Pilazewicz, and Witold Tyloch, eds. *Literatures in African Languages: Theoretical Issues and Sample Surveys*. Cambridge: Cambridge UP, 1985.

1466.   Anozie, Sunday O. *Phenomenology in Modern African Studies*. Owerri: Conch, 1982.

1467.   ———. *Structural Models and African Poetics: Towards a Pragmatic View of Literature*. London: Routledge, 1981. Draws on Jakobson, Lévi-Strauss's structural approach to myth, and other structuralists and poststructuralists.

1468.   Appiah, Kwame Anthony. *In My Father's House: Africa in the Philosophy of Culture*. New York: Oxford UP, 1992. Examines the question of African identity and how the philosophy of culture has addressed it.

1469.   Ashcroft, Bill, Gareth Griffiths, and Helen Tiffin. *The Empire Writes Back: Theory and Practice in Post-colonial Literatures*. New York: Routledge, 1989.

1470.   Baker, Houston A., Jr. *Afro-American Poetics: Revisions of Harlem and the Black Aesthetic*. Madison: U of Wisconsin P, 1988.

1471.   ———. *Blues, Ideology, and Afro-American Literature: A Vernacular Theory*. Chicago: U of Chicago P, 1984.

1472.   ———. *The Journey Back: Issues in Black Literature and Criticism*. Chicago: U of Chicago P, 1980.

1473.   ———. *Long Black Song: Essays in Black-American Literature and Culture*. Charlottesville: UP of Virginia, 1972.

1474.   ———. *Workings of the Spirit: The Poetics of Afro-American Women's Writing*. Chicago: U of Chicago P, 1990.

1475.   Baker, Houston, A., Jr., and Patricia Redmond, eds. *Afro-American Literary Study in the 1990s*. Chicago: U of Chicago P, 1989. Seven essays reflecting current theoretical perspectives.

1476.   Bell, Roseann P., Bettye J. Parker, and Beverly Guy-Sheftall. *Sturdy Black Bridges: Visions of Black Women in Literature*. New York: Harmony, 1980. Critical essays, interviews, selection of poems and stories; with extensive bibliography, including African and Caribbean authors.

1477.   Bhabha, Homi, ed. *Nation and Narration*. London: Routledge, 1990. Fifteen essays present theoretical perspectives on representations of cultural difference in works ranging from Australian and Latin American to African American and English.

1478.   Boelhower, William. *Through a Glass Darkly: Ethnic Semiosis in American Literature*. New York: Oxford UP, 1987. Semiotic approach, draws on Eco and Michel Serres.

1479.   Braxton, Joanne, and Andrée Nicola-McLaughlin, eds. *Wild Women in the Whirlwind: Afra-American Culture and the Contemporary Literary Renaissance*. New Brunswick: Rutgers UP, 1990.

1480.   Calderón, Héctor, and José David Saldívar, eds. *Criticism in the Borderlands: Studies in Chicano Literature, Culture, and Ideology*. Durham: Duke UP, 1991.

1481.   Carby, Hazel. *Reconstructing Womanhood: The Emergence of the Afro-American Woman Novelist*. New York: Oxford UP, 1987. Discusses and draws on theoretical approaches.

1482.   Castillo, Debra A. *Talking Back: Toward a Latin American Feminist Literary Criticism*. Ithaca: Cornell UP, 1992. Aims to construct a feminist criticism that can incorporate the diversity of Latin American feminist theory and writing.

1483.   Cheyfitz, Eric. *The Poetics of Imperialism: Translation and Colonization from* The Tempest *to* Tarzan. New York: Oxford UP, 1990. Develops a conception of translation to analyze the encounter between native culture and imperial invaders.

1484.   Christian, Barbara. *Black Feminist Criticism: Perspectives on Black Women Writers*. New York: Pergamon, 1985.

1485.   ———. *Black Women Novelists: The Development of a Tradition, 1892–1976*. Westport: Greenwood, 1980.

1486.   Davies, Carole B., and Anne A. Graves, eds. *Ngambika: Studies of Women in African Literature*. Trenton: Africa World, 1986.

1487.   Eagleton, Terry, Fredric Jameson, and Edward Said. *Nationalism, Colonialism, and Literature*. Minneapolis: U of Minnesota P, 1990. Collects three essays, one by each author.

1488.   Emenyonu, Ernest N., R. Vanamali, E. Oko, and A. Iloeje, eds. *Critical Theory and African Literature*. Ibadan: Heinemann, 1987. Essays divided into five sections: myth, oral literature, critical theory, stylistic and semantic analysis, and language.

1489.   Evans, Mari, ed. *Black Women Writers, 1950–1980: A Critical Evaluation*. Garden City: Anchor-Doubleday, 1984.

1490.   Frye, Charles A. *Towards a Philosophy of Black Studies*. San Francisco: R. & E. Research, 1978.

1491.   Gates, Henry Louis, Jr., ed. *Black Literature and Literary Theory*. London: Methuen, 1984. Essays applying recent critical theories to African American literature.

1492.   ———. *Figures in Black: Words, Signs, and the "Racial" Self*. New York: Oxford UP, 1987.

1493.   ———, ed. *"Race," Writing, and Difference*. Chicago: U of Chicago P, 1986. Essays by Derrida, Barbara Johnson, Mary Louise Pratt, Said, Spivak, and others.

1494.   ———, ed. *Reading Black, Reading Feminist: A Literary Critical Anthology*. New York: NAL, 1990.

1495.   ———. *The Signifying Monkey: A Theory of Afro-American Literary Criticism*. New York: Oxford UP, 1988. The most widely read and cited study.

1496.   Gurr, Andrew, and Pio Zirimu, eds. *Black Aesthetics: Papers from a Colloquium Held at the University of Nairobi*. Nairobi: East African Literature Bureau, 1973.

1497.   Harlow, Barbara. *Resistance Literature*. New York: Methuen, 1987.

1498.   Harris, Wilson. *The Womb of Space: The Cross-Cultural Imagination*. Westport: Greenwood, 1983. Essays by a leading Caribbean writer and critic.

1499.   Harrow, Kenneth, et al., eds. *African Literature: Critical Theory and Political Commitment*. Washington: Three Continents, 1988.

1500.   Hogue, W. Lawrence. *Discourse and the Other: The Production of the Afro-American Text*. Durham: Duke UP, 1986. Focuses on institutions of literary production, including publishers, bookstores, libraries, and editors.

1501.   Hooks, Bell. *Talking Back: Thinking Feminist, Thinking Black*. Boston: South End, 1989.

1502.   Hord, Fred Lee. *Reconstructing Memory: Black Literary Criticism*. Chicago: Third World, 1991.

1503.   Hull, Gloria T., Patricia Bell Scott, and Barbara Smith. *All the Women Are White, All the Blacks Are Men, but Some of Us Are Brave: Black Women's Studies*. Old Westbury: Feminist, 1981.

1504.   JanMohamed, Abdul R., and David Lloyd, ed. *The Nature and Context of Minority Discourse*. New York: Oxford UP, 1991. Essays develop a paradigm for cultural studies that includes minority and Third World cultures.

1505.   Johnson, Charles. *Being and Race: Black Writing since 1970*. Bloomington: Indiana UP, 1988. Draws on phenomenology.

1506.   Johnson, Lemuel A., Bernadette Cailler, Russell Hamilton, and Mildred Hill-Lubin, eds. *Toward Defining the African Aesthetic*. Washington: Three Continents, 1982.

1507.   Krupat, Arnold. *Ethnocriticism: Ethnography, History, Literature*. Berkeley: U of California P, 1991. Focuses on Native American materials.

1508.   Lionnet, Françoise. *Autobiographical Voices: Race, Gender, Self-Portraiture*. Ithaca: Cornell UP, 1989. Develops theoretical approach to authors of mixed races, cultures, or languages, comparing modern female writers with Augustine and Nietzsche.

1509.   Miller, Christopher L. *Theories of Africans: Francophone Literature and Anthropology in Africa*. Chicago: U of Chicago P, 1990. Tests various theoretical models against African contexts, including the relation of theory to reading African literature, orality and literacy, totemism, dialogism, canonicity and gender theory, ethnicity and ethics.

1510.   Minh-ha, Trinh T. *Woman, Native, Other: Writing Postcoloniality and Feminism*. Bloomington: Indiana UP, 1989.

1511.   Mudimbe, V. Y. *The Invention of Africa: Gnosis, Philosophy, and the Order of Knowledge*. Bloomington: Indiana UP, 1988. Draws on Foucault to analyze knowledge, discourse, power, identity, and otherness.

1512.   Ngara, Emmanuel. *Art and Ideology in the African Novel: A Study of the Influence of Marxism on African Writing*. London: Heinemann, 1985. Surveys Marxist theory and its influence on African literature.

1513.   ———. *Stylistic Criticism and the African Novel: A Study of the Language, Art and Content of African Fiction*. London: Heinemann, 1982. Surveys structuralist stylistic analysis, then applies it to African fiction.

1514.   Nirajani, Tejaswini. *Siting Translation: History, Poststructuralism, and the Colonial Context*. Berkeley: U of California P, 1992. Draws on Benjamin, Derrida, and de Man to develop idea of translation as the "site" for perpetuating unequal power relations.

1515.   Sims, William E. *Black Studies: Pitfalls and Potential*. Washington: UP of America, 1978.

1516.   Smith, Barbara. *Toward a Black Feminist Criticism*. Brooklyn: Out and Out; Trumansburg: Crossing, 1977.

1517.   Sollors, Werner, ed. *The Invention of Ethnicity*. New York: Oxford UP, 1989.

        Soyinka, Wole. *Myth, Literature and the African World*. See entry 1415.

1518.   Spivak, Gayatri Chakravorty. *In Other Worlds: Essays in Cultural Politics*. London: Routledge, 1987. Poststructuralist, Marxist, and feminist essays on Western and non-Western literature and culture.

1519.   ———. *The Post-colonial Critic: Interviews, Strategies, Dialogues*. Ed.

Sarah Harasym. New York: Routledge, 1990. Essays by and interviews with a leading theorist.

1520.   Wall, Cheryl A., ed. *Changing Our Own Words: Essays on Criticism, Theory, and Writing by Black Women.* New Brunswick: Rutgers UP, 1989.

1521.   Wallace, Michelle. *Invisibility Blues: From Pop to Theory.* London: Verso, 1990. Poses questions that emerging black feminist theory must answer.

1522.   Weixlmann, Joe, and Chester J. Fontenot, eds. *Belief vs. Theory in Black American Literary Criticism.* Vol. 2 of *Studies in Black American Literature.* Greenwood: Penkevill, 1986. Essays by Baker, Baraka, and others.

1523.   ————, eds. *Black American Prose Theory.* Vol. 1 of *Studies in Black American Literature.* Greenwood: Penkevill, 1984.

1524.   Weixlmann, Joe, and Houston A. Baker, Jr., eds. *Black Feminist Criticism and Critical Theory.* Vol. 3 of *Studies in Black American Literature.* Greenwood: Penkevill, 1988.

1525.   Willis, Susan. *Specifying: Black Women Writing the American Experience.* Madison: U of Wisconson P, 1987. Marxist approach, establishing context of literary theory and cultural criticism.

15. Feminist and Gender Criticism

The emergence and explosion of feminist criticism is one of the most important developments in literary study in the last fifteen years. Feminist literary criticism developed out of the women's liberation movement, itself an outgrowth of the civil rights and anti–Vietnam War movements. The major figures of women's liberation—including Gloria Steinem, Betty Friedan, Shulamith Firestone, Kate Millett, Germaine Greer, and Robin Morgan—are not listed in this chapter but form the context necessary to understand feminist criticism and its continuing power.

Mirroring the evolution of the wider field of literary study, feminist criticism's initial agenda recalled the philological tradition. The history of literature was combed in search of neglected literary works by women; new editions and reprintings were undertaken; biographical and historical studies sought to establish a tradition of women's writings; literary forms practiced by women, but often excluded from the canon of "great" works—forms like letters, diaries, and British detective fiction—were reexamined and reevaluated. At the same time, critical studies of works by women, of women authors, and of the presentation of women in literature multiplied.

These studies increasingly made use of the whole range of critical approaches, from formalist and structuralist to psychoanalytic, Marxist, and poststructuralist. Prominent women writers such as Margaret Atwood, Tillie Olsen, and Adrienne Rich published essays on literary and other topics. This ferment of study and criticism rapidly began to include reflections on the theoretical issues raised by feminism. The formal and informal professional institutions that previously overlooked women were scrutinized, and an agenda for women's studies emerged. Debate rages over whether there is a body of literature or a tradition that can be labeled "women's literature," and, in a parallel way, some analysts see feminist criticism as a distinctive approach, others as an application of existing approaches to a specific body of material.

A number of male critics and theorists have taken feminist criticism as their starting point and have joined with women to discuss the role men can and should play in relation to feminism. This is one example of the way feminism has raised more broadly the issues of gender and sexuality as socially constructed categories. Following this wider perspective, theorists have drawn on psychoanalysis, psychology, and cultural studies to consider sexual and other bonds between members of the same sex.

Bibliographies

1526.   Gelfand, Elissa D., and Virginia Thorndike Hules. *French Feminist Criticism: Women, Language, and Literature; An Annotated Bibliography.* New York: Garland, 1985.

1527.   Humm, Maggie. *An Annotated Critical Bibliography of Feminist Criticism.* Boston: Hall, 1987.

Introductory Books and Collections

1528.   Belsey, Catherine, and Jane Moore, eds. *The Feminist Reader: Essays in Gender and the Politics of Literary Criticism.* London: Macmillan, 1989. Essays by Spender, Moi, Kristeva, and others, with an introduction surveying the field, a glossary, and an annotated bibliography.

1529.   Cameron, Deborah, ed. *The Feminist Critique of Language: A Reader.* London: Routledge, 1990. Brings together contributions from linguistics and literary criticism on gender and language; with introductions and annotations.

1530.   Eagleton, Mary, ed. *Feminist Literary Criticism.* White Plains: Longman, 1991. Introduces a variety of feminist critics by pairing essays in a "dialogue" form, with equal attention to French and Anglo-American critics.

1531.   ———, ed. *Feminist Literary Theory: A Reader.* Oxford: Blackwell, 1986. Good introductory collection of writing since Virginia Woolf, arranged topically.

1532.   Gilbert, Sandra M., and Susan Gubar. *The Madwoman in the Attic: The Woman Writer and the Nineteenth-Century Literary Imagination.* New Haven: Yale UP, 1979. One of the most widely influential studies.

1533.   Humm, Maggie. *The Dictionary of Feminist Theory*. Columbus: Ohio State
          UP, 1990.

1534.   Kahn, Coppélia, and Gayle Green, eds. *Making a Difference: Feminist
          Literary Criticism*. London: Methuen, 1985. Ten wide-ranging essays intro-
          ducing the field.

1535.   Marks, Elaine, and Isabelle de Courtivron, eds. *New French Feminisms:
          An Anthology*. Amherst: U of Massachusetts P, 1979. Excellent selections,
          many first translated here.

1536.   Mills, Sara, Lynne Pearce, Sue Spaull, Elaine Millard. *Feminist Readings /
          Feminists Reading*. New York: Harvester Wheatsheaf, 1989. Surveys vari-
          ous feminist approaches by discussing each and showing how it can be
          applied to particular texts; approaches include gynocriticism, French femi-
          nism, and Marxist feminism.

1537.   Moi, Toril, ed. *French Feminist Thought: A Reader*. Oxford: Blackwell,
          1987.

1538.   ———. *Sexual/Textual Politics*. New York: Methuen, 1985. Comprehensive
          survey of feminist criticism.

1539.   Ruthven, K. K. *Feminist Literary Studies: An Introduction*. Cambridge:
          Cambridge UP, 1984.

1540.   Showalter, Elaine, ed. *The New Feminist Criticism: Essays on Women,
          Literature, and Theory*. New York: Pantheon, 1985.

1541.   Warhol, Robyn R., and Diane Price Herndl, eds. *Feminisms: An Anthology
          of Literary Theory and Criticism*. New Brunswick: Rutgers UP, 1991.

Books and Collections

1542.   Abel, Elizabeth, ed. *Writing and Sexual Difference*. Chicago: U of Chicago
          P, 1982. Anthology of essays on issues of writing and gender.

1543.   Abel, Elizabeth, and Emily K. Abel, eds. *The Signs Reader: Women, Gen-
          der, and Scholarship*. Chicago: U of Chicago P, 1983. Essays from the
          prominent feminist journal *Signs*.

1544.   Adams, Carol J. *The Sexual Politics of Meat: A Feminist-Vegetarian Critical
          Theory*. New York: Continuum, 1990.

1545.   Armstrong, Nancy, and Leonard Tennenhouse, eds. *The Ideology of Con-
          duct: Essays on Literature and the History of Sexuality*. London: Methuen,
          1987.

1546.   Ascher, Carol, Louise DeSalvo, and Sara Ruddick, eds. *Between Women:
          Biographers, Novelists, Critics, Teachers, and Artists Write about Their
          Work on Women*. Boston: Beacon, 1984. Essays on a variety of women
          thinkers and writers.

1547.   Auerbach, Nina. *Communities of Women: An Idea in Fiction*. Cambridge:

Harvard UP, 1987. Essays on nineteenth- and twentieth-century novels by women.

1548.   ———. *Romantic Imprisonment: Women and Other Glorified Outcasts.* New York: Columbia UP, 1985.

1549.   ———. *Women and the Demon: The Life of a Victorian Myth.* Cambridge: Harvard UP, 1982.

Baker, Houston A., Jr. *Workings of the Spirit: The Poetics of Afro-American Women's Writing.* See entry 1474.

1550.   Barr, Marleen S. *Alien to Femininity: Speculative Fiction and Feminist Theory.* New York: Greenwood, 1987. On science fiction.

Barr, Marleen S., and Richard Feldstein. *Discontented Discourses: Feminism/Textual Intervention/Psychoanalysis.* See entry 958.

Batsleer, Janet, Tony Davies, Rebecca O'Rourke, and Chris Weedon. *Rewriting English: Cultural Politics of Gender and Class.* See entry 1020.

1551.   Battersby, Christine. *Gender and Genius: Towards a Feminist Aesthetics.* Bloomington: Indiana UP, 1990.

1552.   Bauer, Dale M. *Feminist Dialogics: A Theory of Failed Community.* Buffalo: State U of New York, 1988. Bakhtinian approach to novels by Hawthorne, James, Wharton, and Chopin.

Bauer, Dale M., and Susan Jaret McKinstry, eds. *Feminism, Bakhtin, and the Dialogic.* See entry 344.

1553.   Baym, Nina. *Woman's Fiction: A Guide to Novels by and about Women in America, 1820–1870.* Ithaca: Cornell UP, 1978. With an introductory chapter, "The Form and Ideology of Women's Fiction."

Bell, Roseann P., Bettye J. Parker, and Beverly Guy-Sheftall. *Sturdy Black Bridges: Visions of Black Women in Literature.* See entry 1476.

1554.   Benstock, Shari, ed. *Feminist Issues in Literary Scholarship.* Bloomington: Indiana UP, 1987. Thirteen contributions by leading feminist critics.

1555.   ———. *Textualizing the Feminine: On the Limits of Genre.* Norman: U of Oklahoma P, 1991. Discusses works by Derrida, Joyce, Gertrude Stein, and Virginia Woolf.

Berg, Temma F., Anna Shannon Elfenbein, Jeanne Larsen, and Elisa Kay Sparks, eds. *Engendering the Word: Feminist Essays in Psychosexual Politics.* See entry 873.

1556.   Bernikow, Louise. *Among Women.* New York: Harper, 1981. Wide-ranging essays on women in literature.

1557.   Boone, Joseph A., and Michael Cadden, eds. *Engendering Men: The Question of Male Feminist Criticism.* New York: Routledge, 1990. Eighteen male critics retheorizing the male position in culture in the wake of feminism.

1558.   Bowles, Gloria, and Renate Duelli-Klein, eds. *Theories of Women's Studies.* London: Routledge, 1983.

Brennan, Teresa, ed. *Between Feminism and Psychoanalysis*. See entry 879.

1559.   Brown, Cheryl L., and Karen Olsen, eds. *Feminist Criticism: Essays on Theory, Poetry, and Prose*. Metuchen: Scarecrow, 1978. Twenty-one essays on poets and novelists and four theoretical essays.

1560.   Brownstein, Rachel Mayer. *Becoming a Heroine: Reading about Women in Novels*. New York: Viking, 1982.

Carby, Hazel. *Reconstructing Womanhood: The Emergence of the Afro-American Woman Novelist*. See entry 1481.

1561.   Castle, Terry. *Clarissa's Ciphers: Meaning and Disruption in Richardson's Clarissa*. Ithaca: Cornell UP, 1982. Draws on recent hermeneutic theory to analyze Richardson's novel.

Christian, Barbara. *Black Feminist Criticism: Perspectives on Black Women Writers*. See entry 1484.

———. *Black Women Novelists: The Development of a Tradition, 1892–1976*. See entry 1485.

1562.   Cixous, Hélène. *"Coming to Writing" and Other Essays*. Ed. Deborah Jenson. Trans. Sarah Cornell et al. Cambridge: Harvard UP, 1991. On relation between sexual difference and literature; includes previously untranslated essays.

1563.   ———. *Readings: The Poetics of Blanchot, Joyce, Kafka, Kleist, Lispector, and Tsvetayeva*. Ed. and trans. Verena Andermatt Conley. Minneapolis: U of Minnesota P, 1991.

1564.   Cixous, Hélène, and Catherine Clément. *The Newly Born Woman*. Trans. Betsy Wing. Introd. Sandra M. Gilbert. Minnesota: U of Minnesota P, 1986.

1565.   Cixous (book on). Conley, Verena A. *Hélène Cixous: Writing the Feminine*. Expanded ed. Lincoln: U of Nebraska P, 1991. Study of a noted French feminist and writer.

1566.   Cixous (book on). Shiach, Morag. *Hélène Cixous: A Politics of Writing*. New York: Routledge, 1991.

1567.   Cixous (book on). Wilcox, Helen, et al., eds. *The Body and the Text: Hélène Cixous, Reading and Teaching*. New York: St. Martin's, 1990.

1568.   Claridge, Laura, and Elizabeth Langland, eds. *Out of Bounds: Male Writers and Gender(ed) Criticism*. Amherst: U of Massachusetts P, 1991. Essays on how American and British male writers have responded to the confines of a "patriarchal literary code."

1569.   Cornillon, Susan Koppelman, ed. *Images of Women in Fiction: Feminist Perspectives*. Rev. ed. Bowling Green: Bowling Green U Popular P, 1973. Includes section "Feminist Aesthetics" and annotated bibliography.

1570.   Cruikshank, Margaret, ed. *Lesbian Studies: Present and Future*. Old Westbury: Feminist, 1982.

Davies, Carole B., and Anne A. Graves, eds. *Ngambika: Studies of Women in African Literature.* See entry 1486.

1571.   De Lauretis, Teresa. *Alice Doesn't: Feminism, Semiotics, Cinema.* Bloomington: Indiana UP, 1984.

1572.   ———, ed. *Feminist Studies/Critical Studies.* Bloomington: Indiana UP, 1986.

1573.   ———. *Technologies of Gender: Essays on Theory, Film, and Fiction.* Bloomington: Indiana UP, 1987.

1574.   Diamond, Arlyn, and Lee R. Edwards, eds. *The Authority of Experience: Essays in Feminist Criticism.* Amherst: U of Massachusetts P, 1977. Sixteen essays on topics from Chaucer to modern literature, three on theory.

Diamond, Irene, and Lee Quinby, eds. *Feminism and Foucault: Reflections on Resistance.* See entry 1308.

1575.   Doane, Janice, and Devon Hodges. *Nostalgia and Sexual Difference: The Resistance to Contemporary Feminism.* New York: Methuen, 1987. Argues against social commentators, novelists, and critics who have shown alarm at feminism.

1576.   Donovan, Josephine, ed. *Feminist Literary Criticism: Explorations in Theory.* 2nd expanded ed. Lexington: UP of Kentucky, 1989.

1577.   ———, ed. *Feminist Theory: The Intellectual Traditions of American Feminism.* New York: Ungar, 1985.

1578.   Douglas, Ann. *The Feminization of American Culture.* New York: Knopf, 1977.

1579.   Du Bois, Ellen Carol, et al., eds. *Feminist Scholarship: Kindling in the Groves of Academe.* Urbana: U of Illinois P, 1985.

1580.   Duchen, Claire. *Feminism in France.* London: Routledge, 1986. Sets French feminism in its social and historical context.

1581.   Eagleton, Terry. *The Rape of Clarissa: Writing, Sexuality, and Class Struggle in Richardson.* Minneapolis: U of Minnesota P, 1982.

1582.   Ecker, Giesela, ed. *Feminist Aesthetics.* Trans. Harriet Anderson. London: Women's, 1985.

1583.   Eisenstein, Hester. *Contemporary Feminist Thought.* Boston: Hall, 1983. An intellectual history.

1584.   Eisenstein, Hester, and Alice Jardine, eds. *The Future of Difference: The Scholar and the Feminist.* Boston: Hall; New York: Barnard College Women's Center, 1980.

1585.   Ellmann, Mary. *Thinking about Women: Conceptions of Femininity.* New York: Harcourt, 1968.

Evans, Mari, ed. *Black Women Writers, 1950–1980: A Critical Evaluation.* See entry 1489.

Feldstein, Richard, and Judith Roof, eds. *Feminism and Psychoanalysis.* See entry 891.

1586. Felski, Rita. *Beyond Feminist Aesthetics: Feminist Literature and Social Change.* Cambridge: Harvard UP, 1989.

1587. Fetterley, Judith. *The Resisting Reader: A Feminist Approach to American Fiction.* Bloomington: Indiana UP, 1978.

1588. Finke, Laurie A. *Feminist Theory, Women's Writing.* Ithaca: Cornell UP, 1992. Brings together literary theory, feminist criticism, and literature from the medieval to modern eras.

Flax, Jane. *Thinking Fragments: Psychoanalysis, Feminism, and Postmodernism in the Contemporary West.* See entry 895.

1589. Flynn, Elizabeth A., and Patrocinio P. Schweickart, eds. *Gender and Reading: Essays on Readers, Texts, and Contexts.* Baltimore: Johns Hopkins UP, 1986. Twelve essays.

1590. Frye, Marilyn. *The Politics of Reality: Essays in Feminist Theory.* Trumansburg: Crossing, 1983.

1591. Fuss, Diana, ed. *Inside/Out: Lesbian Theories, Gay Theories.* New York: Routledge, 1991.

Gabriel, Susan L., and Isaiah Smithson, eds. *Gender in the Classroom: Power and Pedagogy.* See entry 274.

1592. Gallop, Jane. *Around 1981: Academic Feminist Literary Theory.* New York: Routledge, 1991. History of feminist literary criticism.

1593. ———. *The Daughter's Seduction: Feminism and Psychoanalysis.* Ithaca: Cornell UP, 1982. On Lacan, French psychoanalysis, and feminism.

1594. ———. *Thinking through the Body.* New York: Columbia UP, 1988.

1595. Garner, Shirley Nelson, Claire Kahane, and Madelon Sprengnether, eds. *The (M)Other Tongue: Essays in Feminist Psychoanalytic Interpretation.* Ithaca: Cornell UP, 1985. Combines feminist and psychoanalytic criticism.

1596. Garvin, Harry R., ed. *Women, Literature, Criticism.* Bucknell Review 24. Lewisburg: Bucknell UP, 1978. Twelve essays on topics from Milton to modern literature.

Gates, Henry Louis, Jr., ed. *Reading Black, Reading Feminist: A Literary Critical Anthology.* See entry 1494.

1597. Genova, Judith, ed. *Power, Gender, Values.* Edmonton: Academic, 1987.

1598. Gilbert, Sandra M., and Susan Gubar. *No Man's Land: The Place of the Woman Writer in the Twentieth Century.* 2 vols. New York: Yale UP, 1988.

Grosz, Elizabeth. *Jacques Lacan: A Feminist Introduction.* See entry 968.

1599. ———. *Sexual Subversions: Three French Feminists.* Winchester: Unwin, 1989. On Kristeva, Luce Irigaray, and Michele le Doeuff.

1600. Heath, Stephen. *Representation and Sexual Difference.* Oxford: Blackwell,

1990. Follows Foucault to argue that sexuality is a historical concept rooted in nineteenth-century representations of sexual difference.

1601. Heilbrun, Carolyn G. *Reinventing Womanhood*. New York: Norton, 1979.

1602. ———. *Toward a Recognition of Androgyny*. New York: Knopf, 1973.

1603. Herrmann, Claudine. *The Tongue Snatchers*. Trans. Nancy Kline. Lincoln: U of Nebraska P, 1989. Argues that language is the basic means by which women are oppressed, so that women writers must "steal" or invent a language to express themselves creatively.

Hirsch, Marianne. *The Mother/Daughter Plot: Narrative, Psychoanalysis, Feminism*. See entry 902.

1604. Hirsch, Marianne, and Evelyn Fox Keller, eds. *Conflicts in Feminism*. New York: Routledge, 1990. Essays on literary, philosophical, social, and other aspects of feminism.

Hooks, Bell. *Talking Back: Thinking Feminist, Thinking Black*. See entry 1501.

Hull, Gloria T., Patricia Bell Scott, and Barbara Smith. *All the Women Are White, All the Blacks Are Men, but Some of Us Are Brave: Black Women's Studies*. See entry 1503.

1605. Humm, Maggie. *Feminist Criticism*. Brighton, Eng.: Harvester, 1986.

1606. Hunter, Dianne. *Seduction and Theory: Readings of Gender, Representation, and Rhetoric*. Urbana: U of Illinois P, 1989.

1607. Irigaray, Luce. *The Irigaray Reader*. Ed. Margaret Whitford. Trans. David Macey. Oxford: Blackwell, 1991. Includes first translation of several pieces.

1608. ———. *Speculum of the Other Woman*. Trans. Gillian C. Gill. Ithaca: Cornell UP, 1985. A major text in contemporary French feminism.

1609. ———. *This Sex Which Is Not One*. Trans. Catherine Porter with Carolyn Burke. Ithaca: Cornell UP, 1985. Eleven essays on female sexuality and feminism.

1610. Irigaray (book on). Whitford, Margaret. *Luce Irigaray*. New York: Routledge, 1991.

1611. Jacobus, Mary. *Reading Woman: Essays in Feminist Criticism*. New York: Columbia UP, 1986. Essays about major women writers; develops a Freudian approach to feminist criticism.

1612. ———, ed. *Women Writing and Writing about Women*. London: Croom Helm, 1979.

1613. Jardine, Alice. *Gynesis: Configurations of Woman and Modernity*. Ithaca: Cornell UP, 1985. On contemporary French literary, philosophical, and psychoanalytic works.

1614. Jardine, Alice, and Paul Smith, eds. *Men in Feminism*. London: Methuen, 1987.

1615. Jay, Karla, and Joanne Glasgow, eds. *Lesbian Texts and Contexts: Radical*

Revisions. New York: New York UP, 1990. Lesbianism and the critical interaction among readers, writers, and critics; bibliography.

1616.   Kaplan, Cora. *Sea Changes: Culture and Feminism.* London: Routledge, 1987.

1617.   Kauffman, Linda, ed. *Feminism and Institutions: Dialogues on Feminist Theory.* Oxford: Blackwell, 1989. On legal, academic and professional, and national and international institutions; discusses feminism and deconstruction, the canon, and cultural criticism, setting feminism in a global context.

1618.   ———, ed. *Gender and Theory: Dialogues on Feminist Criticism.* Oxford: Blackwell, 1988. Dialogues between men and women on feminist theory and representation; essays on the gendered body in the act of writing and on the relation of theory to questions of gender, race, and class.

1619.   Keohane, Nannerl O., Michelle Z. Rosaldo, and Barbara Charlesworth Gelpi, eds. *Feminist Theory: A Critique of Ideology.* Chicago: U of Chicago P, 1982.

1620.   Koestenbaum, Wayne. *Double Talk: The Erotics of Male Literary Collaboration.* London: Routledge, 1989. Discusses male collaboration in texts regarded as "female bodies."

1621.   Kofman, Sarah. *The Enigma of Woman: Woman in Freud's Writings.* Trans. Catherine Porter. Ithaca: Cornell UP, 1985. Feminist analysis and critique of Freud's views of women.

1622.   Kolodny, Annette. *The Land before Her: Fantasy and Experience of the American Frontiers, 1630–1860.* Chapel Hill: U of North Carolina P, 1984. Responses of American pioneer women to the frontier.

1623.   ———. *The Lay of the Land: Metaphor as Experience and History in American Life and Letters.* Chapel Hill: U of North Carolina P, 1975.

Kristeva, Julia. See entries 991–97.

1624.   Lakoff, Robin. *Language and Woman's Place.* New York: Harper, 1975.

1625.   Langland, Elizabeth, and Walter Gove, eds. *A Feminist Perspective in the Academy: The Difference It Makes.* Chicago: U of Chicago P, 1981.

Lionnet, Françoise. *Autobiographical Voices: Race, Gender, Self-Portraiture.* See entry 1508.

1626.   MacCannell, Juliet Flower, ed. *The Other Perspective in Gender and Culture: Rewriting Women and the Symbolic.* New York: Columbia UP, 1990. Raises issues about feminism and cultural studies.

1627.   Malson, Micheline R., Jean F. O'Barr, Sarah Westphal Wihl, and Mary Wyer, eds. *Feminist Theory in Practice and Process.* Chicago: U of Chicago P, 1989. Draws from humanities and social sciences; treats black feminist ideology, sexual violence and literary history, mother-daughter relations, female creativity.

1628.   Marcus, Jane. *Art and Anger: Reading like a Woman.* Columbus: Ohio State UP for Miami U, 1988. Collects her essays of the 1970s and 1980s.

1629.   McConnell-Ginet, Sally, Ruth Borker, and Nelly Furman, eds. *Women and Language in Literature and Society*. New York: Praeger, 1980.

1630.   Meese, Elizabeth. *Crossing the Double-Cross: The Practice of Feminist Criticism*. Chapel Hill: U of North Carolina P, 1986. Applies Derrida's deconstruction to feminist theory.

1631.   ———. *(Ex)Tensions: Re-figuring Feminist Criticism*. Urbana: U of Illinois P, 1990.

1632.   Meese, Elizabeth, and Alice Parker, eds. *The Differences Within: Feminism and Critical Theory*. Amsterdam: Benjamins, 1988.

1633.   Miller, Nancy K., ed. *The Poetics of Gender*. New York: Columbia UP, 1987. How gender interacts with literary form and technique.

1634.   ———. *Subject to Change: Reading Feminist Writing*. New York: Columbia UP, 1988.

        Minh-ha, Trinh T. *Woman, Native, Other: Writing Postcoloniality and Feminism*. See entry 1510.

1635.   Minogue, Sally, ed. *Problems for Feminist Criticism*. London: Routledge, 1990.

1636.   Mitchell, Juliet. *Woman's Estate*. New York: Random, 1973. By an eminent feminist critic of psychoanalysis.

1637.   ———. *Women: The Longest Revolution*. New York: Pantheon, 1984.

1638.   Mitchell, Juliet, and Ann Oakley. *What Is Feminism?* New York: Pantheon, 1986.

        Mitchell, Juliet, and Jacqueline Rose, eds. *Feminine Sexuality: Jacques Lacan and the Ecole Freudiènne*. See entry 975.

1639.   Montefiore, Jan. *Feminism and Poetry: Language, Experience and Identity in Women's Writing*. London: Routledge, 1987. Focuses on women poets.

1640.   Monteith, Moira, ed. *Women Reading Women's Writing: A Challenge to Theory*. Brighton, Eng.: Harvester, 1988.

1641.   Mora, Gabriela, and Karen S. Van Hooft, eds. *Theory and Practice of Feminist Literary Criticism*. Ypsilanti: Bilingual, 1982.

1642.   Newton, Judith, and Deborah Roanfeldt, eds. *Feminist Criticism and Social Change: Sex, Class, and Race in Literature and Culture*. New York: Methuen, 1985.

1643.   Orasanu, Judith, Leonore Adler, and Mariam K. Slater, eds. *Language, Sex, and Gender*. New York: New York Acad. of Sciences, 1979.

1644.   Ostriker, Alicia. *Writing like a Woman*. Ann Arbor: U of Michigan P, 1983.

1645.   Pagano, Jo Anne. *Exiles and Communities: Teaching in the Patriarchal Wilderness*. Albany: State U of New York P, 1990. Considers feminist pedagogy in the light of Lacan's revision of psychoanalysis.

1646.   Palmer, Paulina. *Contemporary Women's Fiction: Narrative Practice and Feminist Theory*. New York: Simon, 1989.

1647.   Parker, Patricia. *Literary Fat Ladies: Rhetoric, Gender, Property.* London: Methuen, 1988. Feminist and poststructuralist analysis of rhetoric as a discourse of power and social control.

1648.   Perry, Ruth, and Martine Watson Brownley, eds. *Mothering the Mind: Twelve Studies of Writers and Their Silent Partners.* New York: Holmes, 1984. Feminist investigations of creativity.

1649.   Personal Narratives Group, ed. *Interpreting Women's Lives: Feminist Theory and Personal Narratives.* Bloomington: Indiana UP, 1989.

1650.   Poovey, Mary. *The Proper Lady and the Woman Writer: Ideology as Style in the Works of Mary Wollstonecraft, Mary Shelley, and Jane Austen.* Chicago: U of Chicago P, 1984. Integrates feminism and Marxist literary criticism.

1651.   ———. *Uneven Developments: The Ideological Work of Gender in Mid-Victorian England.* Chicago: U of Chicago P, 1988.

1652.   Rich, Adrienne. *Blood, Bread, and Poetry: Selected Prose, 1979–1985.* New York: Norton, 1986. Prose by the distinguished poet.

1653.   ———. *On Lies, Secrets, and Silence: Selected Prose, 1966–1978.* New York: Norton, 1979.

1654.   Robinson, Lillian S. *Sex, Class, and Culture.* London: Methuen, 1986. With new introduction by the author. American Marxist-feminist criticism.

1655.   Roof, Judith. *A Lure of Knowledge: Lesbian Sexuality and Theory.* New York: Columbia UP, 1991.

1656.   Russ, Joanna. *How to Suppress Women's Writing.* Austin: U of Texas P, 1983.

1657.   Sankovitch, Tilde A. *French Women Writers and the Book: Myths of Access and Desire.* New York: Syracuse UP, 1988. Discusses authors from the Middle Ages to the present, including Beauvoir and Cixous.

1658.   Schor, Naomi. *Reading in Detail: Aesthetics and the Feminine.* New York: Methuen, 1987.

1659.   Sedgwick, Eve Kosofsky. *Between Men: English Literature and Male Homosocial Desire.* New York: Columbia UP, 1985.

1660.   ———. *Epistemology of the Closet.* Berkeley: U of California P, 1990. Argues that questions of heterosexual or homosexual definition are at the heart of forms of representation and knowledge in the twentieth century; includes analyses of writings by Melville, Nietzsche, Wilde, James, and Proust.

1661.   Sellers, Susan, ed. *Feminist Criticism: Theory and Practice.* Toronto: U of Toronto P, 1991.

1662.   ———, ed. *Writing Differences: Readings from the Seminar of Hélène Cixous.* Milton Keynes, Eng.: Open UP, 1988. Essays by Cixous and participants in her seminar; with a list of Cixous's books.

1663.   Sheridan, Susan, ed. *Grafts: Feminist Cultural Criticism*. London: Verso, 1988.

1664.   Sherman, Julia A., and Evelyn Torton Beck, eds. *The Prism of Sex: Essays in the Sociology of Knowledge*. Madison: U of Wisconsin P, 1979.

1665.   Sherry, Ruth. *Studying Women's Writing: An Introduction*. London: Arnold, 1989.

Shevelow, Kathryn. *Women and Print Culture: Constructing Femininity in the Early Periodical*. See entry 1380.

1666.   Showalter, Elaine, ed. *Speaking of Gender*. New York: Routledge, 1989. Fourteen essays on deconstruction, reader-response theory, African American literature, and other topics.

1667.   ———, ed. *Women's Liberation and Literature*. New York: Harcourt, 1971.

Smith, Barbara. *Toward a Black Feminist Criticism*. See entry 1516.

1668.   Spacks, Patricia Meyer. *The Female Imagination*. New York: Knopf, 1975.

1669.   Spender, Dale, ed. *Feminist Theorists: Three Centuries of Key Women Thinkers*. London: Women's, 1983.

1670.   ———. *Man Made Language*. 2nd ed. London: Routledge, 1985. With new introduction.

1671.   ———. *Men's Studies Modified: The Impact of Feminism on the Academic Disciplines*. Oxford: Pergamon, 1981.

1672.   ———. *The Writing or the Sex? or, Why You Don't Have to Read Women's Writing to Know It's No Good*. Oxford: Pergamon, 1989. Argues that the difference between "female" and "male" literature lies not in the work but in the response to it.

Spivak, Gayatri Chakravorty. *In Other Worlds: Essays in Cultural Politics*. See entry 1518.

Sprengnether, Madelon. *The Spectral Mother: Freud, Feminism, and Psychoanalysis*. See entry 931.

1673.   Stambolian, George, and Elaine Marks, eds. *Homosexualities in French Literature: Culture Contexts/Critical Texts*. Ithaca: Cornell UP, 1979.

1674.   Stimpson, Catherine R. *Where the Meanings Are: Feminism and Cultural Spaces*. New York: Methuen, 1988.

1675.   Stratton, Jon. *The Virgin Text: Fiction, Sexuality, and Ideology*. Brighton, Eng.: Harvester, 1987. Adopts the Marxist concept of "commodity fetishism" and shows its effect on reading and sociosexual relations.

Thompson, Ann, and Helen Wilcox, eds. *Teaching Women: Feminism and English Studies*. See entry 301.

1676.   Thorne, Barrie, and Nancy Henley, eds. *Language and Sex: Difference and Dominance*. Rowley: Newbury, 1975.

1677.   Thorne, Barrie, Cheris Kramarae, and Nancy Henley, eds. *Language, Gender, and Society*. Rowley: Newbury, 1983.

1678. Todd, Janet M. *Feminist Literary History: A Defence*. Cambridge, Eng.: Polity, 1988.

1679. ———, ed. *Gender and Literary Voice*. New York: Holmes, 1980.

1680. ———, ed. *Men by Women*. New York: Holmes, 1982. Fourteen essays on male characters in fiction written by women.

1681. ———, ed. *Women Writers Talking*. New York: Holmes, 1983. Essays by fifteen contemporary women writers and feminists.

1682. Tracy, Laura. *"Catching the Drift": Authority, Gender, and Narrative Strategy in Fiction*. New Brunswick: Rutgers UP, 1988. Explores and criticizes the psychoanalytic model of reader-response criticism and raises feminist and cultural issues.

1683. Treichler, Paula A., Cheris Kramarae, and Beth Stafford, eds. *For Alma Mater: Theory and Practice in Feminist Scholarship*. Urbana: U of Illinois P, 1985.

1684. Walker, Alice. *In Search of Our Mothers' Gardens: Womanist Prose*. New York: Harcourt, 1983. Essays by the black feminist novelist and Pulitzer Prize winner.

Wall, Cheryl A., ed. *Changing Our Own Words: Essays on Criticism, Theory, and Writing by Black Women*. See entry 1520.

Wallace, Michelle. *Invisibility Blues: From Pop to Theory*. See entry 1521.

1685. Wandor, Michelene, ed. *On Gender and Writing*. London: Pandora, 1983.

1686. Waugh, Patricia. *Feminine Fictions: Revisiting the Postmodern*. London: Routledge, 1989. Moves from Lacanian psychoanalysis to "object-relations" psychological theory.

1687. Weed, Elizabeth, ed. *Coming to Terms: Feminism/Theory/Politics*. New York: Routledge, 1989. Collects seventeen essays written from 1985 to 1988.

1688. Weedon, Chris. *Feminist Practice and Post-structuralist Theory*. Oxford: Blackwell, 1987. Discusses psychoanalytic and deconstructive theory and Foucault.

Weixlmann, Joe, and Houston A. Baker, Jr., eds. *Black Feminist Criticism and Critical Theory*. See entry 1524.

Willis, Susan. *Specifying: Black Women Writing the American Experience*. See entry 1525.

1689. Winders, James A. *Gender, Theory, and the Canon: From Intellectual History to Cultural Criticism*. Madison: U of Wisconsin P, 1991. Examines five canonical texts in modern European intellectual history that explicitly represent femininity or depend on unstated ideas about gender.

1690. Yaeger, Patricia. *Honey-Mad Women: Emancipatory Strategies in Women's Writings*. New York: Columbia UP, 1989. Uses American feminist and neo-Marxist theory (Frankfurt school) to criticize French feminist theory.

Index